W9-BJN-080

FLORIDA STATE
UNIVERSITY LIBRARIES

JUL 21 1997

TALLAHASSEE, FLORIDA

# Globalization and Autocentricity
## In Africa's Development
## in the 21st Century

# Globalization and Autocentricity In Africa's Development in the 21st Century

### Kidane Mengisteab

## Africa World Press, Inc.

P.O. Box 1892

Trenton, NJ 08607

P.O. Box 48

Asmara, ERITREA

# Africa World Press, Inc.

| P.O. Box 1892 | | P.O. Box 48 |
| --- | --- | --- |
| Trenton, NJ 08607 | | Asmara, ERITREA |

Copyright © 1996 Kidane Mengisteab
First Printing 1996

All rights reserved. No part of this publication may be reproduced, stored in a retrieval
system or transmitted in any form or by any means electronic, mechanical, photocopyir
recording or otherwise without the prior permission of the publisher.

Cover design: Jonathan Gullery

**Library of Congress Cataloging-in-Publication Data**

Kidane Mengisteab.
    Globalization and autocentricity in Africa's development in the
21st century / Kidane Mengistreab.
      p.  cm.
    Includes bibliographical references and index.
    ISBN 0-86543-558-8 (cloth : alk. paper). -- ISBN 0-86543-559-6
(paper : alk. paper)
     1. Africa, Sub-Saharan--Economic policy. 2. Africa, Sub-Saharan-
-Economic integration. 3. Africa, Sub-Saharan--Foreign economic
relations.
HC800.K53  1996
338.967--dc21                         96-48230
                                          CIP

HC
800
K53
1996

# Contents

# Tables

# Abbreviations

| | |
|---|---|
| ACDESS | African Center for Development and Strategic Studies |
| ACM | Arab Common Market |
| AEC | African Economic Community |
| AFTA | ASEAN Free Trade Area |
| ANC | African National Congress |
| APEC | Asia Pacific Economic Cooperation |
| ASEAN | Association of Southeast Asian Nations |
| CACM | Central American Common Market |
| CARICOM | Caribbean Community and Common Market |
| CEAO | Communaute Economique de l'Afrique de l'Ouest |
| CSCE | Conference on Security and Cooperation in Europe |
| DPG | Defense Planning Guidance |
| EAEC | East Asian Economic Caucus |
| EC | European Community |
| ECA | (UN) Economic Commission for Africa |
| ECESAS | Economic Community of Eastern and Southern African States |
| ECOWAS | Economic Cooperation of West African States |
| EEC-ACP | European Economic Community—African, Caribbean and Pacific |
| EPRDF | Ethiopian People's Revolutionary Democratic Front |
| FAO | (UN) Food and Agricultural Organization |
| GATT | General Agreement on Tariffs and Trade |
| GCC | Gulf Cooperation Council |
| GDP | Gross domestic product |
| GNP | Gross national product |
| IFI | International financial institutions |
| IMF | International Monetary Fund |
| LAIA | Latin American Integration Association |
| LDC | Less developed country |
| MERCOSUR | Southern Cone Common Market |
| MFI | Multilateral financial institutions |
| MITI | Japanese Ministry of International Trade and Industries |

| | |
|---|---|
| MMD | Movement for Multiparty Democracy |
| MNC | Multinational corporations |
| MRU | Mano River Union |
| NIC | Newly industrializing countries |
| NAFTA | North American Free Trade Agreement |
| NGO | Nongovernmental organization |
| NPT | Nonproliferation Treaty |
| NWO | New World Order |
| OAU | Organization of African Unity |
| OECD | Organization for Economic Cooperation and Development |
| PTA | Preferential Trade Area |
| SADC | Southern African Development Cooperation |
| SAP | Structural adjustment program |
| SOE | State owned enterprises |
| SPLM | Sudanese People's Liberation Movement |
| TNC | Transnational corporations |
| UDEAC | Union Douanière et Economique de l'Afrique Centrale |
| UN | United Nations |
| UNCTAD | United Nations Conference on Trade and Development |
| UNDP | United Nations Development Programme |
| UNIDO | United Nations Industrial Development Organization |

# Part 1
## Problems with Prevailing Development Strategies

# 1

# Introduction:
# Africa's General Crisis

▼   ▼   ▼

In the 1980s most of the developing countries faced a lingering economic decline. Sub-Saharan Africa (henceforth referred to as Africa) was the hardest hit. Almost all of the countries in that region suffered from economic stagnation, persistent food shortages and famines, rising poverty, declining export earnings, burgeoning debt, and growing marginalization within the global economy. Growth rates of gross national product (GNP) and per capita GNP between 1980 and 1991 were 2.6 and –1.1 percent, respectively, as compared with 4.6 and 3.6 percent for all developing countries. The average annual growth rate of gross domestic investment between 1980 and 1992 was estimated to be –3 percent.[1] Per capita food production was 4 percent lower in 1991 than it was in 1981, while food import dependency ratio rose by about 3.7 percent between 1971 and 1990. In 1990 about 54 percent of the total population of sub-Saharan Africa was in absolute poverty, as compared with 31 percent in all developing countries. By 1991 sub-Saharan Africa's total debt reached 101 percent of GNP, compared with 40 percent in all developing countries. Its debt service rose to about 25.3 percent of exports in 1991, compared with 4.7 percent in 1970.[2] Between 1980 and 1991 exports as percentage of GNP declined by 0.9 percent, compared with 1.2 percent growth for all developing countries. The 1980s, referred to by the UN Economic Commission for Africa (ECA) as the "lost decade,"[3] was a decade of severe regression.

Nor does the picture in the 1990s seem promising. Between 1990 and 1993 African economies grew by merely an average of 1.3 percent. As the ECA notes, this represents an annual decline in per capita income of 1.7 percent.[4] Terms of trade plummeted by about 15 percent between 1987 and 1991, compared with a 1 percent decline in all developing countries during the same period. Between 1991 and 1994 terms of trade continued to decline by an average of 2.87 percent annually. Commodity prices have also continued to decline since 1991, reaching their lowest rates in real terms in 1993. As a result, the debt burden continues to grow, sapping Africa's capacity to import and invest. Commodity prices are expected to see an upturn, leading to a 4 percent annual growth of African exports for the years between 1995 and 2004.[5] Yet according to the World Bank,[6] this upswing, even if it occurs, is not expected to result in improvements in standard of living. For the decade between 1994 and 2003, gross domestic product (GDP) per capita and private consumption per capita are projected to grow only by about 0.9 and 0.3 percent respectively.[7] Industrialization in Africa is also at a standstill: growth in manufacturing output, which averaged 2.3 percent in the 1980s, has fallen below 4 percent in the first half of the current decade. The continent's share of the world's poor was estimated at 30 percent at the dawn of the decade of the 1990s. If present trends continue, and there is every indication that they will under existing development strategies, it is expected that Africa's share of the world's poor will rise to 40 percent.[8]

The economic crisis has been accompanied by crises of governance and state-building,[9] which are manifested by growing sectoral, regional, and social inequalities; ethnic, clan, religious, and social conflicts; gross human rights abuses; widespread corruption; and rising threats of fundamentalism, crime, and anarchy.[10] Such problems have culminated in civil wars and total disintegration in some countries, including Liberia, Somalia, and Rwanda. In several other countries the state is on the brink of dissolution.[11] Despite some progress in the shift from repressive authoritarian regimes to multiparty rule in some countries and an increase in the number of human rights organizations throughout the continent, repression and human rights abuses continue to rise in many countries. Killings, disappearances, imprisonment, and torture of political opponents are widespread and on the rise in countries, such as Kenya, Zaire, Nigeria, and Côte d'Ivoire. The genocide in Rwanda is, of course, the most appalling one. Millions of Africans are also displaced or forced to become refugees. Africa now enjoys the

# Table 1.1. Selected Indicators of Africa's General Crisis

| Indicator | All LDCs | Sub-Saharan Africa | Arab States | South Asia | Southeast Asia | Latin America and the Caribbean |
|---|---|---|---|---|---|---|
| Population in absolute poverty (% of total) | 31 | 54 | 25 | 43 | 35 | 38 |
| Percentage of population with access to health care | 81 | 59 | 88 | 74 | 77 | 88 |
| Daily calorie supply as % of requirements (1988–90) | 109 | 92 | 128 | 103 | 113 | 114 |
| Infant mortality per 1,000 births (1992) | 69 | 101 | 54 | 94 | 55 | 47 |
| Annual population growth rate % (1960–92) | 2.2 | 2.8 | 2.9 | 2.3 | 2.3 | 2.3 |
| Projected population growth rate % (1992–2000) | 1.9 | 3.4 | 2.7 | 2.0 | 1.8 | 1.7 |
| Total fertility rates (1992) | 3.8 | 6.5 | 5.4 | 4.4 | 3.5 | 3.2 |
| Contraceptive prevalence rate % (1985–92) | 53 | 15 | 45 | 39 | 47 | 58 |
| Food import dependency ratio (1988–90) | 10.5 | 10.2 | 49.5 | 6.1 | 9.9 | 18.7 |
| Terms of trade (1991) (1987=100) | 99 | 85 | 87 | 94 | 97 | 106 |
| Exports of primary commodities as % of total exports (1992) | – | 76 | 90 | 27 | – | 62 |
| Total external debt as % of GNP (1991) | 40 | 101 | 55 | 35 | 56 | 40 |
| Debt service as % of total exports (1991) | 21.3 | 25.3 | 32.7 | 26.5 | 18.2 | 30.1 |

*Sources:* UNDP, *Human Development Report 1994*; World Bank, *World Development Report 1994.*

unenviable distinction of producing the largest number of refugees. By the end of 1993 there were 5,825,000 refugees from the African continent, accounting for 35.8 percent of the total number of world refugees.[12]

Population explosion and environmental deterioration have also compounded Africa's problems. Africa's fertility rates are among the highest in the world (see Table 1.1). Africa's population is estimated to have grown by over 140 percent between 1960 and 1992 and it is expected to grow by another 27 percent and reach about 710 million by the year 2000.[13] In concert with general atmospheric changes, periodic droughts, and the communal nature of Africa's land tenure systems,[14] the rapid growth of population has generated severe environmental degradation. Partly triggered by reliance on wood for fuel, deforestation in Africa is estimated to be at the rate of about 0.9 percent per year.[15] Deforestation has in some areas adversely affected the production of coffee and cocoa by making the land too dry. Poor and/or insufficient farming and grazing lands have also become serious problems in many countries of the Sahel and the Horn of Africa. Even water and firewood have become scarce in some of these countries, severely lowering the already woeful standard of living, especially of rural people. Moreover, land degradation and deprivation of access to river banks have generated many internal and international conflicts, such as those between Mauritania and Senegal and Mali and Niger. The countries of the Horn of Africa also face chronic conflicts between nomads and sedentary peasants over access to and control of land.

With growing poverty and malnutrition, Africa is also facing a health-care crisis. The AIDS epidemic is more serious in Africa, especially in the central African region, than in other parts of the world. Although Uganda is said to have made some strides, it is widely believed that the epidemic is beyond the control of the resource-strapped states of the region. Even curable infectious diseases, such as malaria, continue to kill millions of people throughout the continent. The World Health Organization estimates that there are up to 500 million cases of malaria a year with fatalities ranging between 1.5 and 3 million people. About 90 percent of these cases occur in Africa. The emergence of some drug-resistant malaria and other parasitic diseases has made matters worse.[16]

The confluence of these intricately intertwined economic, political, social, and environmental problems has culminated in the continent's general crisis. The toll of the crisis on Africa's population has been extremely high. According to the World Bank,[17] Africa is now the only continent in which poverty is rising. Widespread starvation and malnutrition continue to ravage most Africans. Daily calorie intake is at only 92 percent of requirements, compared with 109 percent in all developing countries.[18] A large number of Africans remain deprived of access to sanitation, clean water, basic health care, and education (see Table 1.1).

Most projections indicate that the crisis either is getting worse or at least is expected to continue for a long time to come. Even in countries that are believed to have made significant progress in the process of adjustment, the growth rates remain very low. The World Bank itself estimated that the average poor in Ghana—the show case of the International Monetary Fund (IMF)/World Bank-sponsored structural adjustment programs (SAPs)—will not cross the poverty line for another fifty years.[19] Needless to say, the implications of prolonged crisis, which may trigger more civil wars and disintegration of states, are frightening.

Engulfed by all these problems, Africa is also facing growing marginalization in the global economic system. Its share of global production and trade is declining. It is also the only region of the world to be adversely impacted by the General Agreement on Tariffs and Trade (GATT)'s Uruguay Round, at least in the short run.[20]

Given the general crisis and the poor projections of Africa's development, it is imperative that the prevailing development strategies and policies be reexamined carefully to determine why they have been difficult to implement and, more importantly, why they have not succeeded in reversing the crisis once implemented. It is also crucial that new alternatives be proposed for serious consideration. As an effort towards that end, this book's overriding objectives are threefold: (1) to identify some of the most important structural conditions that have contributed to generating Africa's general crisis; (2) to examine why the different development strategies and models which African states have attempted, particularly the globalization effort which has been intensified since the early 1980s, have not succeeded in overcoming the crisis; and (3), which is also the principal objective, to outline the essential components of the autocentric development approach that was proposed by Samir Amin a decade ago[21] and examine its potential and feasibility in the era of globalization.

## Structural Underpinnings
## of the General Crisis

The different aspects of Africa's general crisis stem from a number of common structural foundations. The predominance of the subsistence sector in African economies is one such condition. Why the subsistence sector has not undergone a metamorphosis into a surplus-producing exchange economy is a highly contested issue. Some regard the subsistence sector simply as a residue of the traditional society, which persists primarily because of the recalcitrance of the traditional peasantry.[22] Others view the resilience of the subsistence sector as a broader failure of social transformation, related to the nature of peripheral capitalism—which perpetuates the extroversion of African economies, resulting in the bypassing of the needs of the peasantry and in its deprivation from lack of access to resources.[23] Considering the widespread disintegration of traditional values, the high rate of rural-urban migration, and the attempts by the peasantry to participate in the cash-crop production when conditions permit it, the first argument is not very convincing. Even if it has a kernel of truth, it is difficult to sift the impacts of the peasantry's own conservatism, since it remains grossly deprived of access to resources. Differences in access to health care, to clean water, and to educational services between rural and urban areas and differences in fertilizer application between the cash-crop and food sectors are among the obvious indicators of the peasantry's deprivation.

The predominance of the subsistence sector, its marginalization, and the meagerness of its purchasing power generate a number of problems, both in terms of economic development and in terms of state-building. One such problem is the continued dissociation of available resources from social needs. By failing to translate its needs into demand, this sector, largely as a result of its deprivation, fails to influence allocation of resources by the market mechanism. The peasantry, because of its lack of political power, also fails to influence allocation by state policy. Distortions in resource allocation by both mechanisms are, therefore, pervasive.

A related problem is that, as a result of the fragmentation into modern and traditional sectors, the economy is deprived of a domestic market, and thus lacks the internal dynamics to support its own growth and diversification. The modern sector largely bypasses the subsistence sector and relies extensively on the international system for markets, capital, technology, and other inputs. Such dependency, in tandem with the lack of diversification of exports, in turn hinders the growth of dependent economies by limiting their ability to control the national process of capital accumulation. It also renders them highly volatile.

The fragmentation between economic sectors and the consequent lack of interdependence among different regions and ethnic and religious groups also severely undermine the basis for state-building. Lack of economic growth and regional inequalities, which are related to the conditions of fragmentation and extroversion, aggravate the problem by intensifying the competition for and conflict over access to the limited resources among different groups of claimants. More importantly, lack of internal dynamics for the growth of the economy results in lack of interdependence among the different segments of society. Internal fragmentation also restricts the scope of integration with the global economy by limiting both the production capacity and purchasing power of those economies.

## Population and Environmental Problems

The rapid population growth and environmental deterioration that have characterized African countries can also be related to the failure to transform the large subsistence sector. It is widely recognized among analysts that rapid population growth has contributed to the erosion of the standard of living of African societies. However, it is also clear that poverty combined with lack of access to health care and education encourages a higher rate of population growth. Many demographers have linked transformations in fertility and mortality rates to production relations.[24] Mamdani, for example, notes that the decision of an individual family "to have or not to have a child is essentially a judgement of its circumstances. . . ."[25] The subsistence mode of production encourages more births, since children are viewed by individual families as helping hands that increase the family's chances of escaping poverty. Steinhart also notes[26] that, unlike wealthy Western societies, "wealth" in poor African societies "flows from children to parents and children are insurance and capital accumulation" as they provide labor, share their earnings with their parents, and care for them when they are old.

What is a rational decision at the level of an individual family unit clearly worsens the problems of the collective, leading to Hardin's "tragedy of the commons."[27] Yet changing the circumstances by creating access to productivity-raising resources, access to education, and delivery of health-care services to the peasantry is essential for curving population growth. This is abundantly clear from the lack of success of short-cut measures—such as contraceptives—in Africa. Contraceptive demand in most of Africa is too low to impact population growth rates. Notwithstanding significant variations among countries, in the early 1990s the use of contraceptives is estimated not to have exceeded 4 percent.[28] (Zimbabwe, Botswana, and Kenya, with 43, 33, and 27 percent, respectively, are exceptions.[29]) Even in countries where its usage is relatively higher, as in Zimbabwe, it is primarily used for spacing children rather than for reducing the number of births.[30] In Kenya too fertility rates have remained at 6.5, among the highest in the world, despite the increase in contraceptive use from 7 percent to 27 percent between 1977 and 1988.[31]

Rapid growth of the population in concert with a number of other factors—including lack of affordable sources of energy to replace fuelwood, successive droughts, and overgrazing—has led to rapid environmental degradation in much of Africa. The widespread communal land tenure system, which often encourages open access to land and its mismanagement, is another factor that has contributed to environmental deterioration. Privatization of land-ownership has been suggested as a solution to this problem.[32] However, in many areas land tenure reforms are difficult without changing the mode of production of the subsistence sector. It is, for example, extremely difficult to privatize land in nomadic and semi-nomadic areas where seasonal mobility is essential.

Reducing birth rates and livestock size, refraining from cutting trees for various purposes, and fallowing land to restore its vegetation cover are among the essential measures to curtail the rapid process of environmental degradation. However, such measures are unlikely to be acceptable since at the level of individual families they amount to sacrificing one's aspirations (to overcome poverty) for the common good. For the very poor, cutting trees to sell firewood and charcoal is a means of survival. Thus the poorer the subsistence sector is, the less able it is to make such sacrifices and to properly manage its environment.

## Lack of Diversification of Exports

Another structural problem related to the resilience of the large subsistence sector is lack of diversification of production in general and of exports in particular. African economies were the least diversified at the time of their independence in the 1960s, with the manufacturing sector contributing no more than 6 percent of GNP. The level of human resource development in terms of education and technical skills was also among the lowest in the world.[33] Progress toward economic diversification and human development has been very slow since independence. In 1992 the contribution of the manufacturing sector to GNP averaged only 17 percent for all of sub-Saharan Africa.[34] By the late 1980s the ratio of exports of nonprimary commodities (versus total exports) was still less than 14 percent. A number of factors, including the weakness of the domestic market and the difficulty of developing global competitiveness without an internal market to support infant industries and the process of "learning by doing" account for this slow progress. Shortages of capital, technology, and infrastructure, lack of skilled manpower, and lack of access to foreign markets for manufactured products are other constraints.

Unfavorable terms of trade, chronic trade disequilibrium, burgeoning debt, import strangulation, and low growth rates are among the problems associated with lack of diversification of exports. A recent World Bank study[35] reveals that developing countries that are exporters of non-oil commodities grew by an average of 2.8 percent between 1960 and 1992, compared with 7 percent for the exporters of manufactures and 4.9 percent for the countries with diversified exports. Making matters worse, many of Africa's traditional export commodities have lost their importance due to substitutes. For others, it has become increasingly difficult to maintain favorable prices as African states, together with a large number of other developing countries, often oversupply the international market with commodities that are often characterized by low income and price elasticities. Such factors as lack of diversification of exports, the declining relevance of many primary commodities in the global market, and the limited purchasing power of African countries have conspired to intensify the marginalization of African economies in the global economic system.

Despite initial modest progress following independence, human development has been constrained by a number of factors, including limitation and misuse of resources, the debt crisis, concentra-

11

tion of production on primary commodities, and the duality of the economic system. The level of Africa's human resources development remains the lowest in the developing world.[36]

## Regional, Ethnic, Religious, and Class Conflicts

Underdevelopment of state-building is another structural problem facing African states. Considering the rising number of states in the global system that are besieged by ethnic conflicts and civil strife, the problem is by no means limited to Africa. However, widespread regional, ethnic, religious, and class strifes together with the high degree of fragmentation of the economy are manifestations that state-building is, by and large, less advanced in Africa than in other regions. Factors impeding the process of state-building are many and vary greatly from country to country; detailed examination of all of them is beyond the scope of this book. There are, however, some factors that are common to most cases. Among these are the precolonial slave raids, the ethnic classifications, and the divide-and-rule policy exercised by the colonial state (primarily in order to prevent or weaken unified resistance). The added strain on ethnic relations resulting from poverty, extroversion of African economies, the neglect of regions considered less important by the colonial state, and in some cases, appropriation of land and colonial settlements are other important sources of conflict. Relative deprivation of Southern Sudan and Northern Chad by the colonial state are among the obvious examples.

Many of the factors that reproduce suspicions and mistrust among ethnic groups have continued unabated in the post-independence era. By failing to restructure the extroverted economies and thereby to develop interdependence among different economic sectors, regions, and ethnic groups, the post-independence state has largely failed to mend ethnic relations. It has also failed to alleviate poverty and to rectify the uneven access to resources—including political power—among different ethnic groups and geographical regions. In many cases, these problems have been aggravated by leaders who use ethnic divisions as tools in perpetuating their hold on power. Regimes such as those of Idi Amin in Uganda, Siad Bare in Somalia, and Mengistu Hailemariam in Ethiopia, were among the most notorious examples.

   As Zambia's former president Kaunda notes, the post-independence state attempted to create nation-states out of the "sprawling artifacts the colonialists carved out."[37] To attain this objective, most African states adopted centralized administrative structures, often denying ethnic groups the opportunity to manage their local affairs. Even in states where decentralized federal arrangements were initially adopted, including Nigeria, Kenya, Cameroon, and Ethiopia (with Eritrea), centralization and ethnic dominance gradually replaced decentralization.[38] Many regimes pursued policies of assimilating ethnic groups to the dominant culture without addressing the problems of uneven access to resources and to political power. Haile Selassie's Ethiopia and the different regimes in the Sudan are among the best examples. The aim of building a nation-state out of a multi-nation state is, however, an unrealistic goal. The European countries that were believed to have succeeded in this process have not been all that successful. The United Kingdom, France, and Spain, for example, can hardly be regarded as successful nation-states.[39]
   Globalization, which among other things represents openness and state disengagement from economic activity, has also become a factor that obstructs state-building and undermines states. Income inequalities between social classes, ethnic groups, and regions are on the rise, and the state—especially in poor countries—has become powerless to deal with these problems. The state and institutions such as democracy and labor unions are *national* in nature and they are not equipped to deal with the economic system, which is becoming increasingly global.
   Uneven development and deprivation are clearly not the only causes of ethnic conflict, nor do the absence of uneven development or of poverty guarantee successful state-building or harmonious interethnic relations.[40] Uneven development is, however, likely to spark or to aggravate ethnic cleavages.[41] Thus, a state that perpetuates uneven development or fails to correct it is unlikely to succeed in state-building by mobilizing the different ethnic identities for a shared future. Excessive centralization and coercion, which only aggravate ethnic conflicts, have increasingly become the most common means of preserving the territorial integrity of an increasing number of African states.

## Problems with Existing Approaches to Development

The absence of sustained progress in Africa's development and the failure to stem the tide of its present crisis, even with reforms such as SAPs, raises questions about the appropriateness of development strategies and policies that the countries in the continent have pursued. No doubt, different strategies and policies have failed for different reasons. However, the development crisis has a lot to do with the nature of African development strategies. Ever since their incorporation into the global economy, African economies have been characterized by extractive relations or the export of primary commodities. The gold exports of the Guinea Coast states (1400–1800); the exports of ivory, gold, and slaves by the Abyssinian empire (thirteenth to eighteenth centuries) and the states of Zimbabwe and Mutapa (thirteenth to seventeenth centuries); the Atlantic and Indian Ocean slave trade (1550s–1850s); and the exports of ivory, palm oil, and a variety of cash crops from different parts of Africa (replacing slaves after the delegalization of the slave trade) are among the major examples.

The colonial state intensified the extractive relations. Economic strategies and policies largely corresponded to the extractive economic structures and were driven essentially by external demand. The interests of the population were rarely the primary factors in the decisions of the monarchs, chiefs, and the colonial authorities that controlled (or were the middlemen in) such trades. The African masses, in fact, were only marginally involved in the production of these commodities; their benefits from these enclave economies also remained minimal.

The nature of policy changed little under the post-colonial state. A common characteristic of most African policies since independence has been that they are often borrowed from the outside, where structural conditions are markedly different. Such policies have been generally incompatible with the structural context of Africa's problems. Basil Davidson aptly expresses the dependency of African development models as follows:

> Failures and futilities have occurred within a specific context of the attempt to develop Africa out of the history of Europe or America, and primarily for the benefit of Europe and America, rather than out of the history of Africa for the prime benefit of Africa.[42]

14

A number of examples illustrate the problems of dependency and inappropriateness of many of the development strategies Africa has pursued. In the 1960s and 1970s, African states indigenized the bureaucracy but largely maintained the socioeconomic structures established by the colonial state and perpetuated by the urban-biased mainstream-modernization theory. This theory oversimplifies problems of development by associating them primarily with scarcity of some critical resources such as capital, skill, or technology. As a solution it proposes greater integration with the global economy to make diffusion of the scarce resources possible through trade and foreign investment.

Instead of transforming the peasantry and internally integrating African economies, the prescriptions of modernization theory have largely perpetuated the neglect of the peasantry and the extroversion and duality of African economies. During these two decades (60s–70s) some African states officially adopted "African socialism" and "self-reliance" as alternative development strategies. These strategies, which involve considerable structural transformation, can be regarded as efforts toward an *autocentric development approach.* Such efforts, however, remained mostly symbolic, with little actual implementation. A number of factors contributed to the failure of such efforts. In some cases, the leaders were simply dishonest and were not committed to bring about change. In other cases, the balance of class forces was in favor of the status quo. Moreover, African countries also lacked a sufficient number of well-trained and competent bureaucrats to properly implement change. In any case, there were few structural changes that distinguished countries attempting African socialism and self-reliance from those that were guided by the urban-biased mainstream-modernization theory. For example, the peasantry's access to productivity-raising resources under the *ujamaa* villagization scheme of Nyerere's Tanzania—the most celebrated case of African socialism and self-reliance—was little different from those throughout most of Africa.[43] Despite the differences at the level of rhetoric, they all pursued an urban-biased and extroverted development strategy that neglected agriculture and rural transformation. Far from promoting internal integration, state-building, and development, such urban-biased and elite-serving strategies aggravated the problems of food crisis, uneven development, fragmentation, and ethnic and regional conflicts.

Some African states also attempted to adopt a Marxian (Leninist or Maoist) development strategy and nationalized the principal

15

means of production. However, the political, economic, and social preconditions for Marxian socialist transformation were largely absent.[44] In some cases the political elite in the countries of socialist experiment did very little to promote such preconditions by restructuring their political economies. Often socialist rhetoric and nationalization became means of increasing the power of the self-serving custodians of the state by granting them monopoly of both economic and political power. Ethiopia under the military government (*derg*) is a good case in point. Continued neglect and repression of deprived nations and ethnic groups, not to mention general neglect of agriculture in resource allocation manifested by the disproportionate targeting of the available resources in favor of state farms, represented little substantive difference from the strategies of the previous imperial regime.[45]

Other socialist experiments, Angola and Mozambique in particular, were undermined by protracted civil wars, partly fueled by the external intervention typical of the Cold War era. The balance of the social classes in these countries also did not favor the cause of the peasantry. Despite honest commitment on the part of some leaders, the peasantry was too weak to assert its interests. Moreover, civil society, the bureaucracy, and the economy were all too underdeveloped to allow a successful socialist transformation. Resource allocation patterns in these countries also showed little indication of favoring the transformation of the peasantry. Agricultural policies, for example, favored state farms instead of the peasant sector.[46]

With the general neglect of the peasantry, the problems of rapid population growth and poor human resource base have remained unattended or ill conceived. African educational systems are largely incompatible with internal development needs. More importantly, access to education and to productivity-raising technical skills has remained severely limited. Efforts to deal with the problem of population explosion by population control measures have also proven futile since they do not address the conditions that make rapid population growth possible. Without improving access to education for the peasantry, improving the conditions of women and changing the peasantry's mode of production to raise its standard of living and thereby to create circumstances that allow lower birth rates, it remains doubtful that family-planning measures will make a dent on population growth.[47]

Regional integration is another strategy widely adopted by African states. Such schemes have sprouted all over Africa mostly

16

with the objective of promoting intra-African trade and intra-African cooperation on a wide range of issues. African states also adopted a treaty in Abuja, Nigeria, in 1991, establishing an "African Economic Community." As we will see in chapter 3, despite their large numbers, the performance of integration schemes in the continent has remained a dismal failure. Trade among African states has been hampered by a number of structural problems, including the absence of complementarity of their economies. Regional integration without reorienting the dynamics of the production system, especially the export sector, which was created to meet certain demands of the markets of the colonial powers and still responds to the demands of the countries of the Organization for Economic Cooperation and Development (OECD), has remained largely futile.

The effort to integrate African economies with the global economic system has intensified since the early 1980s. This strategy is promoted through SAPs, including export promotion and decontrolling of prices, exchange rates, and imports. There is little doubt that integration with the global economy is essential for Africa's development. In fact, it is a paradox that African economies are the most dependent on the global economy for their growth and they are the most marginalized in the global system. Ironically, the policies that have been implemented to promote integration with the global economy have reinforced marginalization. Policies such as those of SAPs have intensified internal fragmentation by neglecting internal dynamics, and it seems that the more internally fragmented African economies become, the more marginalized they become within the global economic system. This suggests that strategies that integrate African economies internally and equip them to become more active participants in global production need to precede or at least to accompany the strategies of openness and export promotion for successful integration with the global economy. Otherwise, the effort remains at best hollow and at worst distorting, since the exports are primary commodities which are produced with marginal participation of the peasantry and often at the expense of the internal food needs. A key proposition of the present study is that an ingenious *balance* between *global integration* and *autocentricity* is a more promising alternative for Africa's development in the twenty-first century than is the now-predominant globalization strategy.

Expanding the role of the market in resource allocation (marketization) is another reform instituted in the 1980s in many

African countries. Proponents expect that this reform (largely imposed over African states by IMF-World Bank conditionalities as part of the worldwide globalization process) will invigorate African economies through more efficient allocation of resources and more balanced macroeconomic policies. As we will see in Chapter 2, some aspects of the marketization reforms are essential to promote economic efficiency and growth. However, in Africa such reforms are imposed before creating some of the essential preconditions for the proper functioning of the market system, including the transformation of the large subsistence sector into an exchange economy. The state in Africa is also pressured by the multilateral financial institutions (MFIs) and lender countries to disengage from economic intervention without due regard to the market-creating activities of the state. A market system under these conditions, if at all possible, is likely to exacerbate the disparity and malintegration of economic sectors. There is growing evidence that the impacts of marketization and growing disengagement of the state from economic activity have intensified poverty and inequality by lowering the wages and social incomes of lower classes.

As already noted, state-building is a critical challenge facing African states. It clearly involves building political and economic systems that promote *internal integration* among the different *nations, ethnic groups,* and *social classes.* However, the existing African political economy, by and large, discourages centripetal forces, as African economies are excessively dependent on external dynamics. The weakness of the *internal* dynamics of the continent's economy impedes internal interdependence and integration. It also undermines the relevance of the state since it has allowed the sources of economic dynamics to remain largely beyond its control. Under such conditions the state is often viewed as a predator instead of as an institution that enhances the economic security of its citizens.[48] Devoid of legitimacy, the state is characterized by the paradox of being weak and highly authoritarian at the same time.[49] Also, often it is either dominated by ethnic groups or else it largely serves the interests of its custodians and their supporters. In the absence of economic security and integrating economic and political systems, many national groups have challenged the state and in a few cases have attempted to secede from it. African states have increasingly relied on coercive measures to preserve their territorial integrity. State-building through force, however, is unlikely to succeed in the present era, in which the values of democratization and respect for human rights are on the rise globally. The outcome

18

of reliance on coercion has been growing internal strife, anarchy, and sometimes total disintegration.

## Loss of Sovereignty

As the above-listed examples suggest, many of the prevailing development strategies and policies lack the necessary preconditions or are not properly sequenced. Many others, such as the urban bias, excessive extroversion, and state-building by coercive means, are inappropriate. The loss of state sovereignty can be added to this list. The state, which by its failure is largely responsible for Africa's general crisis, is presently under crisis itself. Weakened by dependent economic structures, burgeoning debt, growing marginalization within the global economy, and widespread poverty, the African state has found that internally its basis of legitimacy has been severely eroded. It is increasingly challenged by ethnic or religious rebellions and by increasing protests and demands on the part of the emerging civil society. While some states have responded by reforms of varying magnitudes, some have intensified their repression, in some cases resulting in complete anarchy.

External intervention by multilateral financial institutions (MFIs), the governments of the dominant powers, multinational corporations, and a host of other nongovernmental organizations (NGOs) has also undermined the sovereignty and moral authority of the state. The African state has increasingly surrendered policy-making to external actors, especially the MFIs, the IMF, and the World Bank. The MFIs, which generally (and often correctly) regard the African political elite as incompetent and unaccountable to its populations, have expanded their role in dictating policy to Africa. As Callaghy observes, "[N]owhere else in the world has IMF, World Bank, and [such] private bank advice played such a major public role"[50] as it does in Africa. Every time African leaders come to Washington on their "begging expeditions," they sell a little bit more of their independence as they accept more conditionalities. It is no exaggeration to say that the MFIs, for all practical purposes, have now assumed control of setting the agenda for economic policy-making in Africa. Ghana, for example, was one of the first African states to gain its independence (in 1957). Ironically, the IMF now keeps its own resident representative in an office across the hall from the country's finance minister to keep an eye on the country's reform program. African countries now also face political conditionalities as well as environmental conditionalities since the launching of the National Environmental Action Plan in 1987. Obviously, the more policy is dictated from Washington the less the African population is represented in policy-making.

In much of the literature of the 1980s and thereafter, the erosion of state power by internal and external forces has generally been viewed as a positive development and a condition for democratization and for faster development. As Young notes,[51] it is a welcome development to see an internal civil society come of age and begin challenging the self-serving state for more space. However, there is a fundamental difference between reforming the state and undermining it. The various conditionalities apply to the "reformed" state as they do to the "old" state and they hardly represent progress towards independent policy-making, much less development. As Lipumba notes, while the African state prevented the African masses from influencing policy-making, the MFIs are in the process of taking away local ownership of policy-making altogether.[52] The more sovereignty the African state surrenders, the less likely it is to pay attention to the extroversion of the economy—*and* the less relevant it becomes, complicating the whole process of development and state-building even more.

The penetration by the MFIs, international NGOs, and dominant powers does not stop at the level of the state. Many segments of Africa's civil society are equally compromised and heavily influenced by foreign NGOs and dominant powers. Many African NGOs are, for example, essentially national chapters of international NGOs. Others are financed and cultivated by foreign actors or rely heavily on them for support. No doubt, many of these NGOs play very positive roles. However, relations between international NGOs and national NGOs as well as with the rest of the national civil society are by no means horizontal, and such unequal relations cannot be assumed to promote independent decision-making in Africa.

The growing challenge to the state on the part of civil society does have some promising aspects. It can lead to badly needed reforms and can protect nonstate institutions as well as society at large against the coercive powers of the state. However, weakening the state instead of reforming it poses the danger of exposing Africa to a more overt imperialist domination by undermining the state's ability to resist such tendencies.

"Civil society" is a term that generates a great deal of disagreement as to its meaning.[53] One dominant conception is that it is a

20

sphere of human relations and activity that is outside the sphere of the state. It encompasses a very wide spectrum of nonstate institutions and relations, ranging from trade unions, voluntary associations, hospitals, churches, and capitalist enterprises.[54] Obviously, civil society represents diverse interests and can be dominated by elite interests as much as the state can. Civil society, by itself, is also not equipped to protect society from external domination. This implies that civil society cannot be a substitute for the state. Rather it can only coexist with the state in a relationship characterized by both cooperation and conflict. The state "protects and provides while it dominates; civil society responds with exit, voice, or loyalty."[55] This clearly means that the weakening of the state does not necessarily represent strengthening of civil society, nor does it benefit society or promote democracy. Civil society and the state would thus need to cooperate in liberating policy-making from external dominance since African development is unlikely to occur under conditions of policy dependence. The international bureaucracies of the MFIs and NGOs, despite their technical expertise, are far removed from African realities, even if it could be assumed that their motives included genuinely developing Africa. The MFIs and NGOs are also not any more accountable to the African masses than the African elites. They are not even inclined to assume responsibility when the policies they dictate fail and worsen the conditions of millions of people. Moreover, African development efforts in any event are likely to remain divorced from internal dynamics.]

To conclude this section then, the general crisis that batters African countries seems to be getting more grave, despite SAPs. The global environment also seems to grow increasingly more hostile for African countries. The impacts of GATT's Uruguay Round are ambiguous if not outright contrary to Africa's interests. Terms of trade continue to deteriorate and the debt burden grows heavier and threatens to crush the economies of many African states. African countries are also increasingly drifting to the margins of the global division of labor. As Shaw notes,[56] under these conditions, autocentric development strategies such as local self-help, national self-reliance, and regional collective self-reliance are likely to emerge as alternatives. For such autocentric alternatives to have a chance, African countries require a major overhaul of the state as well as of the state's strategies and policies. In the next section of this introductory chapter an attempt is made to outline some of the essential aspects of an autocentric approach.

## The Nature of the Autocentric Approach

With increased marginalization within the global economic system and the state's heavy-handed intervention, some segments of African economies have withdrawn from the formal sector and taken refuge in the informal sector. This "silent revolution"[57] is often viewed by proponents of SAPs as a rebellion against the interventionist state and an indication of support for a free market system. However, the rise of the informal sector also signifies a return to a self-reliant and autocentric development. The shift from production of export crops to foodstuffs[58] and the relative vigor of the small enterprises that are oriented to meeting internal social needs[59] are clear indications that an autocentric approach to development needs be taken seriously in Africa.

The goal of an autocentric approach is to correct the neglect of internal dynamics in Africa's development effort. One essential aspect of this alternative strategy is for Africans to reclaim ownership of policy-making, which is essential for reorienting policies to deal with specific structural conditions that characterize Africa. Africa needs tailor-made policies since the "one size fits all" type of generic policies imposed by the MFIs have generally proved to be incompatible with African realities. It is also crucial for human and institutional capacity building since it promotes "learning by doing."

Another essential characteristic of an autocentric development strategy is to base African economies primarily on social needs and thereby to promote *internal* dynamics without discarding the benefits of *external* dynamics. Under an autocentric strategy, social needs replace external demand as the primary engine for the production system. The strategy thus aims at transforming the marginalized subsistence peasantry to raise its productivity and levels of consumption, thereby fostering integration between the traditional and the modern sectors of the economy. Such restructuring in the economic arena cannot be implemented properly without corresponding changes in other spheres, including the political and cultural areas. Substantial changes in the economic field without corresponding changes in governance and state-building are unlikely to be feasible. An autocentric approach needs to be implemented in a comprehensive manner.

In this era of globalization, an entirely autocentric approach that approximates autarky is neither desirable nor possible. However, unbridled globalization that neglects internal needs and dynamics is clearly dangerous under the existing structural conditions of African economies. This book attempts to explain how a delicate balance between the two approaches may lead to better results in Africa's development. Since globalization is now the dominant trend and autocentricity is the neglected approach, our emphasis will be placed on the autocentric approach.

An autocentric approach clearly touches upon all aspects of African political economy. This book, however, does not aspire to develop the implications of autocentric restructuring in all areas. Its scope is limited to analyzing how an autocentric approach can transform a few key areas of Africa's political economy. More specifically, the book attempts to answer questions such as how a proper balance between globalization and an autocentric approach would affect African integration, internally, regionally, and globally, what type of democratization would be more conducive for good governance, state-building, and an autocentric development in Africa, what type of economic system (mix between market and state) is likely to be more compatible for African realities, and how would an Africa under a socioeconomic system that balances globalization and autocentricity relate to the rest of the world. Each one of these issues is discussed in a separate chapter.

## Outline of Subsequent Analysis

Taking structural adjustment programs (the most widely implemented package of reforms in Africa since the early 1980s) as a case, Chapter 2 attempts to show the problems of globalization in Africa. So far, SAPs have fallen far short of expectations in invigorating the region's economies. More specifically, the chapter attempts to: (1) outline and critically analyze the neo-liberal diagnosis of Africa's socioeconomic conditions which led to the prescription of SAPs; (2) assess the actual and potential impacts of SAPs on economic growth and macroeconomic imbalances; and (3) explore why SAPs fail to address the most fundamental structural impediments of Africa's socioeconomic development.

Chapters 3 through 6 discuss the most important components of an autocentric approach to overcoming Africa's multifaceted crisis. One aspect of this approach is integration—internal, regional, and global. Chapter 3 attempts to show how an appropriate integration strategy can be instrumental in ending the duality of African economies, cultivating domestic markets, diversifying African production systems, thereby improving Africa's position in the global division of labor and reversing its marginalization.

Another aspect of an integrated autocentric approach is political and economic democratization. Given the marginalization of the subsistence sector, internal fragmentation, uneven development, ethnic conflicts, human rights abuses by self-serving repressive regimes, and rising refugee problems, Chapter 4 examines how and what type of democratization might mitigate some of these problems. The chapter centers around two fundamental questions: (1) What type of democracy would be best suited for promoting state-building and reversing Africa's skid into deepening socioeconomic crisis? (2) What is the likelihood of successful democratization in Africa in the near future?

Chapter 5 examines in greater detail the major reasons for the recurrent failures in resource allocation in Africa, both by the state and by the market mechanism. The chapter then undertakes the difficult question of what roles of the state and the market are indispensable and what mix or type of partnership between these two devices of political economy would be more appropriate for Africa's socioeconomic development. The criteria for appropriateness are stated in terms of overcoming the identified structural bottlenecks of African economies.

Chapter 6 analyzes the most important external constraints facing Africa. Its main concerns are to highlight how *an integrated autocentric approach empowers African states* and enhances their ability to reverse their growing marginalization within the global system, to control the process of capital accumulation, and to more effectively participate in global decision making.

The objectives of the concluding chapter (7) are twofold. The first is to sum up the dynamics of an integrated autocentric approach in overcoming Africa's general crisis. The second is to explore the prospects for widespread adoption of this approach in Africa to form a proper balance with globalization.

## Notes

1.  World Bank, *World Development Report 1994* (Oxford: Oxford University Press, 1994).
2.  UNDP, *Human Development Report 1994* (New York: Oxford

University Press, 1994).

3. Economic Commission for Africa, *Economic Report on Africa 1990* (Addis Ababa: ECA Secretariat, 1990).

4. Roy Laishley, "Faster Growth But No Economic Turnaround," *Africa Recovery* 8, no. 1/2 (April/September 1994): 11.

5. World Bank, *Global Economic Prospects and the Developing Countries* (Washington, D.C.: World Bank, 1995).

6. World Bank, *Global Economic Prospects and Developing Countries* (Washington, D.C.: World Bank, 1994).

7. World Bank, *Global Economic Prospects* (1994), 24.

8. UNDP, *Human Development Report 1991* (New York: Oxford University Press, 1991), 23.

9. The term "state-building" is adopted here instead of nation-building since the latter term is often used in reference to ethnonationalism. For details on distinctions between the two terms, see Walker Connor, *Ethnonationalism: The Quest for Understanding* (Princeton: Princeton University Press, 1994).

10. John Mukum Mbaku, "Bureaucratic Corruption and Policy Reform in Africa," *The Journal of Social, Political and Economic Studies* 19 (Summer 1994): 149–75.

11. Aristide R. Zolberg, "The Specter of Anarchy: African States Verging on Dissolution," *Dissent* 39 (Summer 1992): 303–11; William Zartman, "Introduction: Posing the Problem of State Collapse," in William Zartman, ed., *Collapsed States: The Disintegration and Restoration of Legitimate Authority* (Boulder: Lynne Rienner, 1994).

12. U.S. Committee for Refugees, *World Refugee Survey* (Washington, D.C.: USCR, 1994), 40.

13. UNDP, *Human Development Report 1994*.

14. John M. Cohen, "Land Tenure and Rural Development in Africa," in Robert H. Bates and Michael F. Lofchie, eds., *Agricultural Development in Africa: Issues of Public Policy* (New York: Praeger, 1980); Gershon Feder and Raymond Noronha, "Land Rights Systems and Agricultural Development in Sub-Saharan Africa," *The World Bank Research Observer* 2, no. 2 (July 1987): 143–69.

15. UNDP, *Human Development Report 1994*.

16. Bruce Fetter, "Health Care in Twentieth Century Africa: Statistics, Theories, and Policies," *Africa Today* 40, no. 3 (1993): 9–24.

17. World Bank, *Adjustment in Africa: Reforms, Results and the Road Ahead* (Oxford: Oxford University Press, 1994), 161.

18. UNDP, *Human Development Report 1994*.

19. World Bank, *Adjustment in Africa*, 40.

20. Alexander J. Yeats, "What Are OECD Trade Preferences Worth to Sub-Saharan Africa?" *African Studies Review* 38, no. 1 (April 1995): 81–101; "African Concerns Over GATT Deal," *Africa Recovery* 8, no. 3 (December 1994): 8.

21. Samir Amin, *Delinking: Towards a Polycentric World* (London: Zed

Books Ltd., 1985).

22. Goran Hyden, "The Resilience of the Peasant Mode of Production: The Case of Tanzania," in Robert Bates and M.F. Lotchie, eds., *Agricultural Development in Africa* (New York: Praeger, 1980), 218–43.

23. For details on this debate see Alexander Schejtman, "The Peasant Economy: Internal Logic, Accumulation and Persistence," in Charles K. Wilber, ed., *The Political Economy of Development and Underdevelopment* (New York: Random House, 1988), 364–92.

24. Dennis D. Cordell and Joel W. Gregory, eds., *African Population and Capitalism: Historical Perspectives* (Boulder: Westview Press, 1987); Steven Feierman and John Janzen, eds., *The Social Basis of Health and Healing in Africa* (Berkeley: University of California Press, 1992).

25. Mahmood Mamdani, "Democratization and Marketization," in K. Mengisteab and I.B. Logan, eds., *Beyond Economic Liberalization in Africa: Structural Adjustment and the Alternatives* (London: Zed Press, 1995), 17–22.

26. Peter Steinhart, "Beyond Pills and Condoms: As Africa's Population Mounts, What More Can Be Done?" *Audubon* 93, no. 1 (1991): 24.

27. Garett Hardin, "The Tragedy of the Commons," *Science* 162 (1968): 1243–48.

28. Aaron Segal, "Africa's Population and Family Planning Dynamics," *Africa Today* 40, no. 3 (1993): 25–38.

29. C.L. Kamuzora, "Towards Understanding Low Contraceptive Prevalence in African Societies," *The African Review* 15, nos. 1 and 2 (1992): 1–9.

30. Segal, "Africa's Population," 34.

31. Kamuzora, "Towards Understanding Low Contraceptive Prevalence"; Steinhart, "Beyond Pills and Condoms," 24.

32. Feder and Noronha, "Land Rights Systems," 143–69.

33. World Bank, *Global Economic Prospects*.

34. World Bank, *World Development Report 1994*.

35. World Bank, *Global Economic Prospects*, 32.

36. UNDP, *Human Development Report 1994*.

37. Quoted in Benjamin Neuberger, "State and Nation in African Thought," in John Hutchinson and Anthony D. Smith, eds., *Nationalism* (Oxford: Oxford University Press, 1994), 235.

38. Benjamin Neuberger, "Federalism and Political Integration in Africa," in Daniel J. Elazar, ed., *Federalism and Political Integration* (Tel Aviv: Turtledove Publishing, 1979), 171–88.

39. Connor, *Ethnonationalism*.

40. Connor, *Ethnonationalism*.

41. A.W. Orridge, "Uneven Development and Nationalism," *Political Studies* 29, no. 1 (1981): 1–15, and no. 2 (1981): 181–90; John Breuilly, *Nationalism and the State* (New York: St. Martin's Press, 1982).

42. Basil Davidson, "What Development Model," *Africa Forum* 1, no. 1 (1991): 13.
43. Issa G. Shivji, *Class Struggles in Tanzania* (New York: Monthly Review Press, 1976); C. George Kahama, T.L. Maliyamkono, and Stuart Wells, *The Challenge for Tanzania's Economy* (London: James Currey, 1986).
44. Kidane Mengisteab, "Responses of Afro-Marxist States to the Crisis of Socialism: A Preliminary Assessment," *Third World Quarterly* 13, no. 1 (1992).
45. Kidane Mengisteab, *Ethiopia: Failure of Land Reform and Agricultural Crisis* (New York: Greenwood Press, 1990).
46. Helena Dolny, "The Challenge of Agriculture," in John S. Saul, ed., *A Difficult Road: The Transition to Socialism in Mozambique* (New York: Monthly Review Press, 1985), 211–52; Gillian Gunn, "The Angolan Economy: A Status Report," in Helen Kitchen, ed., *Angola, Mozambique and the West* (New York: Praeger, 1987).
47. Mamdani, "Democratization and Marketization"; Frances Moore Lappe and Rachel Schurman, *Taking Population Seriously* (Oakland, CA: Institute for Food and Development Policy, 1990).
48. Robert Fatton, Jr., *Predatory Rule: State and Civil Society in Africa* (Boulder and London: Lynne Rienner Publishers, 1992).
49. Thomas Callaghy, "The State as Lame Leviathan: The Patrimonial Administrative State in Africa," in Zaki Ergas, ed., *The African State in Transition* (New York: St. Martin's Press, 1987), 87–116.
50. Callaghy, "The State as Lame Leviathan," 107.
51. Crawford Young, *The African Colonial State in Comparative Perspectives* (New Haven: Yale University Press, 1994).
52. Nguyuru H.I. Lipumba, *Africa Beyond Adjustment* (Washington, D.C.: Overseas Development Council [Policy Essay No. 15], 1994).
53. Young, *The African Colonial State*, has provided a concise review of the different meanings. For more details on the different conceptions of civil society see Jean-Francois Bayart, "Civil Society in Africa," in Patrick Chabal, ed., *Political Domination in Africa: Reflections on the Limits of Power* (Cambridge: Cambridge University Press, 1986); Michael Bratton, "Beyond the State: Civil Society and Associational Life in Africa," *World Politics* 41 (April 1989); Patrick Chabal, *Power in Africa: An Essay in Political Interpretation* (New York: St. Martin's Press, 1992).
54. Ellen Meiksins Wood, *Democracy Against Capitalism* (Cambridge: Cambridge University Press, 1995).
55. Young, *The African Colonial State*, 222.
56. Timothy M. Shaw, "The South in the 'New World (Dis)Order': Towards a Political Economy of Third World Foreign Policy in the 1990s," *Third World Quarterly* 15, no. 1 (1994): 17–30.
57. Fautu Cheru, *The Silent Revolution in Africa* (London: Zed Press, 1989), 19.

58. Cheru, *The Silent Revolution*, 19–20.
59. M.S.D. Bagachwa and Frances Stewart, "Rural Industries and Rural Linkages in Sub-Saharan Africa: A Survey," in F. Stewart, S. Lall, and S. Wangwe, eds., *Alternative Development Strategies in Sub-Saharan Africa* (New York: St. Martin's Press, 1992), 145–84.

# 2
# Globalization and Economic Liberalization: Solutions or Problems?

▼   ▼   ▼

## Introduction

The African crisis has triggered a great deal of debate and disagreement on the nature and sequence of reforms appropriate for the continent. Since the early 1980s, economic liberalization (marketization) has emerged as the predominant policy reform worldwide, mostly due to the worldwide globalization trend and its endorsement by the industrialized lender countries and the MFIs in particular. Liberalization is promoted through a package of reforms known as SAPs. These policies are, among other things, expected: (1) to promote a free-enterprise market system and allocative efficiency by disengaging the state from productive and commercial activities through privatization of publicly owned assets, and by decontrolling prices, exchange rates, and interest rates; (2) to achieve macroeconomic balance, including fiscal and trade balances, by retrenchment of public expenditures and promotion of exports respectively; and (3) to integrate economies of developing countries more closely with the global economy by encouraging openness.

Despite frequent uprisings and riots by some segments of their populations, most African governments have largely complied or attempted to comply with the liberalization drive. There are now few African states without some kind of adjustment programs. Over a decade after implementation, the impacts of SAPs have generated as much disagreement as their appropriateness. This chapter is an effort towards a critical assessment of SAPs in particular and globalization in general. First, it briefly outlines and analyzes the neo-liberal diagnosis of the African socioeconomic situation which has led to the prescription of SAPs. Second, it examines the actual and potential impacts of SAPs on economic growth and macroeconomic imbalances. Last, it explores the implications of SAPs for the most fundamental structural impediments to socioeconomic development in Africa. Among such interrelated impediments examined are the predominance of the subsistence peasantry in African economies, internal and regional fragmentation, gross inequalities and dissociation of available resources from social needs, lack of control of the process of capital accumulation, and the growing marginalization of sub-Saharan Africa in the global economy due to its weak position in the global division of labor. These factors are selected because, as noted in the introductory chapter, socioeconomic development is unlikely to advance without improvements in these critical aspects.

## The Neo-Liberal Diagnosis

As Macpherson notes, liberalization refers to a socioeconomic system in which "individuals are free to make the best bargain they could, to offer their services, their products, their savings or their labor, on the market and get the market price which was itself determined by all their independent decisions."[1] The widespread debt crisis, the stagflation of the 1970s, and the growing crisis of socialist economies are among the factors that contributed to the rise of neo-liberalism, which has engulfed the global economy since the early 1980s. This new marketization counterrevolution is essentially predicated on two controversial neo-liberal claims. One is that open-market economies characterized by minimal government intervention outperform economies with active state intervention. The second is the principle that property is private and that state intervention in the economy ought to be restricted so that it does not encroach on private property and individual liberty.

Based on these doctrines, proponents of SAPs have related much of the economic problems of developing countries to pervasive state intervention. Africa's more serious economic crisis relative to those of other regions is attributed to, among other things, the greater magnitude of state intervention, including directly owning assets and fixing of prices, interest rates, and exchange rates, that allegedly characterize the continent.[2] The claim that Africa is more interventionist is not always supported by conclusive empirical evidence. It is, for example, highly contentious that African currencies are significantly more overvalued than those of other developing countries. The real exchange rates of most African currencies, Ghana and Uganda being notable exceptions, appreciated only modestly relative to those of other developing regions and appreciated substantially less than those of industrialized countries between the mid-1960s and the early 1980s.[3] Nevertheless, it is plausible that the claim is largely correct. The private enterprise system and possibly liberalism are much less developed in Africa than in the other regions. As a result, the proportion of the public sector to the private sector is relatively larger in Africa than in other nonsocialist states.[4] By some estimates, the public sector's share of total output is 15 percent relative to 3 percent in (nonsocialist) Asia and 12 percent in Latin America. Its share of investment is estimated at 25 percent relative to about 17 percent and 19 percent in Asia and Latin America respectively. Public enterprises also account for as much as 40 to 45 percent of manufacturing value-added.[5] The continued intervention by the state, despite the frequent failures of its policies is, in turn, attributed to either its self-serving nature or to its commitment to socialist ideology.[6]

The interventionist state diagnosis represents major differences from two other dominant development theories, the radical dependency theory and the orthodox (mainstream) liberal modernization theory, in two related respects. First, it attempts to curtail the regulatory and income redistributive roles of the state much more than these two theories.

Dependency theory relates the problem of underdevelopment to the exploitative relations between the developed and developing areas, which are maintained by the unholy alliance between the international bourgeoisie of the North and its subordinate, the elite in the countries of the South. These structural relations are viewed as diverting production from social needs to external demand and impeding capital accumulation, technical progress, and the development of human resources in developing countries. Dependency theory prescribes the liberation of developing countries from the concerted domination by imperialist countries and the domestic elite, economic democracy through income redistributive measures, and reorientation of the extroverted economy toward meeting domestic social needs. According to dependency theory, a new

31

"reformed" state can play an active role in income redistribution as well as in the promotion of new economic structures.

Mainstream modernization theory also allows considerable role to the state in economic activity, albeit less than what dependency theory does. It essentially attributes the problems of development to the scarcity of some important factors of production, including capital, technology, education, skill, "good government" and, according to some, "development conducive culture."[7] The state is expected to play an active role in the process of capital formation, channeling of investments, and facilitating technical change.[8]

Another characteristic of the neo-liberal theory distinguishing it from the other two theories (dependency theory and mainstream modernization theory) is its emphasis on growth instead of income redistribution. It expects poverty alleviation and income redistribution to come about eventually through a trickle-down process.[9] Dependency theory clearly rejects the growth-first/redistribution-later strategy. Even modernization theory recognizes that growth does not constitute development and that a growth strategy alone does not bring about an adequate reduction of poverty. Kuznets, for example, points out that even if growth takes place, redistribution to alleviate poverty may have a lag time of generations unless promoted by policy.[10]

Since the late 1980s, SAPs have seen some modification for at least two reasons. One is that the widespread concern in the early 1980s that inability on the part of developing countries to service their debts would undermine the international financial system has been largely alleviated. Among the objectives of SAPs had been to ensure availability of foreign exchange for servicing debt.[11] By the late 1980s, this objective became less important. A second reason is intensification of hardship on the poor during the adjustment process, which led to the voicing of opposition to SAPs by many humanitarian organizations and popular protests in many countries.[12] Beginning the late 1980s the MFIs, which are the primary sponsors of SAPs, made some effort to develop policies to mitigate the burden of adjustment on the poor segments of society. The World Bank, in conjunction with other organizations such as the United Nations Development Programme (UNDP), has, for example, launched the Social Dimension of Adjustment project, which involves measures such as food-for-work programs and food subsidies for the poor.[13] As indicated by its last two annual World Economic Reports, the World Bank has also begun to emphasize the importance of expenditures on health, education, and infrastructure for sustained development. Indeed, as Husain observes, there has been some evolution in the World Bank's view of SAPs.[14] However, as Bienefeld notes,[15] true priorities are revealed only when tough choices have to be made during the time of conflict between efficiency and welfare objectives. Despite the apparent shift in its views, efficiency, which is a critical aspect of globalization, remains the World Bank's priority. The social safety-net measures have been severely inadequate and they remain exogenous to the liberalization drive. It is also unclear why the state, to the extent that it is self-serving and responsible for the prevailing political economy of exclusion, would aggressively implement the social safety-net policies to protect the poor. Moreover, increasing the social safety-net mechanisms and public expenditures on education and health care is unlikely without softening the antipublic expenditure zeal of SAPs themselves.

## Laissez-Faire as State Intervention

Ample empirical evidence supports the liberalization school's view that state intervention in Africa has often been self-serving and has led not only to inefficient allocation of resources but also to a reverse income redistribution.[16] Subsidies and regulations of prices, exchange rates, and interest rates which could be used for redistributive purposes have often, under corrupt political leadership, benefited the bureaucracy, the relatively wealthy, and the politically more potent segments of society instead of the poor that need them the most.[17] A good case in point is that no more than 5 percent of African farmers have access to credit from formal financial institutions.[18] Often times, the magnitude of control by the paternalistic state also suffocates innovations and initiatives by individuals and private firms.

State-owned enterprises (SOEs)—which are often established with broad goals such as creating employment, reducing regional inequalities, and generating economy-wide growth through external economies—have been, for the most part, ineffective and inefficient. Contrary to their stated goals, they have frequently become a means of augmenting the power base of self-serving authoritarian regimes and a drain on the national treasury. Their rate of efficiency has also been generally dismal compared with those of the private enterprises. Their more rigidly centralized system of management, which hampers prompt and flexible responses to different kinds of local constraints, is one reason for their inefficiency. Other reasons include less prudent cost control, which generally characterizes public property, and lack of clearly defined incentive systems.

Despite such conspicuous problems with the intervention of the African state in economic activity, the neo-liberal analysis has a number of serious flaws. The implied and stated basic premises that laissez-faire is the natural state of affairs and that economies that closely resemble it outperform those of interventionist states are difficult to sustain.

That laissez-faire is the natural state of affairs is a matter of faith that can hardly be supported by evidence. Private property, the state, laissez-faire, and regulation are all developments of certain epochs of human history, and none of them can be regarded as the natural state of affairs. As we will see in Chapter 4, it is also a matter of belief that laissez-faire is more compatible with individual liberty. Moreover, depending on what the prevailing conditions are, as Gramsci points out, laissez-faire is also a form of state intervention introduced and maintained by legislative and coercive means to change the distribution of the national income in favor of the wealthy.[19] In other words, depending on the pre-existing situation, deregulation and privatization are interventions as much as regulation and nationalization are. SAPs, for example, clearly represent state intervention as they require an active state involvement for implementation. To the extent that the system of production and distribution is a social affair and not disjointed activities of individuals, it can be reorganized and changed by social decisions. Maintaining a laissez-faire system, thus, requires state intervention.

The interventionist-noninterventionist dichotomy is, therefore, neither appropriate nor useful as an analytical tool. The real debate between advocates and opponents of marketization is about different types of intervention and their implications for income distribution.

SAPs do not necessarily reduce the power of the state across the board; they only weaken its redistributive and regulatory roles. They also do not adversely affect the interests of the high-level state functionaries. The political elite, who have accumulated wealth, often through corruption, can relatively easily realign their interests, invest in private enterprises, and join the ranks of the economic elite in order to benefit from liberalization, if they have not already done so. This explains, at least in part, why even the notoriously self-serving states showed little resistance to SAPs. The social groups that have resisted liberalization are mostly workers and low-income consumers.[20] Such groups view SAPs as a permanent intervention against their interests rather than a short-run hardship to be followed by prosperity. Rising unemployment and declining real wages have accompanied SAPs in many African states.[21] This—in concert with trimming of subsidies, with reductions in expenditures on health care and education, and with rising inflation triggered by devaluation and price decontrols—has severely reduced the standard of living of the working class and the urban poor, especially women and children.[22] The number of urban dwellers below the poverty line, which ranged from 30 to 35 percent in the late 1970s, is said to have risen to between 45 and 50 percent in the mid-1980s in Ghana.[23]

Given the unpopularity of SAPs, the state that implements them relies on authoritarian and coercive power to impose and sustain them. This perpetuates the governance and state-building problems of African countries.

A related flaw of the neo-liberal analysis is its implicit generalization that all state intervention in all markets hampers socioeconomic development in all countries and that a liberalized and outward-oriented economy generates faster growth. This claim fails to distinguish between the different types of states and the disparate conditions in different countries. It also suffers from lack of conclusive empirical evidence.[24] Many studies have, for example, shown that the impacts of outward orientation differ significantly between low-income and middle-income countries.[25] Other studies have shown serious doubts that outward orientation works for countries that face adverse world demand conditions.[26]

As already noted, many states clearly impede development by pursuing policies that advance self-interest at the expense of national development and by squandering public funds. Others, due to sheer incompetence, are unable to formulate appropriate policies or to implement them properly. However, as Streeten and Dietz point out, this does not warrant a generalized conclusion that all intervention by the state impedes development.[27] Not all Third World or African states are self-serving or incompetent. Some clearly exercise different forms of regulations with some success to advance broad social interests. Such states promote development by creating access to resources for the deprived segments of their populations, thereby coordinating available resources and social needs. Many observers (including Dietz, Park, Wade, and Sen)

35

attribute the rapid growth of countries like South Korea, Taiwan, and Singapore, at least in part, to active intervention by a developmentalist state although many others have argued that the success of these newly industrializing Asian countries (NICs) came about as a result of their adherence to the free market.[28] At the time of their "takeoff" in the late 1960s and early 1970s, the Asian NICs clearly were market-oriented in the sense that their intervention was to promote capitalist development and not socialism. However, they were by no means laissez-faire economies.

Intervention in these countries took several forms. Despite the neo-liberal argument that interest-rate controls suppress national savings and capital accumulation, these governments intervened to keep interest rates low in order to stimulate investment. Selective protectionism and subsidies and careful scrutiny and control of investments were other forms of intervention undertaken by those countries.[29] Land reform, which entailed redistribution of land and subsidization of many agricultural inputs in both Taiwan and South Korea, also represented another crucial intervention that would not be consistent with the neo-liberal doctrine.

In Africa successful intervention by a developmentalist state is rare. However, relative to most African states, Zimbabwe's intervention can be regarded as moderately successful. The "'land for all' slogan of Independence struggle now rings hollow for most poor Zimbabweans."[30] Nevertheless, Zimbabwe is credited for making some strides toward creating access to productivity-raising resources and to public services for its peasant population.[31] Production increase from the small-scale or communal sector has, for example, been notable more than compensating for the decline in the number of large-scale farms.[32]

The claim that state intervention in all markets (financial, product, and labor) is counterproductive also faces a number of problems, including lack of differentiation. In the first place, there is little evidence that deregulation of exchange rates and interest rates promotes efficiency. Paul Krugman, for example, argued that "belief in the efficiency of the foreign exchange market is a matter of pure faith; there is not a shred of positive evidence that the market is efficient. . . ."[33] State intervention in financial markets is also unavoidable and can make them function better and improve their performance, as Stiglitz notes.[34] Failures of financial institutions and their bailouts by governments are frequent even in the industrialized countries. The prospects for the proper functioning of private financial institutions in developing countries, such as those of sub-Saharan Africa, are much less promising. Governments both in developed and developing nations, as insurers of these institutions, are often compelled to intervene in order to prevent disruptions of financial systems, which have severe consequences on the whole economic system. Furthermore, in developing countries governments can, by creating financial institutions, provide funds for long-term investments, ensure competition, direct resource allocation, and stimulate growth.[35] In low-income developing countries, private financial institutions are simply too weak to play such crucial roles.

Lastly, the neo-liberal thesis fails to explain why African states are more interventionist than others. It appears that the weaker the private sector and the less diversified the economy is, the more the state intervenes. Caporaso's explanation of why the state in developing countries finds it difficult not to intervene is very similar to this hypothesis.[36] If this hypothesis is correct, then intervention in the African case may not be the cause of poor economic performance. Rather it may essentially be a condition dictated by the absence of a reasonably developed private sector and by the fact that African states are late comers to industrialization. This, of course, would have serious implications for the neo-liberal diagnosis and its prescription of SAPs for the African situation. This issue will be discussed in greater detail in Chapter 5.

## Impacts of SAPs on Economic Growth and Macroeconomic Imbalances

The neo-liberal contention that less-interventionist states in developing countries outperform interventionist ones has also faced serious problems. It is quite possible that the private sector, due to its more prudent cost control and higher levels of incentives,[37] may be more efficient than the public sector. However, in the African condition it is likely that the market's inability to overcome the marginalization of the peasantry and gross social and ethnic inequalities, which lead to chronic conflicts, undermine any benefits from allocative efficiency. In any case, conclusive empirical evidence that less-interventionist states outperform more-interventionist ones has been elusive. The findings of studies such as those by Balassa and Landau,[38] for example, are not replicable.[39]

About a decade after their implementation, the impacts of SAPs remain highly contentious. Supporters claim that they have already produced considerable positive results. The World Bank and the IMF claim that countries with improvements in macroeconomic policies outperformed those with little or no adjustments in growth rates, fiscal balance, export performance and even in increasing expenditures in health and education.[40] Ishan Kapur et al. assert that Ghana's adjustment has led to a 94 percent growth of its exports during 1984–1990, compared with 21 percent for the rest of sub-Saharan Africa during the same period.[41] Sharer, Schiller, and Ahmad also attribute Uganda's modest recovery after years of political turmoil to its implementation of structural adjustment programs.[42]

Critics strongly challenge these optimistic claims. The UN Economic Commission for Africa, for instance, argues that there is little difference in the performances of strong and weak or no-reform countries.[43] It claims that nonadjusting counterparts, in fact, have outperformed strong adjusters in the ratio of domestic savings to GDP and in social welfare development.[44] Many NGOs in Africa have also associated SAPs with worsening socioeconomic conditions, especially for the poorer segments of society.[45]

It has proved extremely difficult to empirically test these conflicting claims. Shifting positions of individual countries in terms of implementing adjustment programs and lack of data or their poor quality are among such factors. Correlating indicators of liberalization measures with indicators of performance or even meaningfully classifying countries into strong and weak reformers and comparing their performances have been difficult due to severe data constraint. Statistical data from different sources, such as the World Bank, UNDP, UN Food and Agricultural Organization (FAO), and United Nations Conference on Trade and Development (UNC-TAD), for example, show considerable variation from each other. Results of empirical tests, thus, are at best suggestive. Despite such limitations, significant positive results for SAPs would have been difficult to ignore, even by opponents. SAPs have not produced such results and there is little indication that they have begun to reverse Africa's crisis.

A comparison of economic performances between three groups of twenty-one sub-Saharan African states categorized into three groups by the World Bank on the basis of their progress in macro-economic policy reforms suggests no significant differences. Average economic performances between five years before adjustment (1981–1986) and four years after adjustment (1987–1991) of the three groups of countries do not reveal significant differences (see Tables 2.1 and 2.2). The comparison is undertaken by means of a simple analysis of variance of the performances of the three groups of countries. The indicators for comparison include: GDP per capita growth rates ($x_1$), growth rates of the agricultural sector ($x_2$), growth rates of the industrial sector ($x_3$), gross domestic investment as a ratio of GDP ($x_4$), average per capita food production growth rates($x_5$), and growth rates of exports ($x_6$).

The results show that the impacts of SAPs are, at best, mixed. Some adjusting countries, such as Ghana, have made some strides towards recovery in some areas. The differences between the means of the three groups of countries, in fact, appear to be considerable. The differences within groups are, however, as large. This means that not all adjusting countries have made improvements and not all countries with weak adjustments have failed to register some recovery. The claim that SAPs have already led to significant improvements in economic performance is thus unwarranted, according to these findings. These results are different from those of the World Bank study.[46] Among the reasons are that the World Bank's rigorous tests do not include most of the indicators included in this study.

As already noted, the poor quality of the data renders the evidence on Table 2.2 merely suggestive. There are also significant limitations to the approach of comparing strong and weak (or no-reform) countries since these countries are not consistent on all reform indicators or on the level of commitment to reform over time. As a result, the categorization of countries has often been arbitrary. A comparison of the World Bank study with two other studies shows serious inconsistencies. Two Harvard scholars, Sachs and Warner, who use trade liberalization as a proxy for general liberalization reform, categorize African countries differently than does the World Bank (see Table 2.3). According to the Sachs and Warner study, a country is deemed to be "closed" if:

1. Its nontariff barriers cover 40 percent or more of its trade;
2. Its average tariff levels are 40 percent or more;
3. The country's black-market exchange rate is depreciated by 20 percent or more relative to the official rate, on average during the 1970s or 1980s;
4. The country has a socialist economic system; and
5. If the state has a monopoly on major exports.

**Table 2.1**
**Comparison of Economic Performance Between Strong and Weak Macroeconomic Reform Countries in Africa (1981/86–1987/91)**

|  | $x_1$ | $x_2$ | $x_3$ | $x_4$ | $x_5$ | $x_6$ |
|---|---|---|---|---|---|---|
| **Large Improvements** | | | | | | |
| Ghana | 3.7 | 2.2 | 8.2 | 8.8 | -2.7 | 3.5 |
| Tanzania | 2.9 | 1.9 | 12.1 | 8.7 | -1.8 | — |
| Burkina Faso | -1.7 | -2.3 | 2.5 | 0.9 | -3.8 | 5.4 |
| Nigeria | 7.0 | 2.7 | 10.1 | — | 0.9 | 10.3 |
| Zimbabwe | 0.77 | -4.7 | 3.9 | 1.1 | -1.2 | — |
| **Small Improvement** | | | | | | |
| Madagascar | 1.6 | 0.9 | 3.9 | 3.3 | -2.1 | 13.7 |
| Malawi | 2.2 | 2.3 | 5.0 | 1.1 | -1.5 | 2.0 |
| Burundi | -0.9 | -1.6 | -0.2 | 1.6 | -4.6 | -6.9 |
| Kenya | 1.5 | -0.3 | 2.0 | 0.5 | 1.2 | 4.0 |
| Mali | -1.6 | 2.5 | -9.1 | 4.4 | 0.5 | 4.2 |
| Senegal | -0.6 | -2.2 | 2.8 | 1.7 | -4.2 | -5.2 |
| Uganda | 4.3 | 6.4 | 17.3 | 3.3 | 0.8 | — |
| **Deterioration** | | | | | | |
| Benin | -3.1 | -0.1 | -4.4 | -3.6 | 1.5 | -6.3 |
| C. Af. Republic | -2.6 | -2.9 | 4.7 | 1.0 | -1.0 | -0.8 |
| Rwanda | -5.5 | -0.1 | -4.1 | -1.2 | -3.3 | -2.4 |
| Sierra Leone | 2.9 | 1.4 | 7.8 | -2.3 | -1.8 | 9.7 |
| Togo | 1.4 | -1.8 | 7.4 | -2.6 | 0.8 | 4.1 |
| Zambia | 0.9 | -1.6 | 1.7 | -4.4 | -1.3 | -0.5 |
| Mozambique | 7.6 | 5.2 | 7.8 | 21.8 | -0.7 | — |
| Congo | -4.9 | 1.9 | -4.1 | -23.4 | -1.4 | -3.9 |
| Côte d'Ivoire | -2.6 | 8.2 | -1.1 | -6.4 | -0.8 | 1.0 |

*Sources*: World Bank, *Adjustment in Africa: Reforms, Results, and the Road Ahead* (Oxford: Oxford University Press, 1994); UNDP and World Bank, *African Development Indicators* (Washington, D.C.: World Bank, 1992).

**Table 2.2**
**Results of Analysis of Variance:**
**Comparison of Economic Performances Between Groups[a]**

|                  | $x_1$ | $x_2$  | $x_3$ | $x_4$  | $x_5$  | $x_6$ |
|------------------|-------|--------|-------|--------|--------|-------|
| F Value          | 1.42  | 0.24   | 1.41  | 1.28   | 0.36   | 1.27  |
| PR               | 0.27  | 0.79   | 0.27  | 0.30   | 0.70   | 0.31  |
| $R^2$            | 0.14  | 0.03   | 0.14  | 0.13   | 0.04   | 0.15  |
| Mean             | 0.63  | 0.86   | 3.53  | 0.72   | -1.26  | 1.88  |
| Mean Group 1     | 2.52  | -0.04  | 7.36  | 4.88   | -1.72  | 6.40  |
| Mean Group 2     | 0.93  | 1.14   | 3.10  | 2.27   | -1.41  | 1.97  |
| Mean Group 3     | -0.66 | 1.13   | 1.74  | -2.34  | -0.89  | 0.11  |
| Mean Difference  |       |        |       |        |        |       |
| Group 1–Group 2  | 1.59  | -1.18  | 4.26  | 2.60   | -0.31  | 4.43  |
| Group 1–Group 3  | 3.18  | -1.17  | 5.62  | 7.22   | -0.83  | 6.29  |
| Group 2–Group 3  | 1.58  | 0.01   | 1.36  | 4.62   | -0.53  | 1.85  |

[a]All figures are rounded to two decimal numbers.

A third study in which African countries are ranked differently from the World Bank study is that of the Heritage Foundation (see Table 2.4). In this study the criteria include: capital flows and foreign investment, banking policy, wage and price controls, property rights, regulation policy, and black market.

An alternative approach to ranking and categorizing countries is to correlate indicators of liberalization reforms with those of economic performance. Among the selected indicators of liberalization reforms are exchange rates ($x_1$), changes in total public expenditures as percentage of GDP ($x_2$), changes in real producer price of exports ($x_3$), and changes in fiscal balance ($x_4$). The data for these indicators are derived from the World Bank (see Table 2.5).[47] The same set of indicators of economic performance that were used in the first approach are used in this approach.

The second approach also provides at best mixed results (see Table 2.6). Changes in total public expenditures as percentage of GDP ($x_2$), changes in real producer price of exports ($x_3$), and changes in fiscal balance ($x_4$) appear to be significantly related to gross domestic investment as a ratio of GDP ($y_4$). Exchange rates ($x_1$) also appear to be significantly related to growth rates in GDP per capita ($y_1$). Changes in fiscal balance ($x_4$) is also significantly

**Table 2.3**
**Sachs and Warner's Classification of African Countries on the Basis of Trade Liberalization (Openness)**

| Closed by 1994 | Open by 1994 |
| --- | --- |
| Angola | Botswana |
| Burkina Faso | Gambia |
| Burundi | Ghana |
| Central Afr. Rep. | Guinea Bissau |
| Chad | Uganda |
| Congo | Benin |
| Côte d'Ivoire | Cameroon |
| Ethiopia | Kenya |
| Gabon | Zambia |
| Madagascar | |
| Malawi | |
| Mozambique | |
| Niger | |
| Nigeria | |
| Rwanda | |
| Senegal | |
| Sierra Leone | |
| Somalia | |
| Tanzania | |
| Togo | |
| Zaire | |
| Zimbabwe | |

*Source*: Jeffrey D. Sachs and Andrew Warner, "Economic Reform and the Process of Global Integration," *Brookings Papers on Economic Activity* 1 (1995): 1–118.

but inversely related to growth rates of the agricultural sector ($y_2$). No significant relations are noted between the rest of the indicators. Thus, contrary to the claims of proponents, empirical results do not provide conclusive support that SAPs have already made significant positive differences in African economies. UNDP's human development index figures for 1992 also provide no indication that adjust-

**Table 2.4**
**The Heritage Foundation's Ranking of African Countries on the Basis of Economic Freedom**

| Country | Score | Country | Score |
|---------|-------|---------|-------|
| Botswana | 2.8 | Cape Verde | 3.44 |
| Uganda | 2.83 | Tanzania | 3.45 |
| Swaziland | 2.9 | Cameroon | 3.6 |
| Benin | 2.95 | Lesotho | 3.65 |
| Zambia | 2.95 | Burkina Faso | 3.7 |
| So. Africa | 3.0 | Ethiopia | 3.7 |
| Kenya | 3.05 | Niger | 3.7 |
| Gabon | 3.06 | Zimbabwe | 3.7 |
| Mali | 3.1 | Sierra Leone | 3.75 |
| Ghana | 3.2 | Congo | 3.8 |
| Ivory Coast | 3.25 | Mozambique | 4.05 |
| Nigeria | 3.25 | Sudan | 4.1 |
| Guinea | 3.35 | Zaire | 4.2 |
| Madagascar | 3.35 | Angola | 4.35 |
| Malawi | 3.4 | Somalia | 4.7 |
| Senegal | 3.4 | | |

*Source*: Bryan T. Johnson and Thomas P. Sheehy, *1996 Index of Economic Freedom* (Washington, D.C.: The Heritage Foundation, 1996).

ing countries have made any notable improvement over non-adjusting or poorly adjusting countries (see Table 2.7).

These findings differ starkly from those of the World Bank.[48] One reason for the differences is that the World Bank's study analyzes the impact of macroeconomic policy stance, such as trade liberalization, or taxation of agricultural exports on the performance of specific sectors of the economy. While this method has some advantages, it does not analyze the impacts of specific policy changes on the overall economy. Moreover, this approach does not capture any tradeoffs or even conflicts among the different components of SAPs. The World Bank study also does not provide empirical testing of the impact of macroeconomic policies on agricultural and manufacturing outputs or on investments and savings.

**Table 2.5**
**Selected Indicators of Liberalization Reforms in Selected African States**

|  | $x_1$ | $x_2$ | $x_3$ | $x_4$ |
|---|---|---|---|---|
| Ghana | 283.7 | 2.9 | 96.5 | 4.0 |
| Tanzania | 255.4 | -2.3 | 8.3 | 7.6 |
| The Gambia | — | -5.7 | -25.0 | 7.4 |
| Burkina Faso | -4.7 | -9.9 | 30.6 | 6.0 |
| Nigeria | 404.4 | 5.2 | 46.5 | 1.4 |
| Zimbabwe | 49.9 | 7.1 | -4.8 | -0.1 |
| Madagascar | 99.2 | -2.3 | 5.3 | 0.7 |
| Malawi | 8.4 | -6.7 | -8.8 | 6.0 |
| Burundi | 56.7 | 1.5 | -18.1 | 5.2 |
| Kenya | 42.7 | -0.1 | -26.1 | 1.7 |
| Mali | -9.2 | 0.0 | 5.8 | 2.4 |
| Mauritania | 31.7 | -1.2 | — | 3.4 |
| Senegal | -14.0 | -4.8 | -11.7 | 4.8 |
| Niger | 4.3 | 1.6 | 2.6 | -2.4 |
| Uganda | 46.5 | -0.8 | -36.8 | 1.1 |
| Benin | -12.2 | -9.3 | 21.7 | 2.2 |
| C. Af. Republic | 1.4 | 2.7 | -1.8 | -2.2 |
| Rwanda | 8.1 | 5.0 | -23.3 | -3.3 |
| Sierra Leone | 34.6 | -1.7 | -62.0 | 4.3 |
| Togo | -4.7 | -9.6 | 15.8 | 0.3 |
| Zambia | 65.0 | -3.3 | -42.7 | 5.9 |
| Mozambique | 86.9 | 13.7 | 16.2 | 4.7 |
| Congo | -6.7 | -9.2 | -31.3 | -0.5 |
| Côte d'Ivoire | -20.8 | -0.8 | -49.6 | -6.2 |
| Cameroon | -27.1 | 0.8 | -44.3 | -8.5 |

*Source*: World Bank, *Adjustment in Africa: Reforms, Results, and the Road Ahead* (Oxford: Oxford University Press, 1994).

**Table 2.6**
**Regression Analysis of Relations Between Adjustment and Economic Performance[a]**

| Dependent Variables | Independent Variables Coefficients[b] | | | | F Value | Adjusted $R^2$ | Intercept |
|---|---|---|---|---|---|---|---|
| | $x_1$ $b_1$ | $x_2$ $b_2$ | $x_3$ $b_3$ | $x_4$ $b_4$ | | | |
| $y_1$ | 0.03** (0.01) | -0.10 (0.15) | -0.02 (0.02) | 0.28 (0.18) | 3.44 | 0.39 | -2.41 |
| $y_2$ | 0.02 (0.01) | -0.15 (0.19) | -0.03 (0.02) | -0.44* (0.22) | 1.24 | 0.06 | 0.01 |
| $y_3$ | 0.04 (0.03) | -0.29 (0.34) | -0.03 (0.04) | 0.10 (0.41) | 1.12 | 0.03 | -1.24 |
| $y_4$ | -0.04 (0.02) | 1.12*** (0.32) | 0.12** (0.04) | 0.99** (0.37) | 6.12 | 0.58 | 1.92 |
| $y_5$ | -0.00 (0.01) | -0.13 (0.14) | 0.00 (0.02) | -0.21 (0.16) | 0.66 | -0.10 | -1.49 |
| $y_6$ | 0.04 | -0.25 | -0.03 | -0.17 | 0.36 | -0.21 | -0.51 |

[a]All figures are rounded to two decimal numbers.
[b]Data in parentheses are standard errors of estimated coefficients.
* $p < .1$; ** $p < .05$; *** $p < .01$.

45

**Table 2.7**
**Human Development Index of African Countries**

| | |
|---|---|
| Ghana | 0.382 |
| Tanzania | 0.306 |
| The Gambia | 0.215 |
| Burkina Faso | 0.203 |
| Nigeria | 0.348 |
| Zimbabwe | 0.474 |
| Madagascar | 0.396 |
| Malawi | 0.260 |
| Burundi | 0.276 |
| Kenya | 0.434 |
| Mali | 0.214 |
| Mauritania | 0.254 |
| Senegal | 0.322 |
| Niger | 0.209 |
| Uganda | 0.272 |
| Benin | 0.261 |
| C. Af. Republic | 0.249 |
| Rwanda | 0.274 |
| Sierra Leone | 0.209 |
| Togo | 0.311 |
| Zambia | 0.352 |
| Mozambique | 0.252 |
| Congo | 0.461 |
| Côte d'Ivoire | 0.370 |
| Cameroon | 0.447 |

*Source*: UNDP, *Human Development Report, 1994* (New York and Oxford: Oxford University Press, 1994), 130–31.

## Impacts of SAPs on Structural Bottlenecks

As suggested by Eshag, an evaluation of the merits of economic reforms such as SAPs should take into account not only the impacts on growth rates and macroeconomic equilibria but also on the factors underpinning the economic imbalances as well as their ramifications.[49] Our evaluation of SAPs attempts to follow a similar approach. This section concentrates on the impacts of SAPs on some of the key structural bottlenecks of African economies.

Perhaps a more important problem with the interventionist-state thesis in the African case is that by emphasizing intervention and macroeconomic imbalances it has diverted attention from the fundamental structural obstacles to development. In this way it may have impeded the formulation of more holistic alternative strategies for change. Even if the magnitude of state intervention is a factor, it is not the only or even the major factor distinguishing African economies from those of other developing regions. As already noted, other factors that seriously impair Africa's socioeconomic development yet are neglected by the interventionist-state argument include: the predominance of the subsistence peasant sector, internal fragmentation of the economies of African states, uneven development and the crisis of nation-building (state-building) manifested by chronic internal conflicts, lack of diversification of exports, and Africa's inability to control the process of accumulation.

SAPs do not explicitly claim to deal directly with such intricately related, complex structural problems. It is, however, implied that curtailing state intervention and correcting macroeconomic imbalances would invigorate the economy. Growth, in turn, is expected to bring about a metamorphosis of the structural bottlenecks of socioeconomic development. It is highly presumptuous to expect sustainable growth to take place without arresting the structural problems such as those identified above. It is also very doubtful that growth can, by itself, overcome these problems. Moreover, it may not be possible to implement meaningful economic liberalization (marketization) without some success in overcoming the structural obstacles. We now examine the implications of SAPs for some of the identified structural problems that characterize African economies.

One key structural constraint is the predominance of the subsistence sector in African economies. Despite notable differences between individual countries, as noted in the previous chapter, Africa is dominated more than most other regions of the developing world by the peasant mode of production, which has very weak links with and influence over the modern sector. African farmers are a heterogeneous group ranging from the "resource-poor farmer" and "small-holders and herders" to the "middle or progressive farmers" and "estate" or "settler" farmers. The last group is engaged in cash crops and operates within the market system. By contrast, the first three groups, while by no means self-sufficient or totally insulated from it, are largely marginalized from the profit-driven exchange system and are primarily engaged in subsistence production.[50]

The subsistence peasantry is a source of cheap labor and sells limited quantities of food and livestock products and buys farm inputs and a small group of basic consumer goods such as clothing, oil, and sugar. As Duncan and Howell note, pastoralists in particular are heavily dependent on the market for their subsistence needs.[51] They exchange livestock and livestock products for food and other consumption goods. In its trade with the nonsubsistence sector, the peasantry often faces unequal terms of trade, for a variety of reasons.

Yet the production of the overwhelming majority of the peasantry is essentially use-value oriented. For the subsistence peasant, providing the food needs of the family and not exchange value (profit maximization) is the predominant determinant of allocative decisions.[52] One indirect indicator of this is the small proportion of the marketed portion of agricultural output which is estimated to be no higher than 12 percent of total output.[53] Since it has a limited role in allocation of resources, the nature of exchange in which the subsistence peasantry engages is different from the exchange in a capitalist system.

The peasantry is also marginalized from the public sector, where resources are largely allocated through policy. It has minimal influence on policy. As a result, its access to resources allocated by the state is limited. Therefore, the subsistence segment of the peasantry is, to a large extent, on the fringes of the domains of both the market and the state while, at the same time, it cannot escape operating within the socioeconomic structures established by the market and the state.

The peasantry's weak influence on national resource allocation leads to two types of socioeconomic disarticulation. One is internal fragmentation of African political economies. The modern sector lacks a domestic market and other linkages with the rest of the economy and operates essentially as an enclave relying heavily on the international market for its growth. Its excessive dependence on the international market, in turn, renders the modern sector highly vulnerable to international shocks.

Another aspect of the disarticulation of African economies is the dissociation of the use of available resources from social needs. Political power and economic resources are highly concentrated in the hands of the elite in the modern sector. Policy generally favors the more potent urban dwellers. Market allocation of resources also clearly favors the wealthier segments of society. Consequently, the peasant sector, deprived of resources, remains relegated to a subsistence level of production and unable to raise its productivity and translate its needs into demand. African private enterprises, especially the bigger and the more modern ones, largely bypass domestic social needs and rely on the international market for their process of capital accumulation. The neglect by many African countries of the nonexport sector of their economies, especially the food sector, is a clear reflection of this structural problem. Inputs such as fertilizers are concentrated in the export sector. The ratios of the average amount of fertilizers used in the cash-crop sector to those used in the food sector in 1979–1981, for instance, were 313 to 1 in Mauritius, 63 to 1 in Mozambique, 56 to 1 in Mali, 53 to 1 in Senegal, 32 to 1 in Sudan, 25 to 1 in Burkina Faso, 22 to 1 in Madagascar, 20 to 1 in Burundi, 18 to 1 in Liberia, 16 to 1 in Tanzania, and 10 to 1 in Cameroon.[54]

State control of prices, exchange rates, and credits has certainly contributed to the unfavorable terms of trade and deprivation of the agricultural sector in general and the food sector in particular. In view of this control, the World Bank notes that African agriculture faces the highest rates of taxation.[55] However, the neglect of the food sector and of the subsistence peasantry and the resulting food crisis (see Table 2.8) are not totally attributable to state intervention. They also have a lot to do with the combined effects of the nature of the existing global division of labor and the operations of the free market system.

The weakness of the domestic market and its inability to compete with the international market in attracting resources induces the mechanized commercial farmers to produce cash crops rather than food products. The small, market-oriented middle farmers, as they realize the lower returns from the domestic-market-oriented food products, follow in the footsteps of the mechanized farmers and often switch to cash-crop production after satisfying their own subsistence needs. Frequent food shortages and growing food-import bills are among the outcomes of this situation (see Table 2.8). The continued emphasis on cash crops and the concurrent neglect of the food sector are thus promoted by market forces and not simply by state intervention. Even when the state

**Table 2.8**
**Basic Indicators of Africa's Agricultural Crisis**

| | $x_1$ | $x_2$ | $x_3$ | $x_4$ |
|---|---|---|---|---|
| Ghana | 1.2 | 4.5 | 1.7 | 15.0 |
| Tanzania | -1.5 | 1.8 | 1.0 | 9.0 |
| The Gambia | -2.8 | 0.5 | 3.3 | 43.8 |
| Burkina Faso | 2.8 | 5.7 | 0.5 | 25.7 |
| Nigeria | 2.3 | 5.7 | 1.3 | 18.1 |
| Zimbabwe | -3.4 | 1.2 | 0.0 | 4.3 |
| Madagascar | -1.1 | 1.8 | 0.6 | 17.5 |
| Malawi | -3.1 | 1.0 | -0.2 | 8.1 |
| Burundi | -0.1 | 2.6 | 0.0 | 12.5 |
| Kenya | -0.4 | 2.9 | 0.2 | 9.0 |
| Mali | -0.9 | 2.5 | 0.0 | 24.7 |
| Mauritania | -1.2 | 1.5 | 2.3 | 51.1 |
| Senegal | 0.2 | 3.1 | 3.4 | 31.0 |
| Niger | -1.0 | 2.3 | 1.8 | 28.7 |
| Uganda | 0.2 | 3.2 | 0.8 | 7.3 |
| Benin | 2.2 | 5.6 | 0.9 | 27.1 |
| C. Af. Republic | -0.7 | 1.9 | 0.3 | 22.0 |
| Rwanda | -2.6 | 0.7 | 0.0 | 14.9 |
| Sierra Leone | -1.4 | 1.5 | 0.4 | 51.3 |
| Togo | 0.3 | 3.8 | 1.1 | 26.1 |
| Zambia | -0.6 | 3.2 | 0.5 | 5.5 |
| Mozambique | -1.8 | -0.4 | 1.4 | 26.2 |
| Congo | -1.8 | 1.1 | 1.3 | 16.9 |
| Côte d'Ivoire | -0.3 | 3.1 | 0.0 | 25.4 |
| Cameroon | -1.9 | 0.8 | 0.5 | 15.6 |

$x_1$=average annual growth rates of per capita food production (1980–93)
$x_2$=average annual growth rates of agriculture in % (1980–93)
$x_3$=average annual lag of growth rates of total agricultural production from annual growth rates of demand (1961–85)
$x_4$=food imports as percentage of total merchandise imports

*Sources*: UNDP, *Handbook of International Trade and Development Statistics 1993* (New York: United Nations, 1994); FAO, *Agriculture: Toward 2000* (Rome: FAO, 1987); UNCTAD, *Commodity Yearbook 1993* (New York: United Nations, 1993).

has the political will to correct the deprivation of the food sector, its efforts are often undermined by market forces.

In extreme cases, market forces even lead to large-scale starvation. The rapid growth of mechanized commercial farming and the concomitant evictions of tenants and nomads in Ethiopia in the late 1960s and early 1970s is a case in point. Thousands of tenants who became redundant with mechanization were evicted in many parts of the country. The fertile valley of the Awash river was one of the areas invaded by commercial farmers including multinational corporations which produced sugar cane and cotton. The displaced Afar nomads were forced to rely increasingly on the availability of rain in one of Ethiopia's drier regions. The result was livestock starvation followed by starvation of about 25 percent of the Afar population in the area during the famine of 1973.[56] The failure of the state in this case was twofold: (1) its inability to control the market's devastating impacts on the vulnerable nomads and (2) its failure to curtail market forces by state intervention.

In addition to the neglect and deprivation of the peasantry and the food sector, the emphasis on cash crops by many countries often leads to a general glut of these products on the world market. As a result, the prices of cash crops have faced a general decline. This, in concert with high export taxes and producer price controls, has made the cash crop sector sluggish. Yet it still remains more attractive than the food sector for the market-oriented producers, since the ratios of producer prices for export crops to food crops are generally very high (see Table 2.9).[57]

Basing economic decisions solely on market information and profit incentives may represent efficient allocation of resources on the part of private producers. However, it does not necessarily represent creative organization of national economies, especially when the needs of considerable portions of the population are bypassed. In Africa it has often led to the neglect of the peasantry and consequently to underutilization of the domestic dynamics of economic growth.

Unlike the more diversified economies, in Africa the firms which are engaged in the production of export-oriented products largely fail to perform the classic innovative role of the firm (aptly identified by Schumpeter[58]) as they bypass domestic social needs and have minimal linkages with the rest of the economy. In other words, the market in Africa largely fails to coordinate available resources with social needs. The ability of the market to coordinate resource allocation with social needs improves with increases in the standard of living of the general population and diversification of the economy. At the present stage of African development, however, the peasantry needs to raise its productivity and purchasing power and, with them, its influence on resource

51

**Table 2.9**

**Ratio of Producer Prices of Selected Cash Crops to Those of Maize in Three East African Countries (averages 1975–1985)**

|           | Kenya | Malawi | Tanzania |
|-----------|-------|--------|----------|
| Coffee    | 27.6  | 8.3    | 10.8     |
| Tea       | 18.1  | —      | —        |
| Tobacco   | —     | 6.6    | 9.6      |
| Groundnut | —     | 4.3    | —        |
| Cotton    | —     | 3.4    | 2.6      |

*Source*: Uma Lele, Robert E. Christiansen, and Kundhavi Kadiresan, *Fertilizer Policy in Africa: Lessons from Development Programs and Adjustment Lending, 1970–87* (Washington, D.C.: World Bank, 1989).

allocation for the market to be able to coordinate resources with social needs.

Enabling the subsistence sector to influence the market allocation of resources through improved productivity and purchasing power requires, among other things, downward redistribution of productive services. It also involves providing the peasantry with access to public services such as health care and educational facilities in order to improve its overall quality of life.

Proponents of SAPs expect some components of SAPs such as price decontrols, devaluation, and export promotion to facilitate the transformation of the peasantry. Contrary to expectations, the benefits of these policies to the peasantry have proved to be limited and even negative for several reasons. First, the benefits of devaluation essentially go to a small number of large cash-crop producers. Devaluation of the Ghanaian cedis, for example, raised the producer price for cocoa from c 12,000/tone in 1983 to c 174,000/tone in 1989. However, only 18 percent of Ghana's farmers produce cocoa and 94 percent of the gross cocoa income went to 32 percent of the cocoa producers, who have large operations.[59] The benefits to the cocoa sector failed to spill over to either the subsistence peasantry or the food sector. Terms of trade for food relative to nonfood consumer goods and to cocoa, in fact, declined drastically since 1983.[60]

Some small-holder farmers may switch from food to cash-crop production in response to the altered terms of trade brought about by devaluation. However, the participation of subsistence farmers in the cash-crop sector is limited for a host of reasons.[61] The world market (glut) in cash crops is also unlikely to sustain the transformation of the peasantry through cash-crop production. Furthermore, promotion of export-oriented cash crops may continue to discourage food production as it appears to have already done in Ghana[62] and Nigeria.[63]

The subsistence peasantry is also largely excluded from the benefits of price decontrols by its low productivity. Any such gains essentially go to the large-scale commercial farmers and the market-oriented above-subsistence farmers. The subsistence peasantry needs to improve its productive capacity before it can take advantage of price incentives. Access of subsistence farmers to productivity-raising agricultural research and extension services such as credits and fertilizers in most African countries was already dismal before SAPs. The deprivation of the peasantry in this regard is unlikely to be corrected under severe retrenchment of public expenditures. In the case of Nigeria, Ibeanu notes that devaluation raised the price of inputs to peasants without raising their earnings.[64] Fertilizer prices, for example, rose from N-40 in 1981–82 to N-110 by 1982–83, depressing the productivity and income of peasants. Nnoli also notes that following the devaluation of the naira in Nigeria, prices of improved seeds rose between 200 percent and 500 percent, and herbicides by up to 300 percent.[65]

It is widely believed that SAPs have reduced the welfare-promoting types of public investments (social income) such as in health care and education. However, such reductions have neither occurred in all adjusting countries nor have they been avoided in nonadjusting countries (see Table 2.10). As M. Lutlala, M. Kintambu, and M. Mvudi note, even when retrenchments have occurred in such expenditures they cannot all be attributed to the implementation of SAPs.[66] Rather, they are largely outcomes of the economic downturn and rising debt burden that African states have faced since the middle 1970s. Claims that reforming countries have been able to increase their expenditures on health and education are also untenable. The evidence of the World Bank,[67] for example, which makes such a claim, is highly suspect since Nigeria, a country classified with the reforming group, is conspicuously missing from the analysis although public expenditures have taken a nose-dive in that country.[68]

Aside from the limited social safety net mechanisms, SAPs, as already noted, are intended to promote growth while redistributive measures are mostly left to the market system's trickle-down process. However, it is highly unlikely that the "trickle-down"

**Table 2.10**
**Public Expenditures in Education and Health Before and After[a] SAPs in Three Groups of African Countries with Differences in Macroeconomic Policies (Expressed as Indices, 1980=100)[b]**

| | Education | | Health | |
|---|---|---|---|---|
| | Before | After | Before | After |
| **Large Improvements in Macroeconomic Policies** | | | | |
| Ghana | 58 | 99 | 67 | 132 |
| The Gambia | 57 | 48 | — | — |
| Burkina Faso | 119 | 134 | 105 | 118 |
| Nigeria | 94 | 49 | 81 | 48 |
| Zimbabwe | 152 | 153 | 135 | 133 |
| **Small Improvement in Macroeconomic Policies** | | | | |
| Côte d'Ivoire | 125 | 132 | 97 | 97 |
| Madagascar | 67 | 66 | 61 | 66 |
| Malawi | 112 | 124 | 97 | 100 |
| Kenya | — | — | 100 | 99 |
| Senegal | 72 | 25 | 104 | 113 |
| Niger | 63 | 70 | 84 | 106 |
| Uganda | 103 | 191 | 113 | 155 |
| **Deterioration in Macroeconomic Policies** | | | | |
| Sierra Leone | 104 | 91 | — | — |
| Togo | 109 | 97 | — | — |
| Zambia | 108 | 118 | 100 | 87 |

[a]Before SAPs represents the year the first adjustment loan was signed and the two pervious years. After SAPs refers to three years after the signing of the first adjustment loan.
[b]Considering the rapid rate of population growth, these figures represent relative decline in public services even when they have not declined in absolute terms.

*Source*: David E. Sahn, "Public Expenditures in Sub-Saharan Africa During a Period of Economic Reforms," *World Development* 20, no. 5 (1992): 673–93; World Bank, *Adjustment in Africa: Reforms, Results, and the Road Ahead* (Oxford: Oxford University Press, 1994).

process is capable of correcting the marginalization of large segments of the population, especially the subsistence peasantry. The World Bank itself was highly suspicious of a trickle-down process in the 1970s. This was clearly expressed by its then president, Robert McNamara, who stated:

Without rapid progress in small-holder agriculture throughout the developing world, there is little hope either of achieving long-term stable economic growth or significantly reducing the levels of absolute poverty. The fact is that very little has been done over the past two decades specially designed to increase the productivity of subsistence agriculture.[69]

As John Weeks notes, the World Bank, despite being a "development" bank, has shifted its focus to balance of payments and debt payments.[70] The U.S. Congress in its 1973 Foreign Assistance Act also stressed the need to end the trickle-down approach to development and concentrate on the lower 40 percent of the population of the less-developed countries.[71] SAPs represent a reversal of these antipoverty policies and it is abundantly clear that they have not shown any promising alternatives for transforming the subsistence sector.

Without the peasantry's transformation, it is difficult to envision how some of the other structural bottlenecks African countries face—including internal fragmentation, uneven development, ethnic conflicts, lack of export diversification, and the growing marginalization in the global system—can be surmounted. Real and perceived inequalities have already generated many paralyzing chronic regional, ethnic and religious conflicts in many African countries; Somalia, Rwanda, the Sudan, Burundi, Zaire, and Chad are only the most obvious cases. Needless to say, these problems are not creations of the market system itself. The state (colonial and post-independence) is largely responsible. However, given the inherent tendencies of the market system to promote inequalities, such problems cannot be corrected (at least not quickly enough) without an active role by the state in economic activity.

Despite claims to the contrary, SAPs are also unlikely to reverse Africa's marginalization within the global economy, for several reasons. Attainment of this goal is expected to be facilitated by the dual functions of devaluation—increasing market share for exports, and promoting exports by altering domestic relative prices in favor of exports. However, devaluation is unlikely to be successful in performing these two tasks.

Simultaneous devaluations by many developing countries (as is encouraged by SAPs) are unlikely to improve the market share of developing countries. Given the generally low demand elasticity of many primary commodities,[72] attempts to increase the volume of exports via devaluation by large number of countries is likely to lead to oversupply in the world market, resulting in further fall in prices.[73] A 50-percent increase in the production of cocoa in Ghana between 1983 and 1989, for example, was accompanied by a fall in foreign-exchange receipts.[74] African countries would be especially hurt by such developments due to their already weak market share. By the World Bank's own admission,[75] declining commodity prices, over which SAPs have no control, have already undermined the adjustment process itself in many countries.

Shifting relative prices in favor of exportables made possible by devaluation has also shown no indication of promoting export diversification. Under SAPs, export expansion—if it takes place—is likely to be limited to primary commodities. Industrial diversification in Africa is constrained by both technical and allocative inefficiencies. As Lipumba notes,[76] trade liberalization, which can help improve allocative efficiency, is not likely to remove technical inefficiency. In fact, without considerable improvement in technical efficiency and competitiveness, the import liberalization that SAPs impose is likely to undermine diversification through stiff competition from more established external competitors. Trade liberalization has already led to factory closedowns and workers' layoffs in several countries. Even South Africa, which has a relatively more advanced industrial sector, has suffered from trade liberalization. Footwear imports from China are estimated to have led to a reduction of 6,000 jobs in the country's footwear industry.[77]

As long as industrial diversification is not attained, Africa's unfavorable position in the global division of labor and its marginalization are unlikely to be reversed. The market for most primary commodities, which are supplied by a large number of developing countries, is essentially characterized by free competition, which offers no scope for power over others or to raise terms of trade.[78] By contrast, the market for the imports of developing countries' manufactured products and technology is often oligopolistic in nature. These provide the producers of these products, mostly the multinational corporations (MNCs) from the countries of the North, a great deal of power in tilting the terms of trade in their favor.

Due to their lack of success in transforming the subsistence sector and in placing the population and its needs squarely at the center of development policy, African economies fail to grow and to expand the domestic market significantly on the basis of internal dynamics. Their technical inefficiency and lack of competitiveness also prevent them from growing by relying on external dynamics. SAPs solve neither of these bottlenecks.

Moreover, SAPs tend to have an adverse impact on governance and state-building. High unemployment associated with privatization and reductions in public expenditures and inflation triggered by devaluation and price decontrols, have all contributed to lowering the standard of living of the general population, both in rural and urban areas. As a result, SAPs have encountered serious popular opposition in many countries. Under these conditions, sustaining them is likely to require an authoritarian state, as already noted. With SAPs reducing the state's redistributive and regulatory roles, there is also a danger that the state increasingly becomes an agent of concentration of wealth, losing any potential for playing a balancing role. In tandem with the failure to transform the peasantry and to promote internal integration, this is likely to impede state-building as well.

## Conclusion

Some aspects of SAPs are clearly essential. There is no doubt that governments have to exercise some macroeconomic responsibility. The debt crisis and declines in commodity prices and resource inflows to the continent have made cutbacks in public spending unavoidable for most African countries. Price controls, especially of farm gate prices, often discourage food production, worsening food shortages and raising the bills for food imports. State ownership of enterprises also serves little purpose when such enterprises prevent competition, create few economic externalities, and become a drain on the national treasury due to gross inefficiency.

Yet, despite SAPs, Africa's economic crisis has endured and there is no clear indication that SAPs will reverse the situation. First, they are too narrow in scope to be effective in dealing with Africa's multifaceted crisis. Second, across-the-board retrenching of the redistributive and regulatory roles of the state does not necessarily translate into a workable market system. More importantly, SAPs essentially perpetuate the extractive nature of African economic structures and the corresponding policies that generally bypass social needs, neglect internal dynamics for sustainable development, and accentuate internal fragmentation. As a result, they fail to reverse Africa's marginalization in the global economy.

They also constrain the potential role that the state can play in facilitating general socioeconomic development as well as the development of a market system. State intervention, which is designed to improve the productivity and income of the peasantry and thereby to raise aggregate demand for the overall economy, is not incompatible with marketization. Rather it creates the preconditions for a properly functioning market system. In the African situation, the market remains highly exclusive without such preconditions. We will come back to this issue in Chapter 5.

Finally, in recent years the World Bank has advocated the importance of capacity-building, not only for sustaining adjustment but also for promoting socioeconomic development in Africa.[79] Ironically, the MFIs have expropriated a great deal of policy-making responsibility from the African state by imposing a variety of conditionalities on African countries to ensure adherence to their own policy dictates. The basis for the implicit assumption that the international bureaucracy is more informed about African realities and/or that it is less self-serving than the national bureaucracy is unfounded. On the positive side, as already noted, SAPs seem to be losing their earlier fervor as indicated by the recognition of the importance of expenditures on health care, education, and some social safety-net mechanisms, which allow the state some redistributive role. If this trend proves to be true, developmentalist states are not likely to be severely hampered by SAPs. We now examine the integrated autocentric approach that such states are likely to follow.

## Notes

1. C. B. Macpherson, *The Real World of Democracy* (Oxford: Oxford University Press, 1966), 6.
2. World Bank and UNDP, *Africa's Adjustment and Growth in the 1980s* (Washington, D.C.: World Bank, March 1989); Bruce Bartlett, "The State and the Market in Sub-Saharan Africa," *The World Economy* 12, no. 3 (September 1989): 293–314; Larry Diamond, "Class Formation in the Swollen African State," *The Journal of Modern African Studies* 25 (December 1987): 567–96.
3. Adrian Wood, *Global Trends in Real Exchange Rates, 1960 to 1984*, World Bank Discussion Paper No. 35 (Washington, D.C.: World Bank, 1988). There are frequent claims, including those by the World Bank (see World Bank, *Adjustment in Africa*), that African currencies are relatively overvalued. This assertion is based mainly on the

margin of differences between official and black-market rates. However, this approach has problems. For details see Peter J. Montiel and Jonathan D. Ostry, "The Parallel Market Premium: Is It a Reliable Indicator of Real Exchange Rate Misalignment in Development Countries?" *IMF Staff Papers* 41, no. 1 (March 1994).

4. State ownership does not seem to prevent fast growth in the case of China.
5. Diamond, "Class Formation," 573.
6. Bartlett, "The State and the Market," 304.
7. Henri Anjac, "Cultures and Growth" and David C. McClelland, "The Achievement Motive in Economic Growth"—both in Mitchell A. Seligson, ed., *The Gap Between Rich and Poor* (Boulder: Westview Press, 1984).
8. R. Nurske, *Problems of Capital Formation in Under-Developed Countries* (Oxford: Oxford University Press, 1953); Simon Kuznets, "Towards a Theory of Economic Growth," in Robert Levachman, ed., *National Policy for Economic Welfare at Home and Abroad* (New York: Doubleday and Co. [Bicentennial Conference Series], 1955), 12–85.
9. IMF, "Poverty Reduction and Structural Adjustment Discussed at IMF Seminar," *IMF Survey*, 22, no. 12 (14 June 1993): 178–82.
10. Simon Kuznets, "Economic Growth and Income Inequality," *American Economic Review* 45, no. 1 (March 1995): 1–28.
11. FAO, *The State of Food and Agriculture 1990* (Rome: FAO, 1991), 85–100.
12. Some proponents of SAPs regard the intensified hardship on the poor as a short-run impact until the expected growth materializes. Others deny the relationship between adjustment and the worsening conditions of the poor. See David E. Sahn, "Public Expenditures in Sub-Saharan Africa During a Period of Economic Reforms," *World Development* 20, no. 5 (1992): 673–93.
13. World Bank, *Sub-Saharan Africa: From Crisis to Sustainable Growth* (Washington, D.C.: World Bank, 1989).
14. Ishrat Husain, *The Evolving Role of the World Bank: The Challenge of Africa* (Washington, D.C.: World Bank, 1994), 17.
15. Manfred Bienefeld, "The New World Order: Echoes of a New Imperialism," *Third World Quarterly* 15, no. 1 (1994): 34.
16. For details on the failure of the African state, see Robert H. Bates, *Markets and States in Tropical Africa* (Berkeley: University of California Press, 1981); John A.A. Ayoade, "States Without Citizens: An Emerging African Phenomenon," in Donald Rothchild and Naomi Chazan, eds., *The Precarious Balance: State and Society in Africa* (Boulder: Westview Press, 1988), 100–18; Edmund J. Keller, "The State in Contemporary Africa: A Critical Assessment of Theory and Practice," in Dankwart A. Rustow and Kenneth Paul Erikson, eds., *Comparative Political Dynamics: Global Research Perspectives* (New

York: HarperCollins, 1991), 134–59; and Crawford Young, *The African Colonial State in Comparative Perspective* (New Haven and London: Yale University Press, 1994).

17. Robert H. Bates, *Markets and States in Tropical Africa* (Berkeley: University of California Press, 1981); Sahn, "Public Expenditures."

18. Claudio Gonzaleaz-Vega, "Cheap Agricultural Credit: Redistribution in Reverse," in Dale W. Adams, Douglas H. Graham, and J. D. von Pischke, eds., *Undermining Rural Development with Cheap Credit* (Boulder: Westview Press, 1984), 120–32, esp. 120–21.

19. Antonio Gramsci, *Selections from Prison Notebooks*, ed. and trans. Quentin Moore and Geoffrey Nowell Smith (London: Lawrence and Wishart, 1971), 160.

20. Yusuf Bangura, "Authoritarian Rule and Democracy in Africa: A Theoretical Discourse," in P. Gibbon, Y. Bangura, and Arve Ofstad, eds., *Authoritarianism, Democracy and Adjustment* (Uppsala: Scandinavian Institute of African Studies, 1992). The position of the peasantry is not unified. It is likely, however, that the market-oriented above-subsistence segments would support price liberalization. The subsistence segment, on the other hand, is likely to oppose it since its disadvantages from SAPs outweigh its advantages.

21. Nii Kwaku Sowa, "Ghana," in Aderanti Adepoju, ed., *The Impact of Structural Adjustment on the Population of Africa* (London: UNFPA, Heinemann and James Currey, 1993); F. M. Mwega and J. W. Kabubo, "Kenya," in Aderanti Adepoju, ed., *The Impact of Structural Adjustment on the Population of Africa* (London: UNFPA, Heinemann and James Currey, 1993); Tayo Fashoyib, "Nigeria," in Aderanti Adepoju, ed., *The Impact of Structural Adjustment on the Population of Africa* (London: UNFPA, Heinemann and James Currey, 1993).

22. For details see the different chapter contributions in Aderanti Adepoju, *The Impact of Structural Adjustment on the Population of Africa* (London: UNFPA, Heinemann and James Currey, 1993).

23. Sowa, "Ghana," 17.

24. See Bienefeld, "The New World Order"; Ha-Joon Chang and Ajit Singh, "Public Enterprises in Developing Countries and Economic Efficiency," *UNCTAD Review* 4 (1993): 45–82.

25. Gerald K. Helleiner, "Outward Orientation, Import Instability and African Economic Growth: An Empirical Investigation," in Sanjaya Lall and Frances Stewart, eds., *Theory and Reality in Development: Essays in Honour of Paul Streeten* (London: Macmillan, 1986), 139–53; Sebastian Edwards, "Openness, Trade Liberalization, and Growth in Developing Countries," *Journal of Economic Literature* 31, no. 3 (September 1993): 1358–93.

26. Patricia Gray and Hans W. Singer, "Trade Policy and Growth of Developing Countries: Some New Data," *World Development* 16, no. 3 (March 1988): 395–403.

27. Paul Streeten, "Against Minimalism," in Louis Putterman and Dietrich Rueschemeyer, eds., *State and Market in Development: Synergy or Rivalry?* (Boulder: Lynne Rienner, 1992), 15–38; L. James Dietz, "Overcoming Underdevelopment: What Has Been Learned from the East Asian and Latin American Experiences?" *Journal of Economic Issues* 26, no. 2 (June 1992): 373–83.

28. Dietz, "Overcoming Underdevelopment"; Yung Chul Park, "Development Lessons from Asia: The Role of Government in South Korea and Taiwan," *The American Economic Review* 80 (May 1990): 118–21; Robert Wade, *Governing the Market: Economic Theory and the Role of Government in East Asian Industrialization* (Princeton: Princeton University Press, 1990); Amartya Sen, "Development— Which Way Now?" in Charles K. Wilber, ed., *The Political Economy of Development and Underdevelopment*, 4th ed. (New York: Random House, 1988).

29. World Bank, *The Asian Miracle* (Oxford: Oxford University Press, 1993).

30. *Africa Confidential* 35, no. 20 (7 October 1994).

31. Giovanni A. Cornia and Frances Stewart, "Country Experience with Adjustment," in G. A. Cornia, R. Jolly, and F. Stewart, eds., *Adjustment with Human Face*, vol. 1 (Oxford: Clarendon Press, 1987), 105–27.

32. FAO, *The State of Food and Agriculture 1990*, 53.

33. Paul Krugman, "The Case for Stabilizing Exchange Rates," *Oxford Review of Economic Policy* 15, no. 3 (Autumn 1989): 65.

34. IMF, "Liberalization and the Role of the State Highlighted at World Bank Conference," *IMF Survey* (31 May 1993): 173.

35. IMF, "Liberalization and the Role of the State."

36. James Caporaso, "The State's Role in Third World Economic Growth," *The Annals of the American Academy of Political and Social Science* 459 (January 1982): 103–11.

37. Giovanni Sartori, "Rethinking Democracy: Bad Polity and Bad Politics," *International Social Science Journal* 129 (August 1991): 437–50.

38. Bela Balassa, "Adjustment Policies and Development Strategies in Sub-Saharan Africa," in Moshe Syrguin, Lance Taylor, and Larry E. Westphal, eds., *Economic Structure and Performance* (New York: Academic Press, 1984), 316–40; Daniel Landau, "Government and Economic Growth in Less Developed Countries," in *The Report of the President's Task Force on International Private Enterprise: Selected Papers* (Washington, D.C.: U.S. Government, 1984), 17–41.

39. Kidane Mengisteab and B.I. Logan, "Implications of Liberalization Policies for Agricultural Development in Sub-Saharan Africa," *Comparative Political Studies* 22, no. 4 (January 1990): 437–57.

40. World Bank, *World Bank Annual Report* (Washington, D.C.: World Bank, 1991); World Bank, *Adjustment in Africa: Reforms, Results, and*

*the Road Ahead* (Oxford: Oxford University Press, 1994); IMF, "Closer Integration in Global Economy Vital for Africa," *IMF Survey* 24, no. 14 (17 July 1995): 217–20.

41. Ishan Kapur, Michael T. Hadjimichael, Paul Hilberts, Jerald Schiff, and Philippe Szymczak, "Ghana Adjustment and Growth, 1983–1991," IMF Occasional Paper No. 86.

42. Robert Sharer, Christian Schiller, and Miftah Ahmad, "Uganda's Sustained Structural Reforms Yield Broad Gains," *IMF Survey*, 23, no. 2 (24 January 1994): 21–24.

43. UN Economic Commission for Africa, *African Alternative Framework to Structural Adjustment Programmes for Socio-Economic Recovery and Transformation* (Addis Ababa: E/ECA/CM.15/6/Rev. 3).

44. *Africa Recovery* (December 1991): 21.

45. Nii K. Bentsi-Enchill, "NGOs Widen Anti-Adjustment Action," *Africa Recovery* 6, no. 3 (November 1992): 26–27.

46. World Bank, *Adjustment in Africa*.

47. World Bank, *Adjustment in Africa*, 242–50.

48. World Bank, *Adjustment in Africa*.

49. E. Eshag, "Some Suggestions for Improving the Operation of IMF Stabilization Programmes," *International Labor Review* 128, no. 3 (1989): 297–319.

50. Carl K. Eicher, "African Agricultural Development Strategies," in Frances Stewart, Sanjaya Lall, and Samuel Wangwe, eds., *Alternative Development Strategies in Sub-Saharan Africa* (New York: St. Martin's Press, 1992), 86.

51. Alex Duncan and John Howell, "Assessing the Impact of Structural Adjustment," in Alex Duncan and John Howell, eds., *Structural Adjustment and the African Farmer* (London: Overseas Development Institute, 1992), 7.

52. Eric R. Wolf, *Peasants* (Englewood Cliffs, NJ: Prentice Hall, 1966); Frank Ellis, *Peasant Economies* (New York: Cambridge University Press, 1989); Duncan and Howell, "Assessing the Impact of Structural Adjustment."

53. D. Ghai and L. Smith, *Agricultural Price Policies and Equity in Sub-Saharan Africa* (Boulder: Lynne Rienner, 1987), 60–67.

54. FAO, *Atlas of African Agriculture* (Rome: FAO, 1986).

55. World Bank, *Adjustment in Africa*.

56. Lars Bondestam, "People and Capitalism in North Eastern Lowlands of Ethiopia," *Journal of Modern African Studies* 12, no. 3 (1974): 432–39.

57. Uma Lele, Robert E. Christiansen, and Kundhavi Kadiresan, *Fertilizer Policy in Africa: Lessons from Development Programs and Adjustment Lending, 1970–1987* (Washington, D.C.: World Bank, 1989).

58. Joseph A. Schumpeter, *The Theory of Economic Development* (Cambridge, MA: Harvard University Press, 1934).

59. John Araka et al., "Farmers Adjust to Economic Reforms," *African Farmer* 3 (April 1990): 5–15.

60. Sowa, "Ghana," 13–14.

61. Duncan and Howell, "Assessing the Impact," 6.

62. Sowa, "Ghana."

63. Okechukwu Ibeanu, "The Deteriorating Condition of the Nigerian Peasantry," in Okwudiba Nnoli, ed., *Dead End to Nigerian Development: An Investigation of the Social, Economic, and Political Crisis in Nigeria* (Dakar, Senegal: CODESRIA, 1993), 124–53.

64. Ibeanu, "The Deteriorating Condition," 124–53.

65. Okwudiba Nnoli, "Dead End to Nigerian Development," in O. Nnoli, ed., *Dead End to Nigerian Development: An Investigation of the Social, Economic, and Political Crisis in Nigeria* (Dakar, Senegal: CODESRIA, 1993), 223.

66. M. Lutlala, M. Kintambu, and M. Mvudi, "Zaire," in Aderanti Adepoju, ed., *The Impact of Structural Adjustment on the Population of Africa* (London: UNFPA, Heinemann and James Currey, 1993).

67. World Bank, *Adjustment in Africa*.

68. Sahn, "Public Expenditures."

69. Quoted by John Cohen, *Integrated Rural Development: The Ethiopian Experience and Debate* (Uppsala: Scandinavian Institute of African Studies, 1987).

70. John Weeks, *Development Strategy and the Economy of Sierra Leone* (New York: St. Martin's and Macmillan, 1992), 2.

71. Cohen, *Integrated Rural Development*, 13.

72. Pasquale L. Scandizzo and Dimitris Diakosawas, *Instability in the Terms of Trade of Primary Commodities 1900–1982* (Rome: FAO Economic and Social Development Paper No. 64, 1987); Stewart, Lall, and Wangwe, "Alternative Development Strategies: An Overview," 32.

73. Alfred Maizels, "The Impact of Currency Devaluation on Commodity Production and Exports of Developing Countries," University College London, Discussion Paper No. 86–07, 1986; M. Godfrey, "Trade and Exchange Rate Policy: A Further Contribution to the Debate," in T. Rose, ed., *Crisis and Recovery in Sub-Saharan Africa* (Paris: OECD, 1985), 168–79.

74. Frances Stewart, Sanjaya Lall, and Samuel Wangwe, "Alternative Development Strategies: An Overview," in Frances Stewart, Sanjaya Lall, and Samuel Wangwe, eds., *Alternative Development Strategies in Sub-Saharan Africa* (New York: St. Martin's Press, 1992), 32.

75. World Bank, *Trends in Developing Economies* (Washington, D.C.: World Bank, 1993).

76. Nguyuru H.I. Lipumba, *Africa Beyond Adjustment* (Washington D.C.: Overseas Development Council, Policy Essay No. 15, 1994), 45.

77. *Southern Africa Business Intelligence* 77 (17 November 1995): 6.

78. James A. Caporaso and David P. Levine, *Theories of Political*

*Economy* (Cambridge: Cambridge University Press, 1993), 165–66.

79. See Nii K. Bentsi-Enchill, "Breaking the Expatriate Grip on Africa," *Africa Recovery* 7, no. 1 (June 1993): 13.

# Part 2
## An Autocentric Approach

# 3
# An Autocentric Approach and Economic Integration in Sub-Saharan Africa

▼  ▼  ▼

## Relevance of Integration

Regional integration has received renewed attention in the post-Cold War era. The success of the European Community (EC) and the long delay of the Uruguay Round GATT negotiations (concluded in December 1993) are factors that likely contributed to the revival of regionalism.[1] In the Western hemisphere, the North American Free Trade Agreement (NAFTA) between Canada, Mexico, and the United States has been successfully implemented and there are indications that it may be expanded to include Chile and possibly other Latin American and Caribbean countries in the future.[2] The Southern Cone Common Market (MERCOSUR) between Brazil and Argentina, created in 1990, has been extended to Paraguay and Uruguay. Many of the older regional groupings in Latin America, including the Latin American Integration Association (LAIA), the Central American Common Market (CACM), the Andean Group, and the Caribbean Community and Common Market (CARICOM) have also seen some revitalization. The Enterprise for the Americas Initiative, which aims to achieve hemispheric free trade between the United States and twenty-nine Central and Latin American states, also appears to be in the making.

In Asia, in addition to the growing importance of the Association of South East Asian Nations (ASEAN), there are a number of proposals including ASEAN Free Trade Area (AFTA), East Asian Economic Caucus (EAEC), and an Asia Pacific Economic Cooperation (APEC).[3] Although there are no new initiatives, the Arab Common Market (ACM) and the Gulf Cooperation Council (GCC) have been in operation in the Middle East since 1964 and 1981, respectively. With the disintegration of the Soviet Union, regional integration schemes are also sprouting in central and Eastern Europe as well as in central Asia. The Central European Free-Trade Area, which is comprised of Slovenia, the Czech Republic, Hungary, Poland, and Slovakia, is one of them.

Considerable effort has also been made to rejuvenate many of Africa's regional integration schemes, including the Economic Cooperation of West African States (ECOWAS), the Preferential Trade Area (PTA) of eastern and southern African states, the Southern African Development Cooperation (SADC), and the Communaute Economique de l'Afrique de l'Ouest (CEAO), the Union Douanière et Economique de l'Afrique Centrale (UDEAC), and the Mano River Union (MRU). The PTA and SADC have also begun a merger process to form the Economic Community of Eastern and Southern African States (ECESAS). Discussions are also presently underway to resuscitate the defunct East African Community (EAC). The Organization of African Unity (OAU) has been urging these schemes so as to strengthen their integration and begin a process of merger into a continental full economic union. At an OAU Summit in Abuja in June 1991 African states signed a treaty to establish an African Economic Community (AEC), also known as Pan African Economic Community. The OAU expects a full African Economic Community, with a single currency and a Pan-African parliament, to be realized by the year 2025.

The relevance of economic integration among developing countries is, however, seriously questioned by some. According to de Melo and Panagariya, for example, integration between developing countries does not markedly improve market access since the size of the markets of these countries is limited.[4] These authors also contend that instead of promoting a growth-stimulating environment, regional integration is likely to lead to regional protectionism in developing countries. Skepticism on the relevance of regional integration is greater in the case of sub-Saharan Africa. Some have in fact argued that African countries "are not each others' natural trading partners."[5] One of the aims of this chapter is to refute such a contention by establishing the relevance of regional integration for sub-Saharan African states. Another objective is to examine what type of integration is appropriate for the region and how it relates to internal integration as well as to integration with the global economy. Finally, the chapter attempts to show why regionalism is essential for autocentric development in Africa.

The apprehension about the relevance of regional integration in developing countries emanates in part from the view that there is a tradeoff between regional integration and integration with the global economic system. Many scholars and policymakers view integration with the global economy as the best strategy for promoting faster growth, while they associate regionalism with protectionism, which in turn is linked to slow growth due to the inefficient allocation of resources which regionalism is believed to entail. This view is epitomized by the following statement by Mr. M. Camdessus, the Managing Director of the IMF:

> In fact, open economic relations with the rest of the world provide one of the most reliable generators of growth. The jury is no longer out on this issue: the verdict is clear—the most open economies have been the most successful.[6]

Given the complexity and delays in multilateral negotiations for free trade, some regard regionalism as a second-best as well as a strategy that can allow faster progress towards the ultimate goal of global free trade.[7] The differences between these two views are largely with respect to tactic and thus they can be collapsed into one. Another view contends that, given the differences in levels of economic diversification, the assertion of the benefits of global free trade cannot be generalized to all countries. Instead this view emphasizes regional integration as a strategy for development and not as a different way of getting at global free trade.[8] In Africa, the Organization of African Unity (OAU), the Economic Commission for Africa (ECA), and the African Center for Development and Strategic Studies (ACDESS—an African "think tank" founded by Adebayo Adedeji, the former Executive Secretary of the UN Economic Commission for Africa, and presided over by Julius Nyerere, the former president of Tanzania) share this second view.

The above-identified approaches, especially the first one, manifest some important deficiencies. They both pay inadequate attention to the internal integration that is necessitated by the magnitude of sectoral and regional disparities and fragmentation which characterize African economies. The implicit tradeoffs between global integration and regional integration on which the first (globalist) approach is premised is another problem.

The relationships between the three levels of integration are complex. On the one hand, they all impede the development of each other. As noted in chapter 1, globalism exacerbates internal and regional fragmentation. A regional trading bloc and excessive introversion can also obstruct global integration. On the other hand, all three levels need each other. Internal integration cannot advance without the benefits of globalism, and internal and regional fragmentation clearly hamper proper global integration. A principal hypothesis of this chapter is that in Africa's case all three levels of integration—internal, regional, and global—are, in fact, compatible with each other if implemented in a manner that is properly sequenced and balanced. (None of the three levels of integration can be successfully achieved without sufficient attention to the other two.) Implied in this hypothesis is that the perceived tradeoffs between the three levels are more apparent than real, especially in the longer run.

## Why Internal Integration Is Essential

As noted in the previous two chapters, the domination of their economies by a subsistence peasant sector, which in some cases comprises up to 80 percent of the total population, is a critical structural problem that distinguishes sub-Saharan African countries from most other developing countries. The peasant sector is largely deprived of economic resources, including productivity-raising technological inputs and public services such as health care, education, and transportation facilities. Its influence on decision-making is also minimal. In addition, the peasantry's involvement in the modern economic sector which is closely linked with the global market is limited. The exportable cash crops are essentially produced in estates or plantations. The mining industries also employ a small segment of the population. Only enclaves of African economies are closely linked with the global system.

The origins of this structural distortion go back to the incorporation of African economies into the global capitalist division of labor, mostly through colonialism. With incorporation, African economies were restructured to supply the colonial powers with inexpensive labor, raw materials, and primary commodities. Hardly any production system that would benefit the general population and link it with the global system was introduced. In many cases, the African population was prohibited by law from participation in the production of some cash crops. Kenyan farmers were, for example, barred from producing coffee, which was reserved for white settlers. The production of goods and services for domestic consumption also received little encouragement.

Despite political independence, the distortion and extroversion of African economies largely remained unchanged. The economic sector connected with the global market has continued to engross a lion's share of available resources. As noted in Chapter 2, the proportion of fertilizers used in the cash-crop sector to that applied in the food sector is a case in point. The ratio of producer prices for export crops to food crops is another indicator (see Table 2.9). Yet the ability of the enclave sector to expand on a sustainable basis has been limited. Paradoxically, the more it expands the more it is undermined by gluts of primary commodities and price decreases. Under such conditions the general population has remained largely relegated to the traditional sector bypassed by the modern economic system. The enclave sector has also remained highly dependent and unstable. African economies have essentially reached a dead end as they remain unable to control the process of capital accumulation and to involve the general population in the modern production process by significantly expanding the enclave sector.

With a regional market of negligible size (due to a low standard of living) and a production system that supplies but few primary products (which can be readily and often more cheaply supplied by other producers), Africa's relevance to the global economy has been severely eroded. Africa's share of gross world production in 1990, for example, was less than 1.7 percent.[9] Moreover, internal fragmentation, uneven development, and growing poverty have undermined the process of state-building and encouraged political instability by fostering ethnic and regional cleavages. Instability has, in turn, exacerbated Africa's marginalization within the global economy by hindering ordinary economic activity and by making it unsafe and unattractive for foreign investment.

Under these conditions, neither regionalism nor global integration are likely to succeed. It seems that it is critical for African countries to promote an autocentric development strategy that pays more serious attention to correcting the internal fragmentation by placing the general population at the center of the production process and thereby releasing the internal sources of dynamism. External sources of growth and development are essential complements, but in most cases they are not likely to become substitutes for domestic sources.

71

Internal integration, which is a critical aspect of an autocentric approach to development, involves measures that transform the subsistence sector into a surplus-producing exchange economy by gearing resources to the raising of its productivity and standard of living. Access to such factors as appropriate tools, fertilizers, seeds, educational and training facilities, health care, transportation, irrigation, banking services and credits is essential in transforming the subsistence peasantry. Transformation of the peasantry is also a critical component of the process of state-building and political stability in Africa. Exchange economy in rural areas can foster interdependence not only within the rural sector but also between rural and urban areas. By alleviating the problem of dualism, it can foster internal interdependence, moderate uneven development, and mitigate ethnic strife that has plagued African countries. Improving the purchasing power of the peasantry also has the potential to stimulate economic diversification on the basis of agriculture-led industrialization and to extricate domestic sources of growth by expanding the domestic market. As noted in the previous chapter, Zimbabwe seems to have made some strides in rural transformation.[10] Internal integration has also the potential to create conditions for integrating African economies within themselves as well as with the global economy at a higher level of participation.

## Global Integration

The globalist approach essentially represents an advocacy for decontrolling prices and exchange rates so that domestic prices are aligned with international prices. It also prescribes promotion of exports and liberalization of imports and investment codes. However, it fails to provide any specific strategies for export diversification and transformation of the peasantry. African countries have continued to depend heavily on exports of primary commodities. In 1975 manufactured goods accounted for 7.1 percent of sub-Saharan Africa's exports as compared with 17 percent for developing countries. In 1990 the share of manufactured goods to total exports remained at 12.5 percent in sub-Saharan Africa versus 55.4 percent in developing countries.[11]

As a leading sector, the export sector, which is favored in resource allocation, is expected by the globalist approach to bring about the transformation of the subsistence sector. The expectations have not materialized. Instead, the results have been in many cases internal colonization of the peasantry, including more marginalization, evictions, impoverishment, and migration to urban areas. There is also little diversification of products that is attributable to the export-promotion strategy.

Support for the globalist approach is based on a number of controversial claims. One is that the structural transformation and economic development of countries such as Taiwan, South Korea, Hong Kong, and some of the members of ASEAN have been brought about by closer integration with the global economic system through the export-promotion strategy based on a free market system. As noted in Chapter 2, the NICs are characterized more by a developmentalist state[12] governing the market[13] than by a free market. Most of these countries also started their industrialization process along an import-substitution strategy although their success became more visible after they switched to an export-oriented strategy.[14]

The experiences of the NICs and the debates surrounding them raise two important questions. One is whether the export-oriented strategy is appropriate for African states or if they have to start with a collective import-substitution strategy in order to create a more diversified export basis first. Another related question is whether the export-promotion strategy can work effectively in the absence of a considerable degree of foreign investment and access to foreign markets.

Even if the success of the NICs and ASEAN countries can be attributed to export promotion, the strategy cannot be considered appropriate for African states, for two reasons. One is that the economic structures of the Asian NICs are fundamentally different from those of African countries. The NICs are not exporters of cash crops. Moreover, unlike Africa, their populations are not marginalized from the production process that links them with the global system. A second reason is that the international environment that African states now face has changed significantly from what it was in the 1960s and 1970s. The level of access to foreign markets that was available to the NICs in the 1960s and early 1970s is no longer available. Unlike the ASEAN countries, international capital, by and large, is also inaccessible to African countries. In 1987, for example, the whole of Africa received less foreign investment than Singapore alone. Only about 5.6 percent of direct foreign investment to developing countries went to Africa in the same year and almost 90 percent of that amount went to five countries—Algeria,

Cameroon, Egypt, Nigeria, and Tunisia.[15] As indicated in Table 3.1, sub-Saharan Africa's share of foreign investments as a ratio of the total foreign direct investments in developing countries has declined markedly in more recent years.

Serious theoretical and empirical doubts linger about the relations between the export expansion and economic performance in developing countries.[16] Moreover, in the absence of rapid increase in foreign investments, which can help in diversifying exports, the export-promotion strategy is unlikely to succeed. Whatever diversification occurs is also likely to encounter serious difficulty in market access. It is very likely that the export-promotion strategy would provoke (if it hasn't already) a protectionist response by OECD countries, making its implementation by late comers more difficult.[17] There are a number of reasons why most African states are not likely to be competitive in attracting direct foreign investment in the short run. The real and perceived political instability and lack of developed infrastructure are among them.

Another rationale underlying the export-promotion strategy is that developing countries have a comparative advantage in labor-intensive manufactures. Abundance of low-cost labor by itself does not ensure a comparative advantage, however, since it is only one among many factors. As already noted, few African states are diversified enough to benefit from this advantage. Few have the necessary capital to engage their labor resources productively.

Despite such glaring obstacles, proponents continue to overgeneralize the appropriateness of the globalist approach to all countries, including those that face declining terms of trade, are decapitalized, undiversified, and internally fragmented. This overgeneralization also appears to fail to distinguish between integration with the global economy and openness. Much of the neo-liberal literature of the 1980s has claimed that one of the reasons for the economic malaise of sub-Saharan African economies is that region's failure to integrate itself more closely with the global economy. There is little doubt that Africa is malintegrated with the global economy. The most important criterion used in such analysis, however, is openness, as if openness were the same as integration.[18] If integration means to become an integral part of a system and to be able to influence the system and to make a difference while being impacted by it, then openness is at best only a necessary but not a sufficient condition.

African economies are as open if not more open than most other developing economies. As claimed frequently, many African

**Table 3.1**

**Comparison of Foreign Direct Investment Inflows to Developing Areas (in US$ Millions)**

| Year | Sub-Saharan Africa | East Asia & the Pacific | Latin America & the Caribbean | South Asia |
|------|-------------------|------------------------|------------------------------|------------|
| 1986 | 684.5 | 3,546.3 | 3,553.4 | 260.5 |
| 1987 | 1,392.9 | 4,486.5 | 5,772.2 | 407.5 |
| 1988 | 1,133.8 | 7,602.1 | 7,999.2 | 326.3 |
| 1989 | 2,607.9 | 9,085.9 | 7,982.8 | 486.9 |
| 1990 | 856.0 | 11,038.2 | 7,668.9 | 469.3 |
| 1991 | 1,774.0 | 14,029.5 | 12,374.6 | 475.6 |
| 1992 | 1,613.5 | 20,487.5 | 14,506.5 | 566.0 |
| 1993 | 1,714.0 | 36,481.0 | 16,089.0 | 841.0 |
| 1994 | 2,987.0 | 43,037.0 | 20,811.0 | 1,242.0 |

*Source*: World Bank, *Financial Flows and the Developing Countries* (Washington, D.C.: World Bank, 1994); and World Bank, *Global Economic Prospects and the Developing Countries* (Washington, D.C.: World Bank, 1995 and 1996).

states have lost market share of many of their primary exports.[19] However, this decline does not necessarily indicate that they have become less open. The most commonly cited causes for the decline of market share of Africa's exports include political instability, lack of economic diversity, increased energy costs, drought, inability of governments to respond to adversities, and declining commodity prices.[20] These factors indicate that African states have become less competitive, not less open. Among the appropriate indicators for the degree of openness are the proportion of foreign trade to GDP, the impact of trade on GDP growth rates, exchange rate alignment, and the levels of effective tariff and nontariff barriers to trade. Reliable comparative data are difficult to obtain on the last indicator. However, according to the data provided by Sachs and Warner,[21] in the mid-1980s only Burkina Faso, Nigeria, Malawi, Rwanda, and Zimbabwe would be regarded as protectionist. The first two countries had tariff rates exceeding 40 percent of value while the other three countries had nontariff barriers covering 40 percent or more of trade.

In terms of the proportion of foreign trade to their GDP, African states, by and large, compare rather well with other

**Table 3.2**
**Degree of Openness of African Economies and Other Developing Regions**

| Region | Exports as % of GDP (1990) | % Growth Rates of Column 1 (1980–1990) | Imports as % of GDP (1990) | Exports and Imports as % of GDP (1990) |
|---|---|---|---|---|
| All dev. countries | 19 | 0.1 | 21 | 42 |
| Least dev. countries | 10 | 1.2 | 18 | 29 |
| Sub-Saharan Africa | 25 | 1.4 | 21 | 46 |

*Source*: UN Development Programme, *Human Development Report 1993* (New York and Oxford: Oxford University Press, 1993).

developing countries (see Table 3.2). As Hardy notes, Africa's high score, in fact, understates its openness since subsistence production accounts for between 30 and 40 percent of its total GDP.[22] In terms of the impact of trade on the economy also, growth rates in OECD imports and Africa's barter terms of trade accounted for over 80 percent of the variations in the growth rates of African economies between 1960 and 1990.[23] In addition, Wood's study of exchange rate trends[24] shows that exchange rates of African currencies were, by and large, comparable with those of other countries between the mid-1960s and the mid-1980s (see Table 3.3). Since then, most African countries have been engaged in a frenzy of devaluations. African countries perform poorly when low black-market premiums or their absence is used as a gauge of openness.[25] However, the validity of this indicator is highly suspect.[26]

Despite their relative competitiveness in degree of openness, African countries are clearly the most marginalized within the global economy. Openness (export orientation) per se is not a sufficient indicator of integration with the global economy. Diversification of exports which involves diversification of production, ability to attract foreign investment, and ability to penetrate foreign markets are better indicators. In terms of such indicators, Africa's marginalization becomes glaringly evident (see Table 3.4). Africa can be as open as it wants to, it is not likely to be integrated into the global economy without raising its productive contribution (its

**Table 3.3**
**Actual Real Exchange Rate Trends by Country Groups (1980–1984 Average as Ratio of 1960–1964 Average)**

| Region/Country | Official Rate | Black-Market Rate |
|---|---|---|
| India | 0.62 | 0.83 |
| China | 0.40 | 0.96 |
| Other low-income econ. | 0.60 | 0.58 |
| Low-income Africa | 0.76 | 0.58 |
| Low-income Asia | 0.59 | 0.74 |
| Oil-importing middle-income countries | 0.87 | 0.95 |
| High-income oil exporters | 3.52 | 3.66 |
| Industrial economies | 1.00 | — |

*Source*: Adrian Wood, *Global Trends in Real Exchange Rates, 1960–1984*, World Bank Discussion Paper No. 35 (Washington, D.C.: World Bank, 1988), 66.

value) to the rest of the global community. Africa's share of gross world product, measured in terms of market exchange rates, averaged only about 2.01 percent during 1970–79. This has declined to 1.67 percent during 1980–89.[27]

By using inappropriate indicators for global integration and by failing to clarify under what conditions openness and export orientation become beneficial, the globalist approach has run into a number of problems:

1. It has continued to emphasize an export-promotion strategy when all indications are that the demand and prices of African exports would continue to be bleak.

2. It has not been able to clearly distinguish the differences between dependency (malintegration) and integration with the global economy.

3. It has not been able to devise strategies for integration with the global economy that insulate African countries from net outflow of resources to the countries of the North.

Developing countries differ markedly in their levels of economic diversification and in their ability to benefit from an export-promotion strategy. Thus, the claim that liberalization accompanied by

**Table 3.4**

**Structure of Exports and Terms of Trade in Selected Regions**

| Region | Terms of Trade Averages 1985–1992 | Manufacturing as % of GDP 1991 | Exports of Primary Commodities as % of Total Exports 1991 |
|---|---|---|---|
| Sub-Saharan Africa | -3.85 | 11.3 | 90.7 |
| Asia | -0.20 | 19.21 | 30.0 |
| Western Hemisphere | -3.63 | 18.90 | 73.7 |
| Developing Countries | -2.60 | — | — |

*Source*: Computed from International Monetary Fund, *World Economic Outlook* (Washington, D.C.: IMF, 1993); and World Bank, *World Development Report* (Washington, D.C.: Oxford University Press, 1993).

export promotion may offer the best strategy for enhancing development[28] cannot be generalized to all developing countries. Most sub-Saharan African countries do not presently possess the production capability to take advantage of such a strategy. Moreover, the effectiveness of the export-promotion strategy depends on the global environment which is a variable that undergoes constant change.

The foregoing analysis is not a rejection of integration of Africa with the global economy. There is no doubt that African states need foreign technology, foreign capital and access to foreign markets. Rather, the analysis suggests that: (1) export promotion per se does not promote growth and development since it all depends on what is exported, at what terms of trade, and how involved the general population is in the production of the export products; (2) there is an important distinction between mere openness and integration with the global economy; and (3) when reliance on the global sources of growth are pursued with little regard for internal sources and conditions, they tend to lead to dependency, which undermines the benefits of integration and is not likely to promote export diversification.

## Regional Integration

The regionalist approach faces a problem similar to that facing the globalist approach. It too fails to directly deal with internal integration, without which African countries lack the structural requisites to successfully integrate with each other. Regionalism without internal integration is essentially an effort to integrate the extroverted commercial enclaves of African economies. Integration of this sector, however, is unlikely to succeed since it is dominated by the production of primary products geared to OECD markets and lacks complementarity to allow intra-African integration. The lofty goals of the Abuja Treaty are thus unlikely to be achieved without internal integration of African economies.

As neo-liberals charge, regional integration may also be based on the import-substitution strategy, which has faced a number of serious constraints, including markets and foreign exchange. Pooling their markets together may give African states some relief from market constraint.[29] Collective import substitution would clearly have a higher saturation point than an import-substitution strategy in a single country. Yet in the absence of significant regional markets, due to the marginalization of the masses, this approach is not likely to be dynamic enough to invigorate African economies.

When accompanied by internal integration that transforms the peasantry, however, regionalism has the potential to promote a number of developments. First, it can expand the domestic markets of African states and thereby expand the saturation point for selected collective import-substitution industrialization. Secondly, it promotes complementarity among their economies and mobilizes underutilized internal dynamics of development by coordinating production with social needs and internal resources.

Given the dead end their economies face and their present growing marginalization within the global economy, it is likely that some African countries would begin to turn inwards and restructure their economies by transforming their subsistence sectors and integrating their fragmented economies. One indicator that African countries would benefit by turning their attention to the neglected domestic source of dynamism is that the main impetus to their increased manufacturing output has come from growing domestic demand (including import-substitution industries) rather than exports.[30] Africa's share of world exports of manufactured goods, estimated at 0.36 percent in 1980, has fallen. Its share of total world industrial output, however, increased, albeit modestly, from 0.83 percent in 1970 to 0.97 percent in 1980.

Internal integration through the transformation of the subsistence sector together with regional integration may give African countries a fighting chance in overcoming their overwhelming structural economic problems and their marginalization within the global economic system. Since each country's resource base and domestic market are too small, even with internal integration, a single country's self-reliance strategy is unlikely to be successful. A regional collective self-reliance strategy would, to some extent, enable late comers (such as African states) to complement an export-promotion strategy by a combination of agriculture-led diversification and regional import substitution. This mix of different strategies has a greater potential to provide them with larger markets and a wider resource base to promote economic diversification than either export-promotion or import-substitution strategies on individual country basis. Reliance on internal and regional dynamics for growth also has the potential to reduce their loss of control of the process of accumulation. Moreover, by expanding their markets, it would help make their economies more attractive to foreign investments and enhance their bargaining power both economically and politically. As Wangwe notes, however, collective self-reliance is only a complement to individual country self-reliance.[31]

## What Type of Regional Integration?

There are three principal types (or stages) of regional integration: functional cooperation in limited areas; trade integration (free trade agreement, customs union, and common market); and production coordination. The latter is a higher stage that incorporates the other two types and involves joint ventures and planned distribution of selected industries among members. Most African integration schemes, including the PTA and ECOWAS, follow the trade-integration strategy. SADC was characterized by the limited cooperation approach until 1992, when it adopted the trade-integration strategy.[32] Production coordination, which is the more difficult approach to implement, has not been seriously attempted in Africa, although the 1991 Abuja Treaty embraces it.

It has been widely debated as to which one of these strategies is more appropriate for African countries. Some argue that market integration is more likely to foster development (since it promotes more efficient allocation of resources) than the state-induced production coordination, which involves regional industrial planning.[33] Others claim that diversifying production through production coordination is the more appropriate alternative, given the small size of African markets and the absence of complementarity in their economies, which undermines trade-integration efforts.[34] A third argument is that both the trade-integration (common market) and production-coordination strategies are unlikely to be achieved in Africa. Market integration is undermined by lack of complementarity of African products and also by the unequal distribution of benefits it tends to generate among the members. Production coordination is considered to require too much state involvement in economic activity and a political commitment that is not presently available in Africa. According to this argument, functional cooperation, which is the least ambitious and easiest to implement of the three strategies, is the most realistic one.[35]

The limited cooperation strategy is clearly the easiest to implement since it infringes less on national sovereignty. It also has minimal impact on the revenue governments obtain from tariffs or foreign trade. There are also important benefits from this strategy, including creation of common infrastructure and provision of common services such as common civil aviation and shared universities and research facilities. SADC, for example, has attained notable progress in rehabilitating and developing transportation and communication infrastructure among its members.[36] Developing transportation and communication facilities in the Beira Corridor connecting Zimbabwe and Mozambique is perhaps one of its most notable achievements. When fundamental changes that lead to internal integration are not clearly in sight, this minimalist approach, which does not require internal integration, becomes particularly relevant. However, it is not likely that the rewards of limited area specific cooperation are sufficient to overcome Africa's structural problems and reverse its marginalization.

The debate in respect to the other two strategies is related to the general debates over the appropriate roles of the state and the market, the relative importance of capital formation and efficient allocation of resources, and the appropriateness of export-promotion and import-substitution strategies in enhancing the process of development. As already noted, neo-liberals advance the hypothesis that minimal state intervention, allocative efficiency brought about by a free market, and export promotion supported by free trade promote faster development.[37] However, neither theory nor empirical evidence provide a conclusive support for this hypothesis.[38] The state in Africa has generally been corrupt, compounding market failure with failure of the state. Yet this does not mean that a developmentalist state cannot emerge in Africa, especially if the current democratization struggle in the continent succeeds at least in some countries. These issues will be discussed in greater detail in Chapter 5. There is also no compelling reason why a developmentalist state, which manages the market in order to promote capital formation and poverty alleviation and to initially encourage agriculture-led diversification and collective import substitution in order to create conditions for export promotion, would be any less successful in generating development. Despite widespread claims to the contrary, the East Asian model fits more with the latter hypothesis than with the free-market strategy. There is, therefore, no obvious reason why, given a conducive political framework, trade integration and production coordination cannot complement each other to promote development.

Given the low level of complementarity of African economies and the severe capital constraint they face, production coordination through joint projects and coordinated distribution of some key industries would seem to be more appropriate for promoting economic diversification and complementarity through a more effective utilization of limited resources.[39] Coordinated distribution of industries also has the potential to increase welfare gains and reduce the unequal distribution of benefits which plagues many common market integration schemes.[40] However, trade integration is also an essential component of the division of labor that production coordination entails. Production coordination, therefore, is a higher level of cooperation that incorporates the other two types.

Of course, production coordination does not mean that the distribution of every industry has to be coordinated. Rather the prime candidates for coordination are large industries, especially those of capital goods that require considerable sums of capital and a significant market size to operate efficiently and are essential, due to the economic externalities they generate. Coordination of such industries with freer competition in the areas of agriculture and light industries can promote divergence and complementarity among African economies.

Production coordination is not an easy strategy to implement properly. Agreements on what country is responsible to develop what industries are difficult to reach. However, it is not insurmountable if there is a high degree of political commitment and if economic rationale, such as comparative advantage and ability to sustain such industries, becomes the guiding principle for such allocations. The division of responsibility to develop certain industries among SADC members, for example, is a good beginning.

Production coordination also involves a combination of temporary tariff sheltering and subsidies, including tax relief and preferential access to credit and foreign exchange to selected agriculture-linked and/or import-substituting industries. As proponents of open trade argue, tariff protection may encourage inefficient industries. Subsidies may also exacerbate budgetary deficits. However, liberalizing trade with the rest of the world before some degree of economic diversification is achieved may also undermine the industrialization effort and thereby the whole development process. African states considerably opened up their economies in the 1980s.[41] Yet this has not enhanced their industrialization nor has it reversed their declining access to international markets and international capital. In fact, as Mkandawire argues,[42] trade liberalization in tandem with devaluation may have deindustrialized many of them. Recent experiences of Nigeria, Tanzania, Ghana, and Ivory Coast, for instance, suggest that rapid reductions of trade barriers have undercut local producers by bringing about a flood of cheaper imported products. This happened despite the protection that devaluation provides. In the Ivory Coast, the number of workers employed in textiles dropped from 12,000 in 1982 to 8,000 in 1987 due to imports.[43] In Nigeria also trade liberalization was followed by rampant closures of factories, with manufacturers often blaming the difficulties on the reduction of protectionist barriers and sharp increases in the costs of inputs triggered by devaluation.[44] This is further confirmed by the predictions by an OECD and World Bank-commissioned study that Africa will be the only regional loser from the Uruguay Round GATT agreement. Its losses, primarily due to termination of preferential access to OECD markets of its exports, are estimated to reach $2.6 billion annually by 2002.[45]

There is also no reason why certain agriculture-linked and import-substituting industries cannot become efficient and even expand to become exporters overtime. A sheltered or subsidized collective import-substitution industrialization is essentially a short-run strategy which, through diversification, can be expected to create conditions for more openness and a greater degree of participation in global trade. The strategy of sheltered regional import-substitution industrialization with strategic trading with the rest of the world conflicts with the logic of openness of the emerging global order. It is, thus, uncertain if the current global power structure would allow African countries to pursue such a strategy unless they act as a bloc. Clearly, African countries need to strengthen their political integration to allow independence in policy making. The Organization of African Unity needs to play a more active role in this regard.

## Prospects for Success and Obstacles

African integration schemes—both those of trade integration and those of functional cooperation—have been poorly implemented. Such generally accepted indicators of performance as intraregion trade and growth rates of GDP, agriculture, industry, manufacturing, and per capita agricultural production clearly reflect a disappointing record (see Table 3.5). The poor performance of African integration schemes is accentuated by the presence of untapped potential for intra-African trade and by the continent-wide black-market trade (which is estimated to be about the same size as the official trade, although there are no reliable data).[46]

A number of factors account for the lack of success of African integration schemes. The extroverted nature of their economies, poor infrastructure, lack of communication and information, and the debt crisis and import strangulation (which have halted their process of industrialization) are among the major obstacles to regional integration. A widespread colonial legacy, which has distorted the consumption habits of the relatively wealthier segments of society in favor of imports from industrialized countries, also contributes to the lack of success of African regional integration schemes. Preference of imported synthetic clothing over locally produced cotton fabrics in many African countries is a vivid example. The globalist approach, which advocates export promotion and import liberalization and which is supported by IMF and World Bank conditionalities, has also contributed to preventing African leaders from pursuing a more autocentric development approach.

Absence of monetary cooperation among African states is another serious obstacle that has to be overcome before regional integration can occur in Africa. Integration in these countries cannot attain its potential without a coordinated system of pay-

84

**Table 3.5**
**Performance of Selected African Integration Schemes**

|  | PTA | ECOWAS | SADCC | CEAO | UDEAC |
|---|---|---|---|---|---|
| Avg. Intraregion Exports 1985–1990 | 7.95 | 6.66 | 3.28 | 9.58 | 3.76 |
| Avg. Annual Growth of GDP 1980–1990 | 2.60 | 2.40 | 2.90 | 2.10 | 3.20 |
| Avg. Annual Growth of Agriculture 1980–1990 | 1.80 | 2.80 | 1.70 | 2.30 | 2.70 |
| Avg. Annual Per Capita Growth of Agriculture 1980–1989 | -1.20 | 0.41 | -1.70 | 0.32 | -1.32 |
| Avg. Annual Growth of Industry 1980–1990 | 3.30 | 3.00 | 3.20 | 4.10 | 4.70 |
| Avg. Annual Growth of Manufacturing 1980–1990 | 3.60 | 3.30 | 3.10 | 4.40 | — |

*Source*: World Bank, *World Development Report* (Washington, D.C.: Oxford University Press, 1992); Augusto de la Torre and M. R. Kelly, *Regional Trade Arrangements* (Washington, D.C.: International Monetary Fund, 1992); Ajay Chhibber and Stanley Fischer, *Economic Reform in Sub-Saharan Africa* (Washington, D.C.: World Bank, 1991; and United Nations, *World Economic Survey* (New York: United Nations, 1990).

ments and a financial infrastructure, including export credits and export insurance to support their regional trade. African manufactured products are not likely to be more competitive than the products from elsewhere in the short and intermediate runs. They may, however, become attractive if their purchase is not hindered by foreign exchange constraints. The African Development Bank, the ECA, and the OAU can play leading roles in providing financial, technical, and political support to African regional integration schemes to develop a stable system of payments. It is hard to envision significant progress in African integration without considerable progress in this regard. Continued reliance on OECD currencies for conducting trade among themselves amounts to continued reliance on cash-crop exports in order to obtain hard currencies. It is also equivalent to the colonial infrastructure in which telecommunication linkages among African capital cities were routed through London or Paris.

Loss of revenue that results from significant reductions of tariffs, uneven distribution of the gains and costs of integration, and political instability are other important obstacles to integration. Liberia's political unrest, for example, has undermined the Mano River Union (MRU) between Liberia, Sierra Leone, and Guinea.

Yet lack of political commitment on the part of African governments has to be regarded as a principal factor. As Ravenhill notes,[47] African integration remains largely "an act of faith" and governments have done little to support integration schemes beyond issuing rhetoric. African leaders have continued to give lip service to regionalism for various reasons.[48] (One reason is that since they blame the international environment for much of the economic problems of their countries, the rhetoric of regionalism gives an appearance of commitment on their part to control the destiny of their economies.) Most of these leaders, however, do not translate their rhetoric into deeds. As benefactors of the existing system, many of them are its defenders and not real agents of change and promoters of internal and regional integration.

Despite all these obstacles, there are a number of factors that would provide a ray of hope for genuine regional integration in Africa. One is the growing marginalization of Africa within the global economic system. It has increasingly become clear that continued reliance on the existing extroverted economic structures has led to a dead end. As Kari Levitt notes,[49] the industrialized world has a decreasing need for the countries of the periphery. Under these conditions, reorienting their economies inward and regionally is likely to be seen as the strategic option for survival. ECOWAS, for example, has referred to the 1990s as "Integration for Survival."[50]

The current democratization struggle that has engulfed the continent also gives another reason for optimism. If democratization succeeds, it is likely to have a significant impact on the existing duality and internal fragmentation of African economies. By empowering the general population, genuine democratization can help in transforming the peasantry and reorienting the production system toward meeting internal needs (see Chapter 4).

As noted in Chapter 1, an African civil society is emerging. Part of this civil society is a group of small enterprise owners.[51] A shift toward internal integration and regionalism is likely to be regarded by this social group and by the private sector in general as a new opportunity. The vigor shown by the informal economic sector—and by the small scale enterprises that serve the masses—relative to the formal sector and the bigger enterprises, may be indicative that the private sector is discovering a new source of dynamism. There is thus the potential that both the private sector and the reformed state may become partners in internal and regional integration.

Africa's food crisis and the opportunity it affords potential surplus food producers is another factor for optimism. Africa's deficit of some food products, such as maize, is expected to grow five-fold, from about 10 million tons in 1990 to about 50 million tons in the year 2000.[52] With the Uruguay Round GATT agreements, food prices are expected to rise with the reduction of subsidies. This situation is likely to provide an incentive for greater intra-African trade, especially if the integration schemes can devise a workable system of payments.

Broadening the scope of Africa's integration schemes to areas of security is another factor likely to boost African integration. ECOWAS' modest success in peace-keeping activities in Liberia (although it appears short-lived) is an important step in this direction.[53] African integration schemes also need to act collectively in their dealings with external actors. They can, for example, enhance their position if they negotiate with the MFIs collectively.

The nature of intra-African trade is also promising. Africa's exports to the rest of the world are essentially primary commodities. Intra-African trade, by contrast, is mainly in manufactures, the growth of which is more promising, especially since markets for Africa's manufactured exports are limited elsewhere. Africa's industrialization is thus very much tied to intra-African trade.

Finally, the liberation of South Africa and its entry as a member of SADC may also boost regionalism, at least within the Southern African region if not throughout ECESAS. The level of industrialization of the South African economy is likely to enhance trade complementarity as well as investment opportunities within the region.

In conclusion, despite the well publicized failure of Africa's various global integration schemes, a collective self-reliance development strategy remains a more promising alternative for the development of African countries. Success in modifying the existing economic structures and overcoming the problems of economic crisis and marginalization within the global economic system, if at all possible, is likely to come when African countries integrate themselves internally and regionally. Such an integration has the potential to facilitate the transformation of the subsistence peasantry and thereby to foster state-building by stimulating interdependence among different ethnic groups. It can also promote capital formation, control of the process of accumulation, market expansion, and more efficient allocation of resources. It also makes the simultaneous application of agriculture-led diversification, import-substitution, and export-promotion strategies possible. Internal and regional integration are thus critical aspects of an autocentric approach to development. Debate about the different strategies of integration is not very useful. According to our analysis, cooperation, trade integration, and production coordination are essentially complementary approaches of the same process rather than competing alternatives.

## Notes

1. Augusto de la Torre and M. R. Kelly, *Regional Trade Arrangements* (Washington, D.C.: International Monetary Fund, 1992).
2. "Regionalism and Trade," *The Economist*, 16 September 1995, 23–27.
3. de la Torre and Kelly, *Regional Trade Arrangements*; Helen Hughes, "Does APEC Make Sense?" *ASEAN Economic Bulletin* 8, no. 2 (November 1991): 125–36.
4. Jaime de Melo and A. Panagariya, *The New Regionalism in Trade Policy* (Washington, D.C.: World Bank, 1992).
5. Faezeh Forontan, "Regional Integration in Sub-Saharan Africa: Post Experience and Future Prospects," in Jaime de Melo and Arvind Panagariya, eds., *New Dimensions in Regional Integration* (Cambridge and New York: Cambridge University Press, 1993), 260.
6. International Monetary Fund, "Camdessus Cites Ways to Ease Transition to Market Economies," *IMF Survey* 22, no. 13 (28 June 1993): 195.
7. For details on the debate between multilateralism and regionalism, see Jagdish Bhagwati, "Regionalism Versus Multilateralism," *The World Economy* 15, no. 4 (September 1993): 535–55; David Henderson, "International Economic Integration: Progress, Prospects and Implications," *International Affairs* 68, no. 4 (1992): 633–53; Paul Krugman, "Regionalism Versus Multilateralism: Analytical Notes," in Jaime de Melo and Arvind Panagariya, eds., *New Dimensions in Regional Integration* (Cambridge and New York: Cambridge University Press, 1993), 58–79.
8. The literature on the debate over the benefits of free trade is vast. For good reviews see Sebastian Edwards, "Openness, Trade Liberalization, and Growth in Developing Countries," *Journal of Economic Literature* 31, no. 3 (September 1993): 1358–1393; and Lance Taylor, "Economic Openness: Problems to the Century's End,"

in Tariq Brown, ed., *Economic Liberalization: No Panacea: The Experiences of Latin America and Asia* (Oxford: Clarendon Press, 1991), 99–141.

9. United Nations, *Trends in International Distribution of Gross World Product* (New York: Department for Economic and Social Information and Policy Analysis Statistical Division, 1993).

10. A. M. Hawkins, "Can Africa Industrialize?" in Robert J. Berg and Jennifer S. Whitaker, eds., *Strategies for African Development* (Berkeley: University of California Press, 1986), 288.

11. United Nations Industrial Development Organization, *African Industry in Figures* (Vienna: UNIDO, 1993), 24, 46.

12. Gordon White, ed., *Developmental States in East Asia* (London: Macmillan, 1988).

13. Robert Wade, *Governing the Market: Economic Theory and the Role of Government in East Asian Industrialization* (Princeton: Princeton University Press, 1990).

14. James Dietz builds a strong argument that export promotion per se does not lead to success in economic diversification. He attributes the success of the NICs to their ability to switch from one strategy to the other when conditions were ripe. In the African case, export promotion at the present time may imply continued reliance on the primary commodities. African countries may, thus, require an import-substitution strategy to diversify their products before they can rely on the export-promotion strategy for their growth. James L. Dietz, "Overcoming Underdevelopment: What Has Been Learned from the East Asian and Latin American Experiences?" *Journal of Economic Issues* 26, no. 2 (June 1992): 373–83.

15. United Nations, Industrial Development Organization, *Foreign Direct Investment to Developing Countries* (New York: United Nations, 1990).

16. Taylor, "Economic Openness," 99–141.

17. Mike Douglass, "Global Opportunities and Local Challenges for Regional Economies," *Regional Development Dialogue* 13, no. 2 (Summer 1992): 3–21; Robin Broad and John Cavanagh, "No More NICs," in Gerald Epstein, Julie Graham, and Jessica Newbhard, eds., *Creating a New World Economy* (Philadelphia: Temple University Press, 1993), 326–90; William R. Cline, *Exports of Manufactures from Developing Countries: Performance and Prospects for Market Access* (Washington, D.C.: The Brookings Institution, 1982), 89.

18. Ali Mansoor and Andras Inotai, "Integration Efforts in Sub-Saharan Africa: Failures, Results and Prospects—A Suggested Strategy for Achieving Efficient Integration," in Ajai Chhibber and Stanley Fischer, eds., *Economic Reform in Sub-Saharan Africa, A World Bank Symposium* (Washington, D.C.: World Bank, 1991), 217–232.

19. Stephen R. Lewis, "Africa's Trade and the World Economy," in Robert J. Berg and Jennifer S. Whitaker, eds., *Strategies for African*

*Development* (Berkeley: University of California Press, 1986), 479.

20. Lewis, "Africa's Trade and the World Economy," 479–80. Overvaluation of currencies is one of the factors often regarded as leading to loss of market share. With the exception of a few countries, African currencies were not significantly overvalued relative to those of many other countries. Adrian Wood, *Global Trends in Real Exchange Rates, 1960–1984*, World Bank Discussion Paper No. 35 (Washington, D.C.: World Bank, 1988). The spiraling devaluations of the 1980s have also not begun to show any regaining of market share.

21. Jeffrey D. Sachs and Andrew Warner, "Economic Reform and the Process of Global Integration," *Brookings Papers on Economic Activity* 1 (1995): 1–118.

22. Chandra Hardy, "The Prospects for Intra-regional Trade Growth in Africa," in Frances Stewart, Sanjaya Lall, and Samuel Wangwe, eds., *Alternative Development Strategies in Sub-Saharan Africa* (New York: St. Martin's Press, 1992), 427.

23. Lewis, "Africa's Trade and the World Economy," 480.

24. Wood, *Global Trends*.

25. Sachs and Warner, "Economic Reform,."

26. For details see Peter J. Monteil and Jonathan D. Ostry, "The Parallel Market Premium: Is It a Reliable Indicator of Real Exchange Rate Misalignment in Developing Countries?" *IMF Staff Papers* 41, no. 1 (March 1994): 55–75.

27. United Nations, *Trends in International Distribution*, 313.

28. Henderson, "International Economic Integration," 633–53.

29. As de Melo and Panagariya point out, the size of African markets is limited even with integration and thus the benefits from economies of scale may be limited. (De Melo and Panagariya, *The New Regionalism in Trade Policy*.) However, the market size would clearly be larger under integration than without it. Also, if integration succeeds, one of its dynamic objectives is to expand these markets.

30. Hawkins, "Can Africa Industrialize?" 281.

31. S.M. Wangwe, "A Comparative Analysis of the PTA and SADCC Approaches to Regional Economic Integration," in World Bank, *The Long-Term Perspective Study of Sub-Saharan Africa*, vol. 4, Proceedings on a Workshop on Regional Integration and Cooperation (Washington, D.C.: World Bank, 1990), 37.

32. *Africa Recovery* (November 1992): 35.

33. Mansoor and Inotai, "Integration Efforts in Sub-Saharan Africa." This argument is essentially built on the assumption that the state is self-serving and pursues policies that advance the interests of a given social class at the expense of national development. While this is generally the case at the present time, it does not necessarily imply, as Dietz ("Overcoming Development") points out, that the state inherently retards development. The state can also play a

developmentalist role by representing the interests of those that favor development.

34. A. Ashiabor, "Emerging Complementarities in African Economies," in *The Long-Term Perspective Study of Sub-Saharan Africa*, vol. 4, Proceedings of a Workshop on Regional Integration and Cooperation (Washington, D.C.: World Bank, 1990), 96–101; Nguyuru H.I. Lipumba and Louis Kasekende, "The Record and Prospects of the Preferential Trade Area for Eastern and Southern African States," in Ajai Chhibber and Stanley Fischer, eds., *Economic Reform in Sub-Saharan Africa, A World Bank Symposium* (Washington, D.C.: World Bank, 1991), 233–44.

35. Robert L. Curry, Jr., "Regional Economic Co-operation in Southern Africa and Southeast Asia," *ASEAN Economic Bulletin* 8, no. 1 (July 1991): 15–28; Reginald H. Green, "Economic Integration/Co-ordination in Africa," in James Pickett and Hans Singer, eds., *Towards Economic Recovery in Sub-Saharan Africa* (London and New York: Routledge, 1990), 106–28; John Ravenhill, ed., *Africa in Economic Crisis* (London, New York: Basingstoke, 1986).

36. Curry, "Regional Economic Co-operation."

37. Neo-liberals seem to favor free trade under multilateralism rather than regionalism. If regionalism is unavoidable, however, they seem to favor trade integration over other forms of integration.

38. For details on this argument see Wade, *Governing the Market*.

39. Lipumba and Kasekende, "The Record and Prospects of the Preferential Trade Area."

40. Scott R. Pearson and William D. Ingram, "Economies of Scale, Domestic Divergences, and Potential Gains from Economic Integration in Ghana and the Ivory Coast," *Journal of Political Economy* 88, no. 51 (1980): 994–1008.

41. Mansoor and Inotai, "Integration Efforts in Sub-Saharan Africa."

42. Thandika Mkandawire, "The Road to Crisis, Adjustment and De-industrialization: The African Case," *Africa Development* 13, no. 1 (1988): 5–31.

43. Ernest Harsch, "Privatization: No Simple Panacea," *Africa Recovery* 2, no. 3 (August 1988): 14.

44. Harsch, "Privatization," 14.

45. Ian Goldin, Odin Knudsen, and Dominique van der Mensbrugghe, *Trade Liberalization: Global Economic Implications* (Paris and Washington, D.C.: OECD/World Bank, 1993).

46. Hardy, "The Prospects for Intra-regional Trade Growth," 437–38.

47. Ravenhill, *Africa in Economic Crisis*, 94.

48. Cyril Daddieh, "Structural Adjustment Programs and Regional Integration: Compatible or Mutually Exclusive," in K. Mengisteab and B.I. Logan, eds., *Beyond Economic Liberalization in Africa* (London: Zed Press, 1995).

49. Kari Levitt, "Debt, Adjustment and Development: Looking to the

1990s," *Economic and Political Weekly*, 21 July 1990, 1587.

50. Peter DaCosta, "A New Role for ECOWAS," *Africa Report* 36, no. 5 (September 1991): 37–40.

51. Fautu Cheru, *The Silent Revolution in Africa: Debt, Development and Democracy* (London: Zed Books, 1989).

52. World Bank, *Sub-Saharan Africa: From Crisis to Sustainable Growth* (Washington, D.C.: World Bank, 1989).

53. Obed Asamash, "A New Role for ECOWAS," *Africa Report* 35, no. 5 (October 1990): 17–20; DaCosta, "A New Role for ECOWAS."

# 4

# Democratization and
# Autocentric Development in
# Sub-Saharan Africa

▼   ▼   ▼

## Introduction

Another development that has engulfed most of the African
continent since the second half of the 1980s is a wave of democratization struggle. Africa is clearly at a turn in history, as is much of
the rest of the developing world. Opposition parties are being
formed, dictators are being overthrown, and multiparty elections,
although often faulty, are taking place in a growing number of
African states. According to the Carter Center, which monitors such
developments, only a few African states have not yet jumped onto
the democratization bandwagon.[1]

Despite the setbacks it has already faced in several countries,
including Nigeria, Togo, Brundi, and the Gambia, the new democratization drive has generated a great deal of hope in improving
general human conditions, including civil liberties such as freedom
of speech and association, human rights, human resources, and
standard of living. Many commentators, in fact, see democracy as
a precondition for socioeconomic development. There is little doubt
that, as a political (or socioeconomic) system, democracy would
affect the rate of socioeconomic development. There are, however,
different types of democracy as well as processes of
democratization. Globalization and autocentricity, for example, are
compatible with different types of democracy. The impact of those
different types on socioeconomic development also varies. The
primary concern of this chapter is with two questions: (1) What

type of democratization would have more significant impact in reversing Africa's skid into deepening socioeconomic crisis? And (2) How likely it is that democratization will be successful in Africa in the near future?

The chapter is organized into two parts, each part dealing with the two questions, respectively. The relationships between democracy and socioeconomic development are analyzed by examining the impacts of democracy on the transformation of the subsistence sector, on integration of the fragmented economic sectors, on expansion of the domestic market, and on resolution of internal conflicts. The reasons for selecting these indicators have already been discussed in Chapter 2. The second part evaluates the strengths and weaknesses of the forces that promote democracy in order to determine the prospects for successful democratization in Africa in the near future.

## Impacts of Democracy on Socioeconomic Development

There is a general consensus that democracy is a sociopolitical arrangement that empowers the general population to control the public decision-making process on an ongoing basis.[2] Since there is no country where popular control is complete, democracy is a process towards that goal rather than a finished product. In this respect, the terms democracy and democratization can be used interchangeably. There is, however, little accord on the demarcation of the domains of public and private decisions. This disagreement is a critical source of not only the different views on democracy but also for the emergence of different varieties of it. Decisions on economic activity are to a large extent in the private domain in some societies. In others, public decisions infringe considerably on the economic sphere. One implication of these differences is a tradeoff between property rights and individual liberty, on the one hand, and popular sovereignty (popular control over decision-making) and social equality, on the other.[3]

Isaiah Berlin notes that "[S]ome among the Great Goods cannot live together. . . . We are doomed to choose, and every choice may entail an irreparable loss."[4] Keeping economic decisions entirely private enhances property rights and individual liberty (at least for the propertied class). But it is likely to come into conflict with popular sovereignty, equality, and communal solidarity. Conversely, as Femia points out,[5] the logical conclusion of the premise of popular sovereignty and equality infringes on property rights and on individual liberty. These choices are extremely difficult to make. As Bowles and Gintis claim,[6] "a reasonable political philosophy does not choose between liberty and popular sovereignty." Most societies are likely to avoid the extremes. Yet due to differences in their levels of socioeconomic development, modes of production, and a host of other factors, including culture, it is highly unlikely that all societies would choose the same mix (for example, the liberal form). Moreover, some societies may choose to make decisions on the basis of the choice of the majority while others may adopt a consensual decision-making formula that relies on negotiations, concessions, and power sharing. In any case, the different arrangements that societies choose (or that are imposed over them) would affect their socioeconomic development differently.

In light of this, the impacts and relevance of democracy on socioeconomic development cannot be analyzed without distinguishing the different types of democracy, as is often done in the literature. This chapter identifies three of the most important types of democracy and analyzes the impacts and prospects of each. This does not imply that there can be only three types of democracy. Rather, the three that are identified here are likely to capture the essence of most other varieties.

One type of democracy is liberal democracy, which is the predominant type in the industrialized world today. A second type is consensus (consociational) democracy.[7] It is claimed that consensual democracy has strong roots in most of Africa's traditional political cultures.[8] Lengthy debates aimed at blurring opposites and finding compromises characterize decisionmaking in many traditional African political systems.[9] Some aspects of this type of democracy are also common in many other developing countries.[10] A third type is social democracy. Although the crisis of socialism has largely undermined the Marxian version of democracy, some aspects of socialist democracy have survived in the form of social democracy in many parts of the world, including the Scandinavian countries as well as Eastern Europe.[11] It is possible for some forms of social democracy to play an important role in Africa, as we will see later on. The three types are not mutually exclusive, although their differences are significant enough to justify such a classification. A brief identification of the most important distinguishing characteristics of these three types of democracy follows. We then examine how likely each of them is to foster development in Africa through the transformation of the subsistence sector, promotion of internal integration, expansion of domestic markets, and resolution of conflicts (especially ethnic and religious).

## Liberal Democracy

The crisis of socialism and the collapse of socialist regimes in many countries has been celebrated as the victory of capitalism and its twin, liberal democracy. For some, the crisis of socialism represents the end of history.[12] For others, it represents the end of ideology and of all claims of nonliberal democracy. The following statement by Sartori is a case in point.

> As we enter the last decade of our century liberal democracy suddenly finds itself without an enemy. Whatever else had laid claim on the word democracy, or had been acclaimed as "real democracy," has fizzled out almost overnight.[13]

Sartori goes on to assert that "[N]on-liberal systems also are, by the same token, non-democratic."[14] The crisis of socialism or the end of the Cold War, however, do not necessarily bring about an end to the challenges that liberal democracy faces. Nor do they make liberal democracy the most appropriate form, at least not for all societies. Coexistence with other systems still remains essential. This chapter points out the limitations of liberal democracy to conditions in much of the developing world in general, and Africa in particular. It also attempts to refute the claim of the end of nonliberal democracy. It is, however, beyond the scope of this chapter to counter in detail the claims of the "end of history" and the "end of ideology."[15]

David Beetham provides a very good summary of the essential principles of liberal democracy.[16] They include:

1.  The securing of democratic rights (individual rights) such as freedoms of expression, movement, association and so on;

2.  The institutional separation of powers between executive, legislative, and judiciary in order to ensure the rule of law;

3. The institution of representative assembly elected by popular vote through open competition;

4. The principle of a limited state and a separation between the public and private sectors; and

5. The premise that there is no final truth about what is good for society.

The degree of institutional separation of powers differs in different liberal democratic countries. The most controversial distinguishing element of liberal democracy, however, is the fourth principle, which partitions the spheres of private and public decisionmaking. The line of demarcation is neither clear nor rigid. This has led to the emergence of several variations along a continuum even within liberal democracy. Liberals have both supported and opposed state intervention in economic activity as well as the welfare state, as Bowles and Gintis observe.[17] At one extreme are the minimalists who argue that only a market economy (laissez-faire) creates conditions for sustainable democracy.[18] According to this view, progress towards a laissez-faire economy is essential for progress toward democracy. At the other extreme are the maximalists who view a laissez-faire market system as incompatible with democracy and thus incorporate a great deal of the economic decisions into the sphere or public decisions.[19] This makes liberal democracy a moving target and difficult to pin down as to what it can and cannot do. The maximalist version of liberal democracy, however, would be largely outside the liberal tradition, as it violates the limited state principle. It is also very similar to social democracy and, therefore, it will be treated in that section. The present section concentrates on the minimalist view and varieties close to it.

A truly minimalist liberal democracy rarely exists in actuality. The current wave of neo-liberalism and globalization, however, has pushed liberal democracy in this direction in many countries. For its advocates and for political systems that come close to it, the economic sphere is largely placed outside the realm of public decisions essentially for four reasons. One is because private property is viewed as an embodiment of the rights and freedoms of the individual that cannot be intruded upon by the state.[20] As Macpherson points out,[21] liberal democracy is liberal first and democratic second. In other words, democracy is coterminous with the desired goal of a laissez-faire market system. The primary aim of the tradition of liberal democracy is restricting state power over private property and individual freedom; creating structures that would secure popular control over decisionmaking is secondary. For Friedrich von Hayek,[22] for example, liberalism—the doctrine about what the content of the laws ought to be—is more important than democracy, which is the manner by which the content of the law is determined. In a 1982 interview in Chile, Hayek reasserted his position by stating that he prefers liberalism under dictatorship to democracy without liberalism.[23] From this point of view, the possible tradeoffs between marketization and democratization that we discussed in Chapter 2 disappear. Minimalist liberal democracy is consistent with globalization (and structural adjustment programs) since the latter's primary purpose is to expand the role of the market over that of the state and thereby to narrow the areas of public interest and commonweal that take precedence over private interests.

The second reason for placing the economic sphere largely off limits to public decisions is based on the claim by proponents of liberalism that private enterprises are more efficient than public enterprises. One such forceful claim is made by Sartori,[24] who argues that the private sector ("possessive individualism") has a built-in advantage of engendering caring and cost cutting, qualities that are regarded as essential for good economics, which, in turn, is a requisite for good government.[25] Sartori regards the public sector as a "noneconomical economy" because these qualities are largely absent from it. This argument may be largely correct, considering the problem of incentives in socialist economies. However, even if one concedes that the private sector is more efficient, good economics cannot be reduced to efficiency only. Other issues such as poverty alleviation, human resource development, and environmental protection are critical components of good economics, and the laissez-faire market mechanism is not known to have a shining record in these regards, especially in sub-Saharan Africa, where the majority of the population is on the fringes of the market.

Sartori does not rule out the "public household" altogether. Under certain conditions he sees some merits in regulatory involvement by the state. Despite this opening for some flexibility in state involvement by some segments of its proponents, minimalist liberal democracy is clearly tied to the free-enterprise market system with minimal state involvement.

A third reason is that liberals conceive market allocation of resources as a sphere of freedom and choice, which can offset the state's coercive allocation.[26] This claim has been successfully refuted by pointing out that the separation of capital from labor in a capitalist market constitutes coercion.[27] Moreover, as Macpherson notes, a regulatory welfare state can soothe market coercion. There is little need to engage in this debate at this point since, as noted in Chapter 2, the evidence for such roles of the state through promotion of development is plentiful.

A fourth and perhaps the most fundamental reason for placing economic decisions largely outside the sphere of public decisions by neo-liberals is that capitalism cannot be sustained without some separation of politics and economics and some restriction of public decisions in the economic arena. It is difficult to imagine a capitalist system in which wages, profits, and investments are subject to public decisions. Capitalism, however, does not require the degree of restrictions conceived by the minimalist school. In fact, it is very likely that capitalism would be undermined by strict adherence to a laissez-faire economic system, which tends to self-destruct due to its inherent tendencies to generate labor strife, unemployment, and monopoly.[28] Despite the weakness of its theoretical foundation, the minimalist liberal democracy has been elevated to prominence by the neo-liberal counterrevolution of the 1980s. The crisis of socialism is one factor for this change. Worldwide shift in power relations between capital and labor in favor of capital and between multinational corporations and the state in favor of the former is another factor. Rapid technological change and flexibility, as well as mobility of production and finance across national boundaries, have contributed to shifting the balance of power in favor of capital.[29]

Another controversial characteristic of liberal democracy is its majoritarian rule. Beetham does not identify this as an essential characteristic of liberal democracy. As Lijphart argues,[30] it may also very well be exogenous to liberal democracy. However, as Lijphart admits, it has become synonymous with liberal democracy.

## Limitations of Liberal Democracy

Presently, liberal democracy appears to have reasserted its hegemony. The global resurgence of economic liberalism since the early 1980s is indicative of this. Its apparent resounding victory over other contending forms may, however, turn out to be an "optical illusion" to borrow Etzioni-Halevy's phrase.[31] Despite its apparent victory, liberal democracy continues to face two major problems in its application in most countries of the developing world, especially those with deep societal divisions, less diversified economies, and a market mechanism that fails to coordinate available resources with social needs. Two of its controversial characteristics, namely, its restriction of public decisions from economic activity and its majority rule system are the most important sources of its weakness. In countries where the market mechanism and an autonomous bourgeoisie are underdeveloped, liberal democracy also lacks the institutional basis to sustain it.

## Partition of Economic and Political Life

As discussed in detail in the second chapter, the economies of African countries are dominated by a subsistence sector which is largely deprived of resources and marginalized from economic and political influence. This condition imposes a number of problems, among them: disarticulation of the different economic sectors, underdevelopment of the domestic market, extroversion of the commercial sector, and the failure of the market to coordinate resources with social needs. Correcting these problems necessitates transforming the subsistence sector to a surplus-producing exchange economy. This, in turn, as noted in Chapter 2, requires providing the peasantry with access to resources such as land, fertilizers, credits, appropriate technology, health care, and educational and communication facilities. A critical question that needs to be raised at this juncture is how liberal democracy's sheltering of the economy from public decisions affects the peasantry's access to resources.

Neo-liberals make a strong case that the state, especially in Africa, is a self-serving predator that uses its allocative power to favor the politically more potent segments of society, thereby promoting a negative redistribution of income. This observation is often correct. Yet if we have a "democratic" state stripped of its resource allocative power, how is the existing deprivation of the peasantry to be corrected? How is a post-apartheid "democratic" South Africa, for example, to correct the deprivation of the victims of apartheid if the state's involvement in economic activity is kept at a minimum? If the state gives up or reduces drastically its redistributive role, as the minimalist liberal democracy and proponents of structural adjustment tell us, creating access to resources for the peasantry falls on the lap of the market mechanism.

However, the market allocates resources on the basis of demand—need accompanied by purchasing power—and not on the basis of mere need. Thus, it is not a suitable mechanism for creating access to resources for the deprived who possess little purchasing power.[32] In a strict market mechanism, the benefits to the deprived are essentially limited to the trickles from the growth the market's efficiency might generate. The commercial sector around which the market centers in Africa is too small, too dependent on external sources, and too removed from the subsistence sector to be able to bring about meaningful transformation through a trickle-down process.

Under these conditions, restricting the redistributive role of the state may amount to legitimization and perpetuation of the existing gross deprivation. Without the transformation of the peasantry, the uneven dualism and fragmentation of African economies cannot be corrected. As a result, the domestic market would remain largely confined to the commercial sector. State-building would also be unlikely to succeed, since there is little dynamism for the development of exchange-based interdependence among the different geographical regions and ethnic groups and between rural and urban areas. The inability of the market to bring about the transformation of the subsistence peasantry and other marginalized groups, therefore, severely limits the development impacts of the minimalist liberal democracy in Africa. The classical notion that resolution of distributional conflict precedes accumulation and production remains essential in Africa.

Many commentators have suggested that democracy does not necessarily promote socioeconomic development.[33] Authoritarian developmentalist regimes such as those of South Korea and Taiwan, for example, are considered much more successful than democratic regimes in promoting development. If authoritarian systems can deliver faster development, it would certainly be tempting for many developing countries to discount the relevance of democracy. How can such a choice be blamed under the present conditions of growing poverty? There is, however, a serious problem with the analysis that credits authoritarian regimes with more successful development than democratic ones.

It is possible that popular demand or conflicting interest-group pressures under democracy may constrain the state from pursuing development objectives vigorously. For this reason some have argued for sequencing economic reforms and democratization, with democratization coming last.[34] A compelling counterargument is that an autonomous state may turn out to be self-serving, with potential outcomes far worse than those of the "weak" state. Of course, an autonomous state can also be benevolent and developmentalist, but there are no guarantees of this. This will be discussed in more detail in Chapter 5.

The reasons for the success of the developmentalist regimes are also highly contested.[35] Many have argued that the success of the Asian NICs came about not because of the selective government intervention but despite such interventions.[36] Some also claim that these regimes, due to their authoritarian nature, were able to foster capital accumulation by keeping labor weak and wages low and by shielding a technocratic elite from popular pressure. None of these arguments are convincing. Their success can hardly be attributed to their ability to keep labor weak and wages low, at least initially. This simply was not the case, at least in comparison with their neighbors. The success of these countries was rather due to complex internal policies and unusually favorable external conditions. On the one hand, the state in these countries actively restrained labor. On the other hand, it was able to bring about the transformation of the peasant sectors through redistributive measures such as land and agrarian reforms. The emphasis on human resource development through education and training of the labor force undertaken by these regimes was another indispensable factor in their success. The NICs' industrial policies and interventions in financial markets, which are hardly compatible with the neoclassical view of the market system, are also well documented.[37] These changes cannot simply be attributed to the authoritarian nature of those regimes.

The problem is also related to the restriction of democracy to the political arena. From the perspective of this narrow view of democracy, regimes that implement some aspects of political liberalization with little economic democracy (social justice) are considered democratic while regimes that implement considerable economic democracy with little political liberalization are labeled authoritarian.[38] From a broader perspective of democracy the classification of countries and the conclusions about democracy's impact on development might be different.

Undoubtedly, there are many internal and external factors that affect the development process. As a result, democracy is not a sufficient condition and cannot be a guarantee of economic development. However, development is unlikely to succeed at least in the African context unless the transformation of the peasantry and resolution of ethnic conflicts are major priorities. Democracy has to be clearly linked with redistributive reforms to become relevant in countries such as those of sub-Saharan Africa. Moreover, the international environment has changed considerably since the 1960s and 1970s, when the NICs made tremendous progress in their industrialization process. States are no longer likely, in this age of ethnonationalism, to be able to bring about successful economic development without creating the kind of strong internal cohesion and popular participation that democracy can engender.

If liberal democracy fails to satisfy the basic needs of all citizens and to narrow societal inequalities not only in terms of income but also in terms of the levels of human resource development, it fails to be genuinely democratic in the political sphere as well. Liberal democracy, as noted earlier, involves representation and competition; neither are possible unless gross inequalities are brought under control. As Przeworski points out,[39] in a democracy no single group can be sure that its interests will ultimately prevail, due to the free competition democracy implies. If a given group is sure that its interests either prevail or do not prevail, then democracy is undermined since there is an absence of meaningful competition.[40] The outcome would likely be a facade democracy with growing instability.

In most of Africa the peasantry is grossly deprived of education, information, and many other resources to articulate its interests and to meaningfully compete for attaining them. Furthermore, different economic classes differ considerably in their ability to organize and lobby policymakers to ensure representation of their interests. The peasantry is presently in no position to obtain real representation or to influence policy. Under these conditions, minimalist liberal democracy can only lead to an exclusivist market system and an elitist democracy or to what Owens calls "false democracy."[41] It is entirely possible that under pressure many elitist regimes, such as those of Zaire and Kenya, might liberalize political life relatively and allow elections without fundamentally changing the socioeconomic conditions of their populations. However, if the continued popular protests in post-Kaunda Zambia are any indication, liberal democratic regimes are unlikely to be stable in Africa. The stability that political liberalization is expected to engender is likely to be undermined by the failure to promote economic redistribution. The African condition suggests that the less diversified the economy and the greater societal disparity are, the more difficult it becomes for minimalist liberal democracy to function properly.

## Majority Rule

The second problem of liberal democracy is perhaps less fundamental but important, nonetheless. Considering the dualism, fragmentation, gross uneven development, and pervasive ethnic animosities and cleavages they face, African countries clearly are still grappling with the difficult task of state-building. As Adedeji notes, African economies are also characterized by built-in economy of affection, nepotism, and corruption.[42] Under these conditions, the winner-take-all majority-rule system is dysfunctional and divisive. It leads to the neglect of the interests and concerns of the minority. In extreme cases, majority rule may even lead to civil wars and wars of secession. Sudan, Rwanda, and Burundi are among the obvious examples in this regard. Thus, the less advanced the process of state-building is, the less successful majority rule becomes. Sir Arthur Lewis noted, almost three decades ago, that majority rule may prove to be "immoral, inconsistent with the primary meaning of democracy, and destructive of any prospect of building a nation in which different peoples might live in harmony."[43]

There are arguments that in practice liberal democracy is hardly characterized by majority rule. Lijphart, for example, contends that coalition cabinets, multiparty systems, proportional representation, bicameral legislatures, judicial reviews, and federalism are factors that make it more consensual than majoritarian.[44] However, most of these factors, while they may to some extent reduce the potential dictatorship of the majority, do not make it consensual. In an ethnically, religiously, or even socially polarized society it is possible to have all these and still marginalize a minority (or even a majority). In African countries we may have all of them and still neglect the majority, the peasantry. Multiparty systems, coalitions, bicameral legislatures, and judicial reviews can all be concessions between different interests within the ethnic majority, or even the privileged minority. The impact of federalism would also depend on how it is constituted. Regionally based federalism in cases where ethnic minority groups are spread out among the majority would, for example, have little impact if any.

It is also argued that liberal democracy, despite the facade of majority rule, is dominated by an elite minority. In cases where this allegation is true, the problem is magnified because under these conditions we will have both the majority of the population and ethnic minorities victimized, although it is likely that minorities would be victimized more. In any case, it is likely for protracted conflict to be more prevalent and state-building impeded under these conditions.

## Relevance of Liberal Democracy

The identified limitations do not invalidate liberal democracy altogether. Compared with the existing self-serving authoritarian regimes, as Sandbrook notes, liberal democracy "is worth struggling for."[45] It has the potential to free the producers from the "extra-economic coercion" by separating the market from the state.[46] It can also rationalize and set the rules of the game that would govern political relations among the bourgeois and petty bourgeois elites who, despite their small size, are economically and politically the most potent groups in Africa. Liberal democracy can, for example, bring about smooth transfer of power. The transfer of power in Zambia is a good example. The limited stability gained in this regard may, in turn, have some economic repercussions. Safeguarding civil liberties, such as freedom of speech, press, and association, protecting human rights, and ensuring the rule of law, are also critical achievements of liberal democracy. Compared to other African countries, the "protodemocratic" states of Botswana, Mauritius, Senegal, and the Gambia (before the 1994 coup), for example, are said to have a vastly superior record on human rights.[47] Furthermore, to the extent that liberal democracy engenders some competition within the elite for the votes of the masses, it may have some trickle-down concessions to the general population by way of reforms. However, the combination of minimalist liberal democracy and a laissez-faire economic system is not likely to allow reforms that would significantly impact the standard of living of the peasantry, although variations can be expected between countries. It is unlikely that competition among themselves would lead the elite to surrender significant portions of their privileges to the masses. On the other hand, once the procedures of democracy are established, it is possible although not probable that the elite can be pushed to be more reformist. After all, the classes that would be proponents of liberal democracy do not yet have a strong hegemony over African societies.

## Consensus Democracy

The limitations of liberal democracy do not necessarily imply that more viable alternative forms of democracy presently exist. However, there is no compelling reason why alternative forms cannot be developed. The search for alternative forms of democracy is, therefore, unlikely to die and it does not seem to be futile (as Sartori's claim of the end of nonliberal democracy would imply). Moreover, different types of democracy are likely to be supported and defended by different ideologies, albeit at a lower level of confrontation than that of the Cold War. The claims of the end of ideology and history are indeed groundless.

One possible alternative to liberal democracy is consensus democracy. Among the general characteristics of this type of democracy are that decisions are reached through compromises and concessions rather than through the majoritarian "winner-take-all" (a zero-sum) election formula. This implies that power is shared among different social groups along some criteria. Consensus-based decisionmaking does not eliminate the majoritarian system altogether. Some issues (electing a president from a number of candidates, for example) would of necessity have to be made on majority vote. Many divisive issues can, however, be decided through a consensus-building system.

Some argue that this form of democracy is indispensable in developing societies that suffer from serious internal cleavages and face more sensitive and divisive issues.[48] Others regard consensual democracy as unworkable. Nzouankeu,[49] for example, contends that consensual democracy does not recognize the conflict between private and public interests and, as a result, can only exist in a society of "gods or among slaves." Moreover, he claims that it has already failed in Africa. There are two problems with Nzouankeu's contentions. First, contrary to his claim, no post-independence African state seriously adopted a genuine consensus democracy. This is evident from the rejection of decentralization and federal arrangements by most African leaders in favor of centralized unitary structures.[50] Failure to embrace consensus democracy beyond the level of rhetoric is, in fact, regarded by some as Africa's neglect of its cultural heritage.[51] Second, consensus democracy does not require negation of self-interest in favor of that of the community in an unfree and submissive manner as Nzouankeu claims. On the contrary, it implies negotiations and concessions between different social groups or individuals with competing interests in order to obtain consensus. In many African villages decisions are still made along these lines, and a single dissenting individual can prevent the passage of any decision. Sitting through the endless debates and negotiations in a village assembly makes one wonder, as this author often did, why they do not make decisions on the basis of majority vote. Those communities, however, do not have police forces to enforce majority decisions and to punish violators. The only means available to them for ensuring general observance of village decisions is by basing them on consensus. This makes the villagers neither gods nor slaves.

Nevertheless, Nzouankeu's concerns are not altogether invalid. Consensus democracy in traditional Africa operated essentially within relatively small and homogeneous communities where direct participation in decisionmaking (village assemblies) was possible and where class divisions were not fully developed. In other words, it operated in conditions where precapitalist communalism was predominant.[52] Consensus democracy may also be appropriate under conditions of ethnic or religious diversity, as Arthur Lewis notes.[53] Ethnic groups can compete for their rights and enter into compromises with others without resorting to violence.

Some of the nationalist leaders of the era of decolonization, such as Nyerere[54] and Senghor, argued that a consensus-based single-party political system was appropriate for Africa, since African societies were not polarized along class lines. Zimbabwe's Robert Mugabe has been among the most vocal advocates for a one-party system in more recent years.[55] As a result, consensus democracy has been associated with a single-party system. Nyerere's analysis was, however, flawed on two accounts. First, the assertions that Africa (or Tanzania) was a classless society, or that the relative equality that might have existed at the time could be maintained for long under the existing socioeconomic conditions, were inaccurate. Needless to say, class divisions among African societies have grown sharper since the era of decolonization. Second, ethnic- and religious-based divisions were common among African societies. Third, even in the absence of class and ethnic divisions, consensus democracy does not require a single-party system. Far from promoting a consensual system, single parties have degenerated into suppression of alternative views, ethnic dominance, and authoritarian dictatorships. A multiparty system is more compatible with consensual democracy since it allows ethnic groups to choose their party affiliation and induces political parties to accommodate the interests of diverse groups in order to be competitive. Even if political parties were formed along ethnic lines, as is widely feared, they need not be divisive as long as decisions are made on a consensual basis. Relations among multiple parties can be based on consensual and power-sharing arrangements.

One serious limitation of consensus democracy is that it is unclear if and how it applies to the economic sphere. In traditional agrarian African societies, where land was essentially communally owned, consensual democracy was not restricted to the political arena, although it did not subject all economic matters to public decisions. Individuals decided what to grow in their fields, the size of their livestock, and so on. From the perspective of nationalist leaders like Nyerere also, consensual democracy was not restricted to the political arena. However, under conditions of severe inequality and sharp class divisions (not only between but also within ethnic groups), consensus democracy is unlikely to apply to both the political and economic spheres. It is, for example, highly unlikely that the *gada* system of the Oromo people can function at a higher level in contemporary Oromo society. In any case, since consensus democracy has not been fully developed, the issue of whether it applies to the economic sphere remains unclear.

Nevertheless, consensus democracy is not irrelevant. It can, for example, be rather easily modified to become more like the modern consociational democracy that operates reasonably well in countries such as Switzerland and Belgium.[56] Even under the existing inequalities, it is possible that the elite make decisions along consociational bases among themselves through a combination of proportional representation and decentralization. Consociational democracy, which tries to "share, disperse, restrain, and limit power in a variety of ways,"[57] even if only within the elite and between ethnic and religious groups, would be more conducive to peaceful state-building than majoritarian democracy. As Ake notes,[58] ethnic cleavages are, after all, often instigated by the elite in their quest for power and political support as well as to justify authoritarianism after they have incited the conflicts or threats of them.

Post-apartheid South Africa is one country that has begun implementing some form of consociational democracy. Political parties representing different races, ethnic groups, and social classes are represented in a coalition government with cabinet positions for every 5 percent of the popular vote. The country also seems to have embraced a decentralized political structure, although the power relations between the provinces and the central government are yet to be worked out by the Constitutional Assembly. Ethiopia has also initiated a political system that has the potential to promote some level of power sharing among the country's different ethnic groups. After coming to power in May 1991, the Ethiopian People's Revolutionary Democratic Front (EPRDF) has moved toward a system of proportional representation by allotting seats in the new legislature to different ethnic groups. It has also begun a process of decentralization by instituting a federal arrangement among the newly demarcated and largely ethnic-based ten states, including Addis Ababa, the capital city, which constitutes a separate administrative unit. The new constitution also gives ethnic groups the right to secede if they choose to do so.[59] This novel arrangement, if properly implemented, has the potential to empower minority ethnic groups, enabling them to reduce the power of the majority by controlling their local affairs and by building coalitions even across ethnic lines at the national level. It also has the potential to bring about devolution of authority from the center to local governments and thereby to mitigate the problem of overcentralization that is pervasive throughout Africa.[60]

The Ethiopian experiment has generated a great deal of concern from two sides. On the one hand, many charge that the new ethnic policy may lead to the disintegration of the country along ethnic lines.[61] On the other hand, many accuse the EPRDF government of failing, in sharp contrast to its bold policy declarations, to allow ethnic groups to organize freely. This group of critics argues that the EPRDF manufactures ethnic organizations that march to its orders and suppresses independent organizations.[62] The first charge is unconvincing since ethnic relations in the country were already poisoned by the previous two regimes. Although risky, bold policy measures such as those initiated by the EPDRF were essential to mending ethnic relations and to averting the country's total disintegration. The second charge, which points to the problems of democratization in the country, is more convincing. Reported election irregularities and harassment of opposition parties indicate that the EPRDF has not been as bold in implementing some of its policies as in declaring them. Unfortunately for Ethiopia, the fact that some of the opposition groups are armed is complicating matters. Despite the implementational difficulties, both South Africa and Ethiopia have made encouraging progress toward resolving conflicts and state-building. A combination of power sharing *a la* South Africa and a decentralized political structure similar to Ethiopia's experiment can lead to a consensual political system. It is hard to envision solutions to the conflicts in Ethiopia, Somalia, Sudan, Rwanda, and Burundi without some sort of consensual arrangement.

Political arrangements such as the Ethiopian and South African cases are unlikely to create consensus among different social classes. However, it is not an insignificant achievement if they mitigate ethnic and religious conflicts in those countries as well as in the Sudan, Somalia, Rwanda, Burundi, and Zaire. Moreover, peaceful coexistence and transfer of power among the elite would have some positive economic implications. There are some potential drawbacks to intra-elite consensus. If competition among the elite is mitigated by consociational democracy, then the peasantry and other marginalized social groups may continue to be neglected as they may become even more irrelevant. The African National Congress (ANC) in South Africa clearly faces such a dilemma. The more it compromises with the conservative parties such as the Nationalist Party and the Inkatha Freedom Party to sustain consensus, the more it drifts from the interests of its power base (the marginalized victims of apartheid), thereby endangering itself and the whole transitional arrangement for peaceful change.

## Social Democracy (Maximalist Liberal Democracy)

Marxism provides a theory of democracy that does not partition the political and economic spheres. As Femia notes,[63] there is no single type of democracy that is apparent in Marxist discourse. Participatory, parliamentary, and vanguard are among the possible models, although the Leninist vanguard party model was the most dominant in the actually existing socialist countries. What is common to all these models and distinguishes them from any form of liberal democracy is that they are based on public ownership of the means of production. Like the minimalist liberal democracy, Marxist democracy, especially the Leninist vanguard version, ties democracy to certain outcomes; in this case proletarian dictatorship and social equality.

Whatever the theoretical merits of Marxist democracy, its applicability in Africa at this time of socialist crisis is rather limited. From the experiences of Afro-Marxist states as well as those of other socialist attempts, socialism has proved to be extremely difficult to properly implement in less advanced countries where structures of democracy are unavailable and productivity is low. Socialization of the means of production was essentially replaced by state ownership in these countries. In the absence of democracy, state ownership largely became a means of advancing the interests of those that controlled state power. Under these conditions, the basic objective of socialism—the elimination of all forms of exclusion of the general population from access to decisions on the application of the means of production or access to their fruits— remained unattained.[64]

Lack of democratization and the continued deprivation of large segments of the population combined with intensive conflict between private and social incentive systems during the transition also made the social-based incentive systems of socialism unworkable, resulting in lack of dynamism and in economic stagnation.[65] Some have attributed the socialist crisis in general and socialist democracy in particular to its theoretical foundations. Bowles and Gintis, for example, point out that because of its emphasis on class and social groups, Marxism neglects individual liberty, hides nonclass and noneconomic forms of domination, and therefore cannot fully address the problems of despotism.[66] The socialist experience clearly shows that nationalization of the means of production does not necessarily end domination and exploitation or ensure democracy. Lack of ownership of the means of production did not prevent the political elite in actually existing socialist states from becoming despotic. It is unclear, however, if despotism can arise in a classless society in which equality not only among individuals within a community but also between communities prevails. Actually existing socialist states could hardly be considered classless.

In any case, the crisis of socialism has almost rendered capitalist development the only game in town, at least for now. Yet democratization and humanization of capitalism, as well as its adaptation to transitional societies, are surely possible. Social democracy, which has built-in elements of corporatism, can provide a compromise by balancing conflicting demands between different classes such as unions and the organized private sector.[67] Unlike the minimalist liberal democracy, social democracy does not strictly confine democracy to the political sphere. At the same time, unlike Marxism, it does not attempt to socialize all of the means of production and, consequently, does not rely on the presently unworkable socialist incentive system for its dynamics.

Social democracy, which is a variant of maximalist liberal democracy, is by no means revolutionary. There is little doubt about its commitment to preserving the capitalist socioeconomic system. It clearly shelters economic decisions from the sphere of public decisionmaking, since it is doubtful that capitalism can be sustained if the economy is fully exposed to public decisions. Surplus extraction by the owners of capital would be undermined under economic democracy.[68] However, social democracy is relatively more flexible in the demarcation of the boundaries of the private and public decisions. In other words, social democracy does not fix *a priori* the confines of democracy. As a result, it allows the possibility for a welfare state to attempt to satisfy the essential human needs by providing basic resources for all citizens by means of government-operated or government-financed services. In other words, by not placing the economy entirely under the sphere of public decisions, social democracy makes capitalism possible. Yet by not letting the market mechanism have a free hand, as neoliberals wish, it mitigates the market's coercive powers and its adverse impacts on equity.

Comparing developed capitalist economies indicates that those with social democracy show "less income inequality, and more extensive welfare services" while their economic performance is at least comparable.[69] It is also reasonable to expect that the flexibility of social democracy would enable a developmentalist state to more vigorously create access to resources for the peasantry and thereby to facilitate its transformation. Moreover, the compromise of social democracy may be essential in countries—such as those of Africa—where the transition from precapitalist communalism to capitalist possessive individualism is incomplete.

One of the most likely candidates for social democracy in Africa is post-apartheid South Africa. The ANC over the last few years has significantly moderated its radical economic program. Nevertheless, from its election platform, the Reconstruction and Development Program, it maintains that the magnitude of deprivation of the African people is unlikely to be corrected by a market mechanism alone.[70] Although the process of their democratization is (perhaps with the exception of Zimbabwe) at a rudimentary stage, Ethiopia, Mozambique, Angola, and Zimbabwe are also poised in the direction of social democracy.

## Weaknesses of Social Democracy

Social democracy, however, faces two problems. One is that, although it is rooted in the principle of compromise, in its present formulation it is largely based on majoritarian decisionmaking, which can undermine its relevance in ethnically divided societies. Social democracy in Africa could be more appropriate if it adopts the consensual (consociational) decision-making formula for reasons already discussed. The second problem is more fundamental. Considering the power disparity between the elite and the peasant masses, how do we obtain the compromise that social democracy entails? And how is consensual social democracy to be implemented? Here we have to rely on Cabral's theory of social change. The recent alliances and coalitions of social classes in Africa's pro-democracy movements and the fluidity of the state also provide some hint in overcoming this riddle.

Cabral regards the radical petty bourgeois, especially the intelligentsia, as a potential agent of social change, capable of adopting the cause of the masses and organizing them.[71] Cabral expects that this class would sacrifice its own short-term interests ("commit class suicide") in order to bring about societal transformation, which would also bring about its own development as a class in the longer run.

The petty bourgeois saviors did not emerge during the last three decades of Africa's history, shaking the promise of Cabral's theory. However, the role that different segments of the petty bourgeoisie in particular, and civil society in general, are playing in the current democratization struggle gives cause for some optimism. Civil society, which encompasses a wide range of institutions and relations—trade unions, voluntary associations, hospitals, churches, women's movements, the media, and capitalist enterprises,[72] or citizens with some level of organization[73]—is not cohesive, as it represents different interests. Nevertheless, it can rally around a minimum common ground, such as safeguarding basic civil rights. Presently, it seems that civil society in Africa has forged a common front against the widespread abuses by the self-serving and authoritarian state functionaries. It also appears that many segments of the pro-democracy movement, including the middle-class professionals, student organizations, the media, women's movements, church groups, labor unions, and the urban dispossessed, favor development programs that protect the poor and the peasantry.[74] These social groups view the transformation of the peasantry not as a class issue but as a broader social interest that is a requisite for national development. Thus, it is still possible that certain segments of civil society can champion the struggle for social democracy and provide farsighted leadership that relates the plight of the peasantry to the predicament of the national economy.

An assessment of what type of democracy is likely to emerge in Africa (assuming the democratic struggle succeeds) requires disaggregation of civil society and examination of the balance of the forces of its different components. Empirical research is badly needed in this area, yet it is clear that so far the bourgeois class that champions liberal democracy has not established a hegemony over other classes in most of Africa. The potential for compromises between different social classes that would lead to social democracy remains a good possibility. Undoubtedly, the likelihood for and the manner in which consociational social democracy can be implemented is likely to vary from country to country depending on specific conditions, especially in terms of ethnic and class relations.

However, African countries, unlike most other countries, are engaged in state-building and democratization simultaneously. The fusion between the two processes together with the military and economic vulnerability of African states rules out force as a viable option for state-building. It also implies that the nature of democracy and the terms for state-building are subject to the outcomes of negotiated compromises among the disparate ethnic and social groups. Some combination of a genuine decentralization[75] and proportional representation with some form of social democracy is one likely outcome. As indicated earlier, proportional (ethnic) representation, a federal system, and power-sharing arrangements embarked upon by Ethiopia and South Africa indicate possibilities in this direction. In any case, as Sklar notes,[76] there is no ready-made and transferable formula of democratic process that is suitable for African conditions. African countries have to invent one for themselves.

To conclude this section of the chapter, then, our analysis shows that any form of democracy is preferable to the existing self-serving authoritarian regimes that dominate Africa's political landscape. However, Africa has to become autocentric in developing a democratic system that suits its own socioeconomic and cultural conditions. Some form of social democracy that adopts the consociational decision-making formula would seem to be more conducive for enhancing socioeconomic development. Because of its greater ability to redistribute resources in favor of the poor, this combination has greater potential to promote the transformation of the subsistence sector. Its consensus-building mechanism (via extensive decentralization, proportional representation, and power sharing) is also better equipped to produce a more legitimate system of governance that is conducive to state-building. Such an autocentric arrangement portends some conflict with the unfolding globalization process, which curtails state engagement in economic activity. It is also a difficult combination, with delicate balancing of different classes, ethnic groups, internal and external dynamics, and market and state relations. But in countries where class, ethnic, and religious tensions are very high, anything less may not be sufficient to bring about peaceful state-building and transition.

## Prospects for Sustainable Democracy

During the period of "decolonization" of Africa, the colonial state created democratic institutions in many countries in an effort to leave behind liberal democracies. However, these institutions, created hurriedly at the eleventh hour, had little chance of survival since there were no foundations to sustain them. The colonial state did not allow the development of human resources and socioeconomic structures necessary to sustain a democratic political system. The general population was essentially uneducated and the middle and working classes were numerically negligible. In the absence of a civil society to keep it accountable, the elite, by and large, used the state to advance its own interests instead of transforming the structures of the state so as to advance social interests. Under these conditions, those institutions had little chance of survival and quickly crumbled like a house of cards. Given the autonomy of the self-serving elite, a genuine pursuit of development also became largely impossible.[77] As social opposition intensified with gradual emergence of a small civil society, the African elite increasingly preoccupied itself with its own survival.

The conditions for democracy have now improved notably from what they were in the 1960s: awareness of the relevance of democracy is greater, and the pro-democracy social classes are stronger. The post–Cold War global climate is also in some regards more conducive to democracy than it was throughout the Cold War.

The causes for the recent wave of pro-democracy movements may help shed some light on the improved conditions for democratization. Over the last thirty years some changes—such as higher degree of urbanization, greater access to education, some degree of industrialization, and a relative expansion of the working class and the petty bourgeoisie—have taken place, albeit at a much lower pace than in most of the rest of the developing world. These changes have been accompanied by deepening economic crisis and a widespread dissatisfaction, especially since the late 1970s. Moreover, the African state has surrendered a great deal of its sovereignty in economic policymaking to the MFIs and other aid donors since the early 1980s.

The abuses of the state and the general socioeconomic crisis, in tandem with the growing loss of national sovereignty, have encouraged many social groups to coalesce in seeking greater accountability and transparency in the management of economic affairs. The elite that had little organized opposition at the time of decolonization is now facing greater demands for rights, social justice, and multiparty democratic political systems.

External factors have also contributed to the current democratization drive. The revolution in Eastern Europe and the former Soviet Union is one of the external factors. Authoritarian rule in the name of "proletarian dictatorship" (as was the case in some countries, such as Ethiopia) has now lost its currency. As Huntington notes,[78] it is also likely that the events of 1989 in Eastern Europe may have acted as a catalyst in Africa's democracy movement by emboldening democratic opposition groups and encouraging frightened authoritarian regimes to allow opposition parties elsewhere. The end of the Cold War is another important external factor. Many regimes, such as those of South Africa and Zaire, had milked their anticommunist position to acquire Western support in sustaining themselves in power. With the end of the Cold War they have lost an important tool of diversion.

## Obstacles to Democratization

Despite the relatively improved conditions, predicting the prospects for democracy in Africa remains an extremely difficult task. One key source for this difficulty is the fluid nature of the state itself. As Cardoso notes,[79] the state represents a pact of domination that exists among social classes. In Africa this pact is not yet firm. Despite its relative dominance over the other classes in some countries, the African bourgeoisie has not yet succeeded in establishing a firm hegemony. The petty bourgeois has also been incapable of establishing a hegemony, largely due to its class nature. It is a fluid class whose membership ranges from the owners of small enterprises to the intelligentsia and other professionals. This class has no common ideological affiliation or type of political regime. The masses also are in no position to establish a hegemony of any sort over society. Thus, it can be argued that the state in most of Africa does not truly represent any particular class. Often it represents a fragile coalition of the small bourgeoisie and some segments of the petty bourgeoisie; in other cases, it merely represents a social strata such as the military or individuals that rely heavily on the military and/or ethnicity for their support.

Given this unstable nature of the "African state," it is difficult to determine the rules of the game (i.e., the type of regime) that will emerge. The prospects for democracy and the types of democracy will depend largely on the type of pact that emerges in Africa following the current wave of struggle. On the other hand, the absence of a clear hegemonic class may be conducive to democracy, which (as Przeworski notes[80]) requires a class compromise. It is, however, likely to remain unstable, considering the unstable nature of the balance of power among the different classes in Africa.

Democracy in Africa also faces a number of other formidable obstacles. Africa's socioeconomic distortions—which, to be overcome, require democracy—constitute a major impediment to the democratization process. Lack of access to education, information, and resources largely marginalizes the peasantry from the crucial struggle for democratization. As Yusuf Bangura notes,[81] these low levels of national integration restrict democratization to the level of an urban phenomenon. Ethnic conflicts and the violence involved also impede democratization, although the struggle by oppressed national groups for their rights does have democratizing impacts. In other words, the pro-democracy forces are stronger now than they were at the period of decolonization, as noted earlier. Yet it is uncertain that they are strong enough to win the struggle and to sustain democracy in the short term. Poor economic performance—which, given the existing internal and external socioeconomic structures, is likely to persist—may also prove a threat to sustained democratization.

External influence is another potential impediment to the democratization process in Africa. According to some, external impact may be positively decisive.[82] Claude Ake, for example, argues that political conditionality for aid by the MFIs and donor governments can promote democracy in Africa by strengthening pro-democracy forces and weakening authoritarian regimes.[83] Clearly, the potential positive impacts of external influence cannot be denied. However, aid and economic conditionality have not promoted economic development in Africa. Political conditionality is not likely to have different results. The Western powers and most of the democratic forces in Africa also have different notions of democracy. By attempting to shape the process in their own image, the Western powers may in fact obstruct democratization in Africa. Furthermore, the stark global inequality and the undue influences and rigid conditionalities by the MFIs may impede democratization.

One critical external obstacle to the success of democracy is the marketization drive, which is largely imposed upon African states by the IMF, the World Bank, and lender countries. As noted earlier, from the liberal point of view, marketization and democratization are compatible processes. From the perspective of social democracy, however, there are tradeoffs between the two processes. The marketization drive strengthens the position of the economic elite (and of those with the potential to become an economic elite) while it further squeezes the lower economic classes, including the workers and the peasantry. In many countries this has driven the lower classes, especially those in the urban areas, to engage periodically in riots and other actions that intensify political instability. Intervention by a reformed state to implement income redistribution and agrarian reform is indispensable for empowering the masses and for bringing about stability. It also can make African economies less dependent by cultivating internal dynamics for their growth. The marketization and globalization drives constrain such intervention by the state. It is only from this point of view that we can understand why many of the same social forces that are active in the pro-democracy movement in Africa are strongly opposed to the structural adjustment programs.[84]

Moreover, whatever the merits of SAPs, their imposition from outside is counter to the development of democracy. This is evident from the experience of Zambia. Frederick Chiluba, who was a strong critic of SAPs, complained in 1987 that "the IMF had set the government on a collision course with the people."[85] Since he took office, however, his government has chosen to adopt SAPs despite their impacts on the general population. This policy in conjunction with many other things has helped to break up the pro-democracy coalition that swept the Movement for Multiparty Democracy

(MMD) to power in Zambia. There is even the danger that it may fragment the fragile civil society in that country.

## Conclusion

The pro-democracy movement presently underway is a mass movement that incorporates different social groups with different notions and expectations of democracy. This unity of different forces may succeed in bringing down many authoritarian regimes. Such unity is, however, likely to break up over the type of democracy that emerges during the consolidation stage of democracy, thereby endangering the whole process.

To the extent that the democratic process survives in some countries, it is unlikely to be of the same kind in all of Africa. Considering the significant differences among African countries with respect to the level of state-building, the degree of diversification of the economy, the magnitude of uneven development and ethnic conflict, and the relative balance of power among different social classes, different varieties of democracy are likely to be adopted in different countries.

Furthermore, whatever success is registered in democratization, it is unlikely to come in a single wave or even in a linear progression. Rather it is likely to be in successive waves or even in a cyclical manner of alternating authoritarianism and democracy. As Robert Michels notes,[86] democratic changes in history often resemble "successive waves," with the old leaders betraying the causes of democracy and developing authoritarian tendencies and new accusers leading the struggle against the "traitors." Shifting balance of power between the competing social classes in Africa is likely to lead to such cyclical changes.

Finally, in terms of the relations of democracy to socioeconomic development, our analysis suggests that consociational social democracy is likely to be more effective than the other types of democracy in transforming the subsistence peasantry and thereby enhancing general socioeconomic development as well as in accommodating the interests of different ethnic groups. Given the magnitude of the deprivation of the peasantry and the consequent internal fragmentation of African societies, a democratic state that is active in the redistribution of resources is likely to have more significant impact in advancing human resource development and state-building than a liberal and majoritarian democratic system in which market coercion is left unchecked as the state largely leaves resource allocation to the market mechanism. It is also more likely to promote autocentric development by transforming the peasantry and thereby expanding internal dynamics for growth. For the same reasons, consociational social democracy is also likely to be more stable than liberal democracy.

## Notes

1. The Carter Center, "The Promise of Democracy," *Africa Démos* 3, no. 4 (March 1995): 1–4.
2. David Beetham, "Liberal Democracy and the Limits of Democratization," *Political Studies* 40 (Special Issue, 1992): 40–53.
3. There is a great deal of disagreement on the relationships between property rights and individual liberty. As Macpherson notes, democracy in its original sense of government in accordance with the will of the common people was regarded as a leveling doctrine and "fatal to individual freedom" by the elite until about a century ago. Crawford B. Macpherson, *The Real World of Democracy* (Oxford: Oxford University Press, 1966). Economic democracy is still viewed as bad for individual freedom mostly by the economic elite. There is no compelling reason why individual liberty for the common people would be enhanced if economic decisions were private.
4. Isaiah Berlin, *The Crooked Timber of Humanity: Chapters in the History of Ideas* (New York: Alfred A. Knopf, Inc., 1992).
5. Joseph V. Femia, *Marxism and Democracy* (Oxford: Clarendon Press, 1993), 10.
6. Samuel Bowles and Herbert Gintis, "Democracy and Capitalism," in Philip Green, ed., *Democracy: Key Concepts in Critical Theory* (Atlantic Highlands, NJ: Humanities Press, 1993), 168–74.
7. As we will see later on in this chapter, consensus democracy can be modified to approximate consociational democracy.
8. Jacques-Mariel Nzouankeu, "The African Attitude to Democracy," *International Social Science Journal* 128 (May 1991): 373–85.
9. Naomi Chazan, "Between Liberalism and Statism: Africa Political Cultures and Democracy," in Larry Diamond, ed., *Political Culture and Democracy in Developing Countries* (Boulder and London: Lynne Rienner Publishers, 1993), 67–105.
10. Raul S. Manglapus, *Will of the People: Original Democracy in Non-western Societies* (New York: Greenwood Press, 1987).
11. Social democracy, as we will see later on in this chapter, involves compromises between classes; for example, between the bourgeoisie and the working class. The nature of the compromises depends on

the relative balance of power between the contending classes. Whether Eastern European social democracy will differ significantly from the West European version would also depend on the ability of the East European working class to assert its interests, given the communist experience.

12. Francis Fakuyama, "The End of History," *The National Interest* 16 (September 1989): 3–18.
13. Giovanni Sartori, "Rethinking Democracy: Bad Polity and Bad Politics," *International Social Science Journal* 129 (August 1991): 437.
14. Sartori, "Rethinking Democracy," 448.
15. Many scholars both from the left and even the right have strongly challenged the claim of the end of history. Samuel Huntington, "Why International Primacy Matters," in Sean M. Lynn-Jones and Steven E. Miller, eds., *The Cold War and After* (Cambridge: MIT Press, 1993), 310.
16. Beetham, "Liberal Democracy."
17. Samuel Bowles and Herbert Gintis, *Democracy and Capitalism* (New York: Basic Books, Inc., Publishers, 1986).
18. F.A. Hayek, *The Constitution of Liberty* (London and Henley: Routledge and Kegan Paul, 1960); Milton Friedman, *Capitalism and Freedom* (Chicago: Chicago University Press, 1962); Larry Diamond, "Promoting Democracy," *Foreign Policy* 87 (Summer 1992): 25–46.
19. Charles E. Lindblom, "The Market as Prison," *Journal of Politics* 46, no. 2 (May 1982): 324–36; Robert Dahl, "Why All Democratic Countries Have Mixed Economies," in John W. Chapman and Ian Shapiro, eds., *Democratic Community* (New York: New York University Press, 1993), 259–82. The flexibility of liberal democracy in terms of drawing the demarcation line between the private and public decisions is another point that creates a problem in terms of isolating the characteristics of liberal democracy. This vagueness may allow consensual and social democracies to be regarded as simply variants of liberal democracy. This, however, would outstretch liberalism and shift the debate from different types of democracy to different types of liberal democracy.
20. The individual, by living under the state and by obeying its laws, has already submitted to limitations of his freedom. Why the economic decisions would be particularly intrusive on his freedom is not very clear. More importantly, it is unclear why enslavement of society is more tolerable than the enslavement of the individual.
21. Macpherson, *The Real World of Democracy*, 6.
22. Hayek, *The Constitution of Liberty*.
23. Bowles and Gintis, *Democracy and Capitalism*, 11–12.
24. Sartori, "Rethinking Democracy."
25. It is doubtful that Sartori's "possessive individualism" applies to all types of private enterprises. In the era of large corporations there is considerable distinction between ownership and management.

26. Friedman, *Capitalism and Freedom*.
27. Crawford B. Macpherson, *Democratic Theory* (Oxford: Clarendon Press, 1973).
28. Benjamin Barber, *Jihad vs. McWorld* (New York: Random House, 1995).
29. For details see Robert W. Cox, "Global Restructuring: Making Sense of the Changing International Political Economy," in Richard Stubbs and Geoffrey R.D. Underhill, eds., *Political Economy and the Changing Global Order* (New York: St. Martin's Press, 1994), 45–59; Gary Teeple, *Globalization and the Decline of Social Reform* (Toronto: Garamond Press, 1995).
30. Arend Lijphart, "Majority Rule in Theory and Practice: The Tenacity of a Flawed Paradigm," *International Social Science Journal* 129 (August 1991): 483–93.
31. Eva Etzioni-Halevy, *The Elite Connection: Problems and Potential of Western Democracy* (Cambridge, U.K.: Polity Press, 1993), 1.
32. Charles Edward Lindblom, *Politics and Markets: The World's Political Economic Systems* (New York: Basic Books, 1977); Edgar Owens, *The Future of Freedom in the Developing World* (New York: Pergamon Press, 1987).
33. Richard Sandbrook, "Liberal Democracy in Africa: A Socialist-Revisionist Perspective," *Canadian Journal of African Studies* 22, no. 2 (1988): 240–67; Alain Touraine, "What Does Democracy Mean Today?" *International Social Science Journal* 128 (May 1991): 259–68; Georg Sorensen, *Democracy and Democratization* (Boulder: Westview Press, 1993).
34. Donald Emmerson, "Capitalism, Democracy, and the World Bank: What Is to Be Done?" in Lual Deng, Markus Kostner, and Crawford Young, eds., *Democratization and Structural Adjustment in Africa in the 1990s* (Madison: University of Wisconsin, African Studies Program, 1991), 9–12.
35. World Bank, *The East Asian Miracle: Economic Growth and Public Policy* (Washington, D.C.: World Bank, 1993).
36. "Asian Model Attests to Value of Openness and Minimal Policy-Induced Distortions," *IMF Survey* 22, no. 21 (8 November 1993): 338–41.
37. Paul P. Streeten, "Against Minimalism," in Louis Puttermann and Dietrich Rueschemeyer, eds., *State and Market in Development: Synergy or Rivalry?* (Boulder: Lynne Rienner, 1992).
38. Social justice generally refers to income redistribution for purposes of reducing inequality. It is, however, a vague term. Justice is a juridical term which refers to what is in compliance with the existing legal system. If inequality is not illegal then it can also be just.
39. Adam Przeworski, "Democracy as a Contingent Outcome of Conflicts," in Jon Elster and Rune Slagstad, eds., *Constitutionalism and Democracy* (Cambridge: Cambridge University Press, 1988).

40. Such a group can easily form a dictatorship which is characterized by having an effective control over political outcomes that would have adverse impacts on one's interests. Przeworski, "Democracy as a Contingent Outcome of Conflicts," 60.
41. Owens, *The Future of Freedom.*
42. Adebayo Adedeji, "Sustaining Democracy," *Africa Report* (January-February 1992): 29–32.
43. Arthur W. Lewis, *Politics in West Africa* (London: Allen and Unwin, 1965), 64–66. Unlike for Hayek, for Arthur Lewis the primary objective of democracy is "that all who are affected by a decision should have a chance to participate in making that decision, either directly or through chosen representatives." Lewis, *Politics in West Africa*, 64.
44. Lijphart, "Majority Rule in Theory and Practice."
45. Sandbrook, "Liberal Democracy in Africa," 250.
46. Mahmood Mamdani, "Peasants and Democracy," *New Left Review* 156 (March/April 1986): 48. This is not to suggest that the market is not coercive as Friedman claims (Friedman, *Capitalism and Freedom*). The coercion of the market has already been discussed. It simply means that if the state is self-serving, promoting a negative income redistribution, retrenching its involvement in economic matters, to the extent that it is possible, would reduce the magnitude of coercion to that of the market.
47. Sandbrook, "Liberal Democracy in Africa," 243.
48. Lewis, *Politics in West Africa*; Lijphart, "Majority Rule in Theory and Practice."
49. Nzouankeu, "The African Attitude to Democracy."
50. Donald Rothchild, *Politics of Integration—An East African Documentary* (Nairobi: East African Publishing House, 1968); Benjamin Neuberger, "Federalism in Africa: Experience and Projects," in Daniel J. Elezar, ed., *Federalism and Political Integration* (Tel Aviv: Turtledove Publishers, 1973), 171–88.
51. Maxwell Owusu, "Democracy and Africa—A View from the Village," *The Journal of Modern African Studies* 30, no. 3 (1992): 369–96.
52. Not all African states were characterized by precapitalist communalism. The Abyssinian Empire, for example, is known for its feudal hierarchical social relations. Consensus democracy was little known in feudal Abyssinia.
53. Lewis, *Politics in West Africa.*
54. Julius Nyerere, *Ujamaa: Essays on Socialism* (Dar es Salaam: Oxford University Press, 1968).
55. W. Shaw, "Towards the One-Party State in Zimbabwe: A Study in African Political Thought," *Journal of Modern African Studies* 24 (1986): 373–94.
56. For details on consociational democracy see Gerhard Lehmbruch, "Consociational Democracy and Corporatism in Switzerland,"

*Publius* 23, no. 2 (Spring 1993): 43–60.
57. Lijphart, "Majority Rule in Theory and Practice."
58. Claude Ake, "Rethinking African Democracy," in Larry Diamond and Marc F. Plattner, eds., *The Global Resurgence of Democracy* (Baltimore: Johns Hopkins University Press, 1993), 70–82.
59. For details see Articles 39 and 47 of the 1994 Constitution of the Federal Republic of Ethiopia.
60. James S. Wunsch and Dele Olown, "The Failure of the Centralized African State," in James S. Wunsch and Dele Olown, eds., *The Failure of the Centralized State: Institutions and Self-Governance in Africa* (San Francisco: Institute for Contemporary Studies, 1995), 1–22.
61. For details see Marina Ottaway, *Democratization and Ethnic Nationalism: African and Eastern European Experiences* (Washington, D.C.: Overseas Development Council, 1994); Walli Engedayehu, "Ethiopia: Democracy and the Politics of Ethnicity," *Africa Today* 40, no. 2 (Second Quarter, 1993): 29–52.
62. Mohammed Hassen, "Ethiopia Missed Opportunities for Peaceful Democratization Process," paper presented at the Annual Meeting of the African Studies Association, Toronto, 1994; Tecola W. Hagos, *Democratization? Ethiopia (1991–1994): A Personal View* (Cambridge, MA: Khepera Publisher, 1995).
63. Femia, *Marxism and Democracy*, 69.
64. Kidane Mengisteab, "Responses of Afro-Marxist States to the Crisis of Socialism: A Preliminary Assessment," *Third World Quarterly* 13, no. 1 (1992): 78.
65. The social incentive system is the realization by individuals that their well-being is enhanced only when that of the society is advanced.
66. Bowles and Gintis, *Democracy and Capitalism*, 17–20.
67. Yusuf Bangura, "Authoritarian Rule and Democracy in Africa: A Theoretical Discourse," in P. Gibbon, Y. Bangura, and Arve Ofstad, eds., *Authoritarianism, Democracy, and Adjustment* (Uppsala: Scandinavian Institute of African Studies, 1992); A. Cawson, "Is There a Corporate Theory of the State?" in G. Duncan, ed., *Democracy and the Capitalist State* (London: Cambridge University Press, 1989); A. Carter, "Industrial Democracy and the Capitalist State," in G. Duncan, ed., *Democracy and the Capitalist State* (London: Cambridge University Press, 1989).
68. Ellen Meiksins Wood, *Democracy Against Capitalism* (Cambridge: Cambridge University Press, 1995).
69. Adam Przeworski, *Democracy and the Market* (Cambridge, MA: Cambridge University Press, 1991), 131.
70. African National Congress, *The Reconstruction and Development Programme: A Policy Framework* (Johannesburg: Umanyans Publications, 1994).
71. Amilcar Cabral, *Revolution in Guinea: An African Peoples' Struggle* (London: Monthly Review Press, 1969).

72. Wood, *Democracy Against Capitalism*, 242–43.
73. Michael Bratton, "Civil Society and Political Transitions in Africa," in John W. Harbeson, Donald Rothchild, and Naomi Chazan, eds., *Civil Society and the State in Africa* (Boulder and London: Lynne Rienner Publishers, 1994), 51–81.
74. Bangura, "Authoritarian Rule and Democracy in Africa."
75. Richard Vengroff, "The Transition to Democracy in Senegal: The Role of Decentralization," *In Depth* 3, no. 1 (Winter 1993): 23–51.
76. Richard Sklar, "Developmental Democracy," *Comparative Studies in Society and History* 23, no. 4 (1987): 686–714.
77. Georges Nzongola-Ntalaja, *Revolution and Counter Revolution in Africa* (London: Zed Books Ltd., 1987); Ake, "Rethinking African Democracy."
78. Samuel Huntington, "Democracy's Third Wave," in Larry Diamond and Marc F. Plattner, eds., *The Global Resurgence of Democracy* (Baltimore: Johns Hopkins University Press, 1993), 8.
79. Fernando Enrique Cardoso, "On the Characterization of Authoritarian Regimes in Latin America," in David Collier, ed., *The New Authoritarianism in Latin America* (Princeton: Princeton University Press, 1979).
80. Przeworski, "Democracy as a Contingent Outcome of Conflicts."
81. Bangura, "Authoritarian Rule and Democracy in Africa," 51.
82. Samuel Huntington, "Will More Countries Become Democratic?" *Political Science Quarterly* 99, no. 2 (1984): 205.
83. Ake, "Rethinking African Democracy."
84. Bangura, "Authoritarian Rule and Democracy in Africa."
85. Quoted in Callaghy, "Civil Society, Democracy, and Economic Change in Africa," 232.
86. Robert Michels, "Political Parties," in Philip Green, ed., *Democracy: Key Concepts in Critical Theory* (Atlantic Highlands, NJ: Humanities Press, 1993), 68–73.

# 5

# Mixed Economic Strategy in an Autocentric Development Approach

▼  ▼  ▼

## Introduction

The previous two chapters have attempted to identify the types of democratization and integration (internal, regional, and global) that form the cornerstones of a development strategy that balances globalism and autocentricity. Those chapters also hinted at the type or mix of the two devices of resource allocation—the state and the market—that would be compatible with such a development approach. The present chapter attempts to examine in greater detail the market-state relations that are more likely to facilitate overcoming the structural bottlenecks of Africa's socioeconomic development, including the resilience of the subsistence sector, internal fragmentation, lack of diversification of exports, and problems of state-building.

This chapter is organized into three parts. The first part reviews the major reasons for the recurrent failures of the state and the market in Africa and discusses why some of the roles of these two institutions are indispensable despite their failures, and despite the prevailing overblown claim that wholly unregulated markets can do no wrong and states can only do harm. The second part attempts to sketch what constitutes a mixed economy and how it may mitigate some of the failures of the state and the market and thereby help in pulling African economies out of their present quagmire. The concluding part discusses briefly the essential conditions for a workable mixed economic system.

## What Are the Indispensable Roles of the State and the Market?

There is little dispute that, for a market system to operate, the state needs to perform certain basic functions: (a) protecting citizens from external aggression and from internal disorder, (b) safeguarding private property, (c) enforcing private contracts and adjudicating disputes, (d) providing a reasonably stable monetary framework, and (e) creating and promoting competition. State intervention beyond these minimum requirements has been highly controversial.

Opponents of state intervention argue that any expanded involvement by the state in the economy beyond the identified basic functions is counterproductive and only undermines the market's effectiveness. Income redistribution measures by state policy, for example, are generally perceived by opponents as adversely affecting growth. They contend that in any war against poverty the government always loses and that the benefits to the poor from economic growth are much larger than those from policy-instigated redistribution. Irrespective of its implications for growth, many conservatives oppose, in principle, any state involvement in expropriating wealth from the rich for redistribution to the poor. They view it not only as beyond the scope of the appropriate role of the state but also as a violation of the sanctity of private property and an intrusion on individual liberty.

By contrast, proponents of greater state involvement claim that the market does not, by itself, bring about redistribution that is justified either on the basis of social justice or on the grounds of human resource development.[1] They also insist that without redistributive measures, growth is often undermined by aggregate demand constraints as well as by low productivity of unskilled workforce, especially when large segments of the population are deprived. In addition, they contend that the state can perform a number of other services that are market-creating and growth-enhancing. The promotional activities of the Japanese Ministry of International Trade and Industries (MITI) in the 1950s are cited as an example of market-creating state activities. The MITI is said to have organized a massive research-and-development effort to identify the best areas in which Japan could be competitive. The identified industries—optics, electronics, and automobiles—were then given a number of incentives. The magnitude of research and information processing required for such a projection was clearly beyond the reach of individual private firms.[2] Other examples of market-creating activities of the state include the formation of trading companies by the South Korean government. These companies are responsible for integrating a large number of exchange-related activities such as marketing and the transfer of technology. It is claimed that such companies gave a tremendous boost to Korea's export-oriented industrialization.[3]

The idea that industrial development in the West was primarily due to the roles of capitalist entrepreneurs in a free market in western societies is also largely a myth. The Dutch "Golden Age" of the seventeenth century was clearly accompanied by strong state support in raw material imports and exports of manufactures.[4] During the eighteenth century, Britain not only imposed tariffs on textile imports from India and China but also made the wearing of such imports illegal in order to stimulate British textile industry.[5] In the nineteenth century, countries like Germany, France, and the United States counteracted British hegemony through nationalist economic strategies that included protective tariffs and credit facilities from state banks in order to develop national industries.[6] In the case of Russia also, Gerschenkron observes that despite the incompetence and corruption of the bureaucracy, the impact of the policies pursued in promoting industrialization is "undeniable."[7]

Proponents of active state involvement warn of the potential adverse impacts of restricting state policy too much or subordinating it to the private-enterprise market system, even if the market's alleged superiority in productive efficiency and growth were established. The dangers are not only in unmitigated inequality but also on sustained growth, on the environment, on the safety and health of workers, and even on democracy. Lindblom,[8] for example, alerts us that state policymaking may be increasingly subordinated to the decisions of managers of private enterprises for the sake of efficiency and growth, making democracy increasingly more hollow. Bienefeld also warns that "it is foolish and dangerous to create circumstances in which the economic demand for efficiency is privileged above all others because economic survival demands certain levels of efficiency at any social or political cost. . . . Such a world will ultimately be neither efficient, nor stable, nor desirable as a place to live in."[9]

The relative levels of coercion associated with the state and the market are another source of controversy. According to Milton

Friedman, for instance, state intervention beyond the identified minimum roles only undermines the market mechanism's "cooperative exchange."[10] Hayek also warns that state intervention leads to a totalitarian control of life.[11] Critics like Macpherson and Wood,[12] on the other hand, reject these claims by noting that the separation between capital and labor has made a capitalist market system highly coercive. Moreover, these critics view state regulation as a potential mitigator of such market coercion.[13]

The relations between individual liberty and resource-allocative roles of the two devices of political economy have also contributed to the controversy. Opponents of state intervention claim that private property is an expression of individual liberty and that the private-enterprise market system safeguards liberty while state interference infringes on it. On the other hand, proponents believe that intervention to promote human resource development and to mitigate gross inequalities, in fact, enhances individual liberty.

These debates have characterized socioeconomic policymaking since at least the days of the classical economists, if not since the rise of capitalism. They are also unlikely to go away as neither side is likely to convince the other. Furthermore, despite the intensive debates, reality is in most cases a mixed bag. Przeworski, for example, notes that "all capitalist economies are 'mixed.'"[14] The role of the state ranges from policy intervention to directly owning industries, especially those with externalities and increasing returns to scale. Some even claim that "the market-versus-government dichotomy" is a "fake one" in the sense that the roles of both institutions are indispensable.[15] The market-state mix that emerges in different countries may also depend on the relative strength of different social classes with competing interests. Yet the appropriateness of the state-market mix is likely to hinge, among other things, on the levels of socioeconomic development. The mix that is appropriate for the industrialized or semi-industrialized nations, for example, is unlikely to be suitable for African states. Thus, the debate on the appropriate proportion of each of these institutions for economies at different levels of development remains a useful one, especially considering the current neo-liberal marketization counterrevolution. In addition, the virtues attributed to the market and the state by their respective proponents do not always exist in reality. The appropriate mix between the two when neither one of them operates properly also becomes relevant.

This chapter attempts to identify the essential components and strengths of the state and the market and to explore a mix between the two suitable for the African situation. The chapter by no means claims to provide a conclusive solution to this difficult issue. Rather it is an exploratory discussion that draws tentative conclusions to encourage further research. The performances of the market and the state in Africa are now briefly assessed.

## The Limitations of the Market in Africa

One essential function of the market is to relay to producers information on effective actual and expected demands on the basis of which they make investment decisions and formulate plans. Private resource allocation is believed to more closely correspond to market information than state allocation, due to the penalties of lower profits or even bankruptcy that may result from wrong decisions. As a result, private allocative decisions are often claimed to represent a superior efficiency than allocation by the state in terms of putting resources into more highly valued use.

A corollary role of the market is that it furnishes consumers with what they need and at the same time enables them to influence decisionmaking on what the economy produces, provided that they can translate their needs into demand through their purchasing power. In other words, purchasing power is the means by which members of a society individually satisfy their needs and wants for goods and services and collectively, through their aggregate effective demand, influence economic decisions on the types and quantities of goods and services produced. Through the identified two roles, the market also coordinates the activities and energies of a multitude of economic units into a more or less coherent system of production and distribution.

The market performs these functions reasonably well in the diversified and more advanced economies where the market infrastructure is fairly developed, and where the purchasing power of even the relatively poorer segments of society is significant enough to allow them to participate. In low-income undiversified economies such as those of Africa—where a large segment of the population is mostly outside of the exchange economy, the modern sector is essentially an outward-looking enclave, and the market infrastructure is rather rudimentary—the market does not perform these three essential functions properly. While compounded by factors such as inappropriate state intervention, unfavorable international conditions, and natural disasters, this failure is due not simply to exogenous factors but also to the inherent forces of the market itself.

Market allocation neglects needs that are not accompanied by purchasing power or goods and services whose production does not generate a certain profit rate to suppliers. As noted in Chapter 2, the needs of the subsistent peasantry in most African states are mostly neglected due to the inability of this social group to translate its needs into demand via purchasing power. "Market democracy" or popular influence on economic decisions by producers is extremely weak in Africa. This is in part why African economies lack internal dynamism and are dependent on external demand for their growth.

At the micro level, private enterprises may be relatively efficient in utilizing resources to maximize their profits, although their ability to expand their productive capacity and effectively compete in the global market is often limited by a number of factors, including technical know-how and marketing skills. At the macro level, however, private firms do not necessarily put resources into a more highly valued use and promote national development when they bypass social needs and depend on the international market instead of cultivating a domestic market. As noted in Chapter 1, the colonial experience has largely separated the African masses from the commercial sector (cash crops and mining), which was created to meet the needs of the markets of the colonial powers. When social needs do not influence allocative decisions, the market also largely fails to coordinate the activities of the multitude of economic units. This is reflected by the perverse internal fragmentation of African economies.

As noted in the previous chapter, the deprivation of the African masses in post-apartheid South Africa is highly unlikely to be corrected by the market system alone. Likewise, the deprivation of the peasantry and the resultant resilience of the large subsistence sector and the duality of African economies are unlikely to be corrected by the market system alone, at least not any time soon. As long as large segments of the population are marginalized, allocation of resources by private economic units (via the market) remains essentially elitist, drawing resources toward those with purchasing power. It relegates the transformation of the subsistence sector to the generally ineffective trickle-down process. Even in the advanced countries, it is the countries with strong social democratic tradition, such as the Nordic countries, that have registered more success in alleviating poverty.[16] Thus, contrary to the expectations of the liberalization school, the market mechanism cannot be a panacea for Africa's economic crisis, at least until its preconditions are established. The growth that neo-liberals expect to occur as a result of the micro-level efficiency is likely to be undermined by the weakness of the domestic market as well as by political conflicts that often accompany pervasive uneven development. Even if some growth is achieved, it is likely to bypass those on the fringes of the market, such as the peasantry.

The individual liberty and cooperative exchange that opponents of state intervention expect the market system to engender are also seriously undermined by the distortions that characterize African economies. It requires little discussion that the existing market system that bypasses social needs, marginalizes the large subsistent sector and many ethnic groups, and, in many cases leads to evictions and starvation of peasants cannot be regarded as promoting cooperative exchange and individual liberty.

The identified three principal roles of the market are clearly indispensable. However, in the African conditions these roles are not performed properly. Instead we have a vicious circle in which the deprived peasantry, due to its lack of purchasing power, fails to influence market decisions. As a result, producers bypass the needs of the peasantry and this, in turn, perpetuates the deprivation of the peasantry. There is also no clear indication that the market's self-correcting mechanism is effective enough to break this cycle.

## The Failure of the State and Different Types of Intervention

The performance of the state has been even more dismal than that of the market in Africa. The post-independence African state, in most cases, emerged as a result of popular struggle for self-determination. It was expected by the general population to play a liberating role, which included not only national independence but also basic civil rights and freedom from poverty, disease, hunger, and illiteracy. Active participation in economic activity was thus considered imperative by the newly independent state. As noted in Chapter 2, state intervention in economic activity has since been significant in Africa. Needless to say, intervention has not been a sufficient condition for attaining the goals of liberation.

In order to fulfill the promise of liberation, the disarticulated economic structures that were established during Africa's colonization and incorporation into the global economy had to be modified and access to resources for the deprived general population needed to be created. The post-independence state largely failed to bring about these essential changes for a number of reasons. The post-independence African state was simply too weak to fundamentally change the colonial economic structures. Where attempts to bring structural changes and to control the national process of accumulation were manifested, the leaders were either overthrown and/or murdered—as in the cases of Lumumba in the Congo and Cabral in Guinea Bissau—by the combined forces of imperialism and the domestic elite who benefited from the system and naturally wanted to maintain it. Others, realizing their inabilities to challenge the power of imperialism, chose not to endanger their survival and abandoned the goals of social change.

In most other cases, the leaders of the post-independence state have shown neither the commitment nor the competence to bring about such changes. As Ake notes,[17] they saw the advantages the inherited social order provides for self-enrichment and chose to embrace it. Accordingly, the elite has intervened in the economy, to a large extent, in order to advance its own economic interests and to create patronage with certain politically influential social groups or segments of the population. State ownership or control of some of the means of production, which could have enhanced the state's ability to create access to the deprived and to develop human resources, became largely a means of reverse income redistribution and a means of monopolizing political power by depriving opponents economic power.[18] Zaire's government under Mobutu was, for example, declared in 1981 by Zairian bishops as representing an "organized pillage for the profit of the foreigner and his intermediaries."[19] While Mobutu's regime is often regarded as the epitome of squandering public funds by the elite, many African states are characterized by this self-serving intervention.[20]

Ensuring the minimum state commitment necessary for achieving the goals of economic liberation and human resources development requires some degree of control of decisionmaking by the general population. Given the lack of political empowerment of the African masses due to their lack of education and organization, the African elite, for the most part, used the state like the colonialists, for extracting wealth from society for self-enrichment instead of for liberating society at large. The state thus became paternalistic, unaccountable, and authoritarian, often suppressing individual liberty and resorting to brute force and foreign support to maintain order when challenged. The literature on the failure of the state is abundant.[21] A well-known scholar describes the failure of the post-independence state and its resemblance to the colonial state as follows:

> Nationalist revolution in Africa had less sweeping goals, and thus by silent incorporation it [the state] retained more of the operational code of its defeated enemy in the postcolonial polity. In metamorphosis the caterpillar becomes butterfly without losing its inner essences.[22]

Having essentially substituted the colonial bureaucracy, the self-serving elite has preoccupied itself primarily with accumulation of private wealth and maintenance of itself in power. As Nzongola-Ntalaja observes,[23] very limited supply of governmental energy and resources were committed for development purposes beyond the level of rhetoric. As a result, the deprivation of the general population's access to resources, the gap between the urban and rural areas, as well as the inequalities among ethnic groups and regions have by-and-large remained unresolved. In many cases they have even deteriorated since independence, leading to chronic conflicts. The conflicts in Rwanda, Burundi, Uganda, Somalia, Liberia, Sudan, and Chad are only the most obvious cases.

Clearly the disarticulated economy, uneven development, and ethnic strife were largely inherited from the colonial experience. The post-independence state was also ill-equipped to deal with all these problems. Limited bureaucratic capability (absent proper training and experience) and lack of infrastructure undermined its ability to deal with the problems of uneven development and to promote state-building. Continued unfavorable international conditions such as declining commodity prices and terms of trade have also contributed to the failure of the state. State-building and economic transformation under these conditions are difficult to attain.

The lack of success in restructuring the economy, in controlling the process of accumulation, and in creating conditions for socio-economic development also undermined national independence from foreign domination. With deepening economic crisis in the 1980s, the African state has increasingly surrendered economic policymaking to the IMF, World Bank, and bilateral lenders. In terms of economic policymaking, the African state seems much less independent in the 1990s than it was at the time of formal independence.

Under these conditions, the redistributive, market-creating, and human resource-developing roles that proponents of state intervention attribute to the state hardly apply to most of the existing state in Africa. Moreover, far from mitigating the coercion of the market mechanism, as expected by the critics of neo-liberalism, the state in fact has compounded the market's coercion. Its regulations, such as price controls, are usually anti-peasantry, which continues to be deprived not only of resources allocated by the market but also of those allocated by the state. Access to public services such as schools and health care as well as to subsidized credits and productive services, for example, is severely limited.

When both the market and the state fail, the failure of the state is more detrimental than that of the market. First, despite its importance, the market is essentially a device that cannot operate properly without the right conditions—which can only be established by the state. We will come back to this point in the next section of this chapter. Second, as we have already seen, the market's failure is primarily in terms of coordinating available resources with social needs. At the micro level, there are sufficient empirical indications that the private sector is generally more cost-effective than public enterprises. When state policy fails, however, in addition to failing to coordinate resources with social needs, it also usually fails in terms of micro-level efficiency. The private sector is certainly not a guarantee for superior efficiency. Generally, however, excessive centralization, incentive problems, and multiplicity of goals tend to make the public sector relatively less efficient than the private sector. Moreover, when state policy fails it hampers the efficiency of the private sector through various measures.

Considering its superior micro-level efficiency, the market is likely to generate relatively faster growth and greater trickle-down than the public sector under a self-serving state or under a state that suffers from technical incompetence. Expanding the domain of the market at the expense of that of the state would clearly be a superior option or a "second best" choice. However, the dynamics of this "second best" are also fundamentally limited. As already discussed, it is highly unlikely that the market's trickles will be sufficient to alleviate poverty or transform the subsistence sector in African countries. More importantly, marketization is unlikely to be sustained under a self-serving state. Such a state is likely to tolerate a market system only to the extent that the market does not adversely affect its interests or if the alternatives are more adverse to its interests. As already noted, to the extent that the elite wants to maintain a monopoly of political power, it cannot allow a free market that may lead to economic empowerment of its opponents unless forced to do so by opposition forces and other members of civil society.

The African condition, therefore, provides us with the challenge of what to do when both the market and the state fail. Restricting the role of the state in favor of that of the market, as neo-liberals suggest, is a poor choice for a number of reasons. First since the market operates within the rules of the game set by the state it is unlikely to function properly when the state is malevolent.

Second, the balance of social classes in most of Africa does not allow significant and sustainable restriction of the role of the state. As noted in the previous chapter, the African state is fluid with no firm hegemony of any particular class. The development of the African bourgeoisie as a class has been impeded by its inability to control and expand the process of accumulation and to develop a domestic market where it could ascertain its independence. Its ability to create jobs and a working class that depends on it for its economic livelihood is quite limited. Consequently, it is largely incapable of imposing a free market hegemony over the rest of society.

The petty bourgeoisie has also been incapable of establishing a hegemony due to its class nature. This is a fluid class whose membership ranges from the owners of small enterprises to the intelligentsia and other professionals. This class has no common ideological affiliation and no common position on how to restructure the African economy. The masses (the urban poor and the peasantry), on the other hand, are largely excluded from access to resources, including political decisionmaking. As a result, they are incapable of forming a hegemony. However, to the extent that they can exert any influence, they are unlikely to be supporters of a free market system, given their dismal purchasing power. The frequent riots against IMF imposed conditionalities are indicative of this.[24]

Finally, as noted in Chapter 2, the state in less diversified economies, unlike the state in advanced countries, faces a number of compelling reasons to intervene in economic activity even when it is not self-serving. Among these reasons are: (a) fragmentation of the economy, (b) weakness of the private sector, (c) the difficult international competition that newcomers to industrialization face, (d) the domination of the modern private sector by foreign concerns, which is often perceived as hampering economic independence, and (e) rapid population growth that undermines their economies and threatens their political systems.[25]

Considerable across-the-board disengagement of the state, therefore, is not likely nor is it a sustainable solution to Africa's general crisis. There is no strong demand for such curtailment of the state among social classes in Africa. The small bourgeoisie expects investment incentives, such as tax breaks and tariff protection from international competition; the petty bourgeois and urban dwellers expect subsidies on food, health care, and educational facilities; the peasantry requires subsidies on productivity-raising resources, although it rarely gets them. The drive to limit the role of the state and to impose a private enterprise is essentially an external imposition by the powerful actors of the global economy, which has come to be known as the "Washington consensus."[26] In other words, the anti-state neo-liberal ideology is essentially an external imposition with little internal foundation in Africa. It is thus unlikely to succeed since it does not correspond with the social and structural conditions of the receiving societies. If it succeeds, it is likely to continue to promote Africa's marginalization, since it neglects internal dynamics. Development is a complex process and the strategies designed to promote it have also to correspond with the social context. Otherwise they may become inappropriate, as importation of technology often turns out to be inappropriate for a number of reasons. Sustaining structural adjustment programs has already proved to be difficult in Africa.

The solution to the dilemma lies in reforming the African state and in expanding its capability in order to promote a society-serving developmentalist intervention in place of the self-serving intervention that largely characterizes it at the present time. Promoting a developmentalist intervention does not imply weakening the market. On the contrary, it involves coordinating the roles of the state and the market in such a way that the benefits from the strengths of each are maximized. Given the failures of the state and the market and the absence of any hegemonic class in Africa's socioeconomic landscape, a mixed economic strategy—a partnership of the essential components of the two devices of political economy—seems to be a more appropriate strategy. As we saw in Chapter 4, the African state is already under growing popular pressure for much wider social change than mere economic liberalization. An attempt is now made to define the anatomy of a mixed economy.

## Anatomy of a Mixed Economy and its Appropriateness

Critical distinctions between the market and the private sector and between price policy and laissez-faire, to which Paul Streeten[27] draws attention, are helpful in identifying the essential components of the market that need to be incorporated into a mixed economic strategy. The market is all too often associated with the private sector. However, it is not necessarily limited to the private sector nor is the public sector inherently incompatible with the market mechanism. There is ample evidence that public firms, like private firms, can be operated along market lines.[28] Laissez-faire and price policy are also two very different concepts. Laissez-faire refers to the free play of market forces without or with minimum state intervention. By contrast, distribution of goods and services through a price system can be an instrument of state policy.

One implication of these distinctions is that the price policy, which is critical in guiding resource allocation by providing information to producers, can operate in an economy where state intervention is significant or even dominant. Another implication is that public firms, if they are run as profit seekers, like private firms, can operate efficiently and do not undermine the price mechanism. Moreover, public firms can create economic externalities when they operate in areas where private firms do not exist and they can be instrumental in promoting competition when they coexist with private firms.

With this clarification, a mixed economy can be defined as an economic system which, like the private-enterprise market system, mostly relies on the price mechanism but in which, unlike the private-enterprise market system, the state largely defines long-term economic goals and actively participates in both the distribution and production systems in order to create access to resources to the deprived segments of society, to create economic externalities, and to better coordinate and promote development. In other words, in a mixed economy, unlike in a private-enterprise (laissez-faire) market system, state policy is not subordinated to market forces.

139

Instead, the market is a policy instrument of the state. Moreover, in a mixed economy, the market is largely subject to and not outside the collective decisions of society (democracy).

This definition does not provide specific guidelines on the magnitude of state involvement in distribution, in setting of economic goals, or in direct participation in production. The reason is that the desirable mix between the state and the market is likely to hinge on the degree of social inequality and the transformation of the peasantry, on the level of development of the private sector, and on the level of diversification and international competitiveness of the economy. The less the general population is able to influence economic decisions through its purchasing power, the less the market is able to coordinate resources with social needs and the more essential the role of the state becomes in distribution, in setting economic goals, and in guiding the effort to attain them. In addition, the less advanced the private sector and economic diversification are, the more the state needs to engage in direct production for purposes of creating economic externalities and promoting international competitiveness. In this case a mixed economy is essentially a corporatist system, in which, as Milner notes, policy is a negotiated outcome between different social groups.[29] This negotiated economy is made possible by the weakness of the private sector, which reflects the inability of the bourgeoisie or any other class to establish hegemony over the rest of society. A mixed economic strategy is also compatible with social democracy, which (as we saw in the previous chapter) is also a compromise among different social classes. Moreover, a mixed economy allows a delicate balance between globalism and autocentricity, and between national capitalism and global capitalism.

## Possibilities a Mixed Economy Creates

For less developed economies such as those of sub-Saharan Africa, a mixed economic system creates a number of possibilities that laissez-faire and statist systems do not. In terms of allocative efficiency, the relative performances of the private enterprise system and a mixed economy with considerable state ownership are difficult to determine. As Stiglitz notes,[30] contrary to the general perception, only under exceptional circumstances are markets Pareto efficient—an optimum allocation in which no further improvement in the economic conditions of individuals is possible without making other individuals worse off. This gives the state the scope to engage in welfare-enhancing intervention. In theory, it can also enhance efficiency by correcting some of the most important failures and imperfections of the market.[31] However, in actuality there are many factors that undermine the efficiency of the state. Multiplicity of objectives, equity concerns, problems of information, and immunity from competition often granted to public enterprises are among the most important.[32] Nevertheless, in less diversified economies where the market system is underdeveloped, a mixed economy can be more effective in coordinating economic activity with social needs, and thereby in developing human resources in general and transforming the peasantry in particular, as well as in promoting economic diversification.

As a principal actor in a mixed economy, the state can formulate economic policies that improve the peasantry's access to resources. Only the state can provide peasants with access to productivity-raising resources such as fertilizers, appropriate tools, better quality seeds, research services, training, human and livestock health care services, and marketing facilities. The private-enterprise market system lacks the mechanisms to provide these services to the peasants who have not attained the necessary level of purchasing power. The state can use a combination of measures such as subsidized prices and long-term loans in providing such services. No doubt that resource limitation is a serious constraint on such measures, however, gradual progress is possible provided there is the political will that gives priority to the peasant sector. Ensuring that the benefits go to the targeted groups is another technical obstacle. But such problems also can be largely overcome, especially if peasants are organized into some sort of cooperatives and are empowered with the distribution of such resources.

Additionally, the state can play a major role in creating an atmosphere conducive for mobilizing peasants to assume responsibility for their own transformation. The experience of the post-reform Chinese village complex is extremely valuable in this regard. The village complex in many parts of China is engaged not only in agricultural production but also in industrial and commercial activities. Land, property, and enterprises are owned by the village collectively but they are run along the lines of a price system by a unified management of the village committee.[33] Empowerment of the peasantry, utilizing the price system and collective enrichment, are the lessons that can be learned from the Chinese village complex. Such an arrangement—which is consistent with a mixed

economic strategy and which develops partnership not only between the state and the market but also between the state, civil
society, and the market—can become a reality only with active
involvement of the state.

In the short to intermediate runs, such policies designed to
transform the peasantry imply a rural-biased development strategy.
However, without such rural transformation, the modern sector
is likely to remain an enclave, and control of the national process
of accumulation and reversing the growing marginalization of
African economies in the international economic system are
unlikely to be achieved. At the present level of African economies,
transforming the subsistence sector, which implies expansion of
the domestic market, is probably the most important economic
externality that the state can create for the entire economy.

Transforming the peasantry can also lead to a major redefini-
tion of urban–rural relations. It can promote small-scale rural
industrialization, creating alternative employment for peasants and
reducing rural poverty. As a result, it can curve rural–urban migration and better integrate the two sectors to complement each other.
It may also mitigate the alarming rate of environmental degradation that many African states presently face partly due to the
growing impoverishment of the peasantry. Massive environmental
degradation has already led to severe yield decline and deterioration
of pasture land in many African countries.

Furthermore, transforming the peasantry has critical implications to the rehabilitation and development of the food sector which
is unlikely to be brought about by the market system alone. The
market system's price incentive which encourages only the capable
commercial and above-subsistence farmers has largely failed to
invigorate the food sector. This failure has a lot to do with the
market's encouragement of production by the few without raising
the productive capability and purchasing power of the multitude.
The commercial farmers often switch to the production of the more
attractive cash crops and, even when food production rises, the
poor that are largely left out of the production process are unable
to afford to buy food. A mixed economic strategy, which retains the
price incentives and creates access to productivity-raising resources
to the peasantry, has a higher potential to alleviate poverty and to
reverse Africa's declining per capita food production and its rapidly
rising food import bills.

Another area where state involvement is crucial in Africa is in
supporting industries that have the potential to improve a country's

position in the global division of labor. One aspect of this involves support for diversifying the export sector and making it more competitive on the international market. Considering the magnitude of the influence multinational corporations and governments of advanced countries wield in determining the structure of global competition, it is farfetched to expect industrialization to succeed in Africa and other developing countries without active state involvement. It is thus critical that the state in Africa support carefully selected export activities. Another aspect of the same objective is supporting selected import-substituting industries to build a domestic industrial base. Some complications are likely to arise in pursuing these two sides of the same objective. Export promotion may, for example, require measures such as devaluation of national currencies, tax relief, and other subsidies. Support for import substitution, on the other hand, may require lowering import duties for selected industries and preferential access to foreign exchange to facilitate the importation of intermediate goods and other inputs. In an attempt to overcome such conflicts many countries use a multiple-exchange-rate system and exchange-rate controls which often are additional administrative burdens on the economy. As a result of these complications, many have argued against import substitution. It is, however, unclear how to promote exports in manufacturing without some experience in agriculture-led industrialization and collective import substitution, especially in the absence of notable foreign investments.

While not easy, considerable industry-specific and nonconflicting incentive systems can be developed to carefully pursue both tracks. Direct and indirect subsidies, direct and indirect lending, publicly provided services, including research and marketing support are among the measures available for the state. Such involvement of the state in the African situation would clearly represent market-creating and market-facilitating activities. As discussed in Chapter 3, regionalism and collective self-reliance can make possible—at least initially—the simultaneous implementation of agriculture-linked industrialization, import-substitution, and export-promotion strategies.

In areas where there is no private-sector investment or there is an oligopolized market, the state can directly participate in production to provide economic externalities and to provoke competition. Such activities, especially in industries that are essential for the development of the national economy, do not hurt the operations of the market or the private sector. Rather, as

Rueschemeyer and Evans note, they elicit entrepreneurial behavior from otherwise too comfortable oligopolists.[34] As the private sector grows, however, its participation in state-owned industries (as shareholders with the state or as full owners and competitors) should be open in order to engender competition and efficiency.

It goes without saying that state activity is clearly required in providing infrastructure such as schools, hospitals, roads, railways, power stations, and telecommunication facilities. Investments in these areas do not attract private capital as they do not render quick returns. They are, however (needless to say), essential for national-development-creating external economies for all sectors of the economy. Thus, the criteria for economic reforms in Africa should be how to use the state and the market effectively to solve problems and not simply to reduce the role of the state at any cost as the current counterrevolution attempts to do.

## Essential Conditions for a Mixed Economy

The foregoing discussion attempted to establish the advantages of a mixed economy over laissez-faire and statism. This section of the chapter attempts to identify the most important preconditions for the success of a mixed economic strategy. One critical requisite on which the argument for a mixed economy rests is that the state acts in the social interest instead of in a self-serving manner. Opponents of state intervention claim that government policies generally reflect self-interest and/or the interests of the dominant social groups. James Buchanan, for example, raises the question of "why the state should be assumed to act in the social interest when everyone else is more or less self-seeking."[35] A mixed economic system under a self-serving state essentially leads to a mixture of an inefficient sector controlled by a self-serving state with another sector under an exclusivist private-enterprise market system. This combination—which is presently predominant in most African states—has produced the worst of both worlds.

There are, however, theoretical and empirical indications that the state serves evolving interests and that, under certain conditions, can act largely in the social interest.[36] One theory states that there is a symbiotic relation between state and economy which can make the state act in the social interest.[37] This implies that realization that their own long-term interests are best served by national development would induce state functionaries to act in the social interest. Among the reasons for the success of the developmentalist state in the Asian NICs, for example, is claimed to be its autonomy from undue influence by powerful interest groups which enabled it to act in the interests of society at large. As Zia Onis notes,[38] the logic of the developmental state rests on the combination of bureaucratic autonomy with a high degree of public–private cooperation.

State functionaries as well as the national bourgeoisie, like other segments of society, can benefit from increased control over the national process of capital accumulation. There is, thus, a reason for them to be part of a national front for structural change to avert national self-destruction. However, this has not happened with Africa's present leadership. This may be due to the weakness of the national bourgeoisie or its compradorized nature. In any case, the theory of state–economy symbiotic relations provides no guarantees that the state functionaries would have the consciousness to identify their long-term interests with social interests. There is also no compelling reason to believe that they would choose to sacrifice short-term gains for long-term interests.

The emergence of civil society, which has been treated as the defender of society from the malevolent state by much of the literature, also provides no guarantee. As noted in the previous chapter, civil society, which can rally in the safeguarding of civil rights, is not free from functional divisions as well as class and ethnic conflicts. There is thus no compelling reason to expect that civil society as a united force would be the defender of broad social interests. The relative strength of classes that may lead to the compromises of social democracy may, however, lead to some protection of social interests.

A more reliable condition for the protection of broad social interests is democratization—empowering the general population to control decisionmaking. Democratization fosters governance, which Robert Charlick[39] defines as an effective management of public affairs through the generation of a widely accepted set of rules for promoting societal values. Genuine democratization promotes a high degree of state autonomy from the domination by special interests and allows the state to act in the social interest and to become developmentalist.

Democracy does not necessarily provide a full proof against the domination of the state by the interests of the elite. However, democracy provides the best chance for the masses to curtail the undue power of the elite, to influence policy, and thereby to advance social interests. The economic system that emerges from such a democratic social compromise is essentially a mixed economy. Robert Dahl advances a compelling argument that democracies are characterized by mixed economies.[40] Our analysis shows that mixed economies also require democracy to succeed.

The conditions essential for successful democratization, including the development of the masses, the ability of the lower classes to curtail the domination by the elite, and the resurgence of civil society, which plays a critical role in safeguarding civil rights, are all essential for the proper functioning of a mixed economic strategy. In this regard too, the African condition faces a vicious circle. As noted at the beginning of this chapter, among the reasons for the need of an active state and a mixed economy was the weakness of the private sector and civil society and the disenfranchisement of the masses. Paradoxically, the more the role of the state is needed due to the underdevelopment of civil society, the more prone the state is to becoming authoritarian and self-serving, hindering the development of civil society. Thus, as already argued, the state is not to be given a blank check of support. However, the development of civil society and the empowerment of the masses is also unlikely to take place without the active involvement of the state. Hence, prematurely removing the state from economic activity or weakening its role also threatens the development of the private sector, civil society, and the masses. Civil society in Africa now is clearly more developed than it was at the time of independence. The prospects for breaking the vicious circle which impedes democracy and a mixed economy are thus better. Yet a reformed state remains a critical partner in any further progress.

Another important condition for the success of a mixed economy is the presence of a certain level of capability of the state to act coherently and effectively. If it does not, it would be, as Putterman notes, "a prescription for disaster to assign major policy tasks to it."[41] Even when it has the minimum required level of bureaucratic capability, it is critical for the state to avoid excessive centralization. As already noted, the state generally lacks effective means of acquiring information. African states also lack a number of other crucial factors, including technically sophisticated managerial capability and the technical level necessary for timely processing of information. Under these conditions decentralization is, as Stiglitz notes, a form of risk diversification.[42] It is also, as noted in the previous chapter, a critical aspect of democratization and state-building. It is a mechanism that can contribute in curtailing the state's tendency to degenerate into an elite or self-serving device.[43]

In conclusion, the analysis in this chapter affirms the relevance of the role of the state. The market cannot be an alternative or a substitute for the state since it cannot function properly under a malevolent state and it cannot perform the roles of the state. The primacy of political reforms over economic reforms—or at least the recognition that both have to take place simultaneously—is also affirmed. The argument that economic reforms should precede democratization is misguided.[44] A malevolent state can always impede and undermine any economic reforms. Finally, the role of the state within a democratic context is not to replace the market; rather, as Mamdani notes, it is the best venue to promote a functional market system.[45]

## Notes

1. Paul P. Streeten, "Against Minimalism," in Louis Putterman and Dietrich Rueschemeyer, eds., *State and Market in Development: Synergy or Rivalry?* (Boulder, Lynne Rienner, 1992), 15–38.
2. Mrinal Datta-Chaudhuri, "Market Failure and Government Failure," *Journal of Economic Perspectives* 4, no. 3 (Summer 1990): 25–39.
3. Datta-Chaudhuri, "Market Failure."
4. Wim F. Wertheim, "The State and the Dialectics of Emancipation," *Development and Change* 23, no. 3 (July 1992): 257–81.
5. Wertheim, "The State and the Dialectics of Emancipation," 261.
6. Wertheim, "The State and the Dialectics of Emancipation," 262. For further details on the role of the state in economic development see Thomas Callaghy, "The State and Development of Capitalism in Africa: Theoretical, Historical, and Comparative Reflections," in Donald Rothchild and Naomi Chazan, eds., *The Precarious Balance: State and Society in Africa* (Boulder: Westview Press, 1988), 67–99; Dietrich Rueschemeyer and Peter Evans, "The State and Economic Transformation: Toward an Analysis of the Conditions Underlying Effective Intervention," in P.B. Evans, D. Rueschemeyer, and T. Skoçpol, eds., *Bringing the State Back In* (New York: Cambridge University Press, 1985), 44–77. Robert B. Reich, *The Work of Nations: Preparing Ourselves for the 21st Century Capitalism* (New York: Alfred A. Knopf, 1991) also provides very useful insights on the role of the state in the industrialization of the United States.
7. Alexander Gershenkron, *Economic Backwardness in Historical Perspective* (New York: Praeger, 1962), 20.

147

8.  Charles E. Lindblom, "The Market as Prison," *Journal of Politics* 44, no. 2 (May 1982): 325–36.
9.  Manfred Bienefeld, "The New World Order: Echoes of a New Imperialism," *Third World Quarterly* 15, no. 1 (1994): 40.
10. Milton Friedman, *Capitalism and Freedom* (Chicago: Chicago University Press, 1962).
11. Friedrich A. Von Hayek, *The Road to Serfdom* (London: Routledge and Sons, 1944).
12. Crawford B. Macpherson, *Democratic Theory: Essays in Retrieval* (Oxford: Clarendon Press, 1973); Ellen Meiksins Wood, *Democracy Against Capitalism* (Cambridge: Cambridge University Press, 1995).
13. Macpherson, *Democratic Theory.*
14. Adam Przeworski, *Democracy and the Market: Political and Economic Reforms in Eastern Europe and Latin America* (Cambridge: Cambridge University Press, 1991), 125.
15. Datta-Chaudhuri, "Market Failure."
16. Henry Milner, *Social Democracy and Rational Choice: The Scandinavian Experience and Beyond* (London: Routledge, 1994).
17. Claude Ake, "How Politics Underdevelops Africa," in Adebayo Adedeji, Owodunni Teriba, and Patrick Bugembe, eds., *The Challenges of African Economic Recovery and Development* (London: Frank Cass, 1991), 316–29.
18. Ake, "How Politics Underdevelops Africa."
19. Quoted in Crawford Young, *The African Colonial State in Comparative Perspective* (New Haven and London: Yale University Press, 1994), 4.
20. For details on the failure of the state, see Robert M. Bates, *Markets and States in Tropical Africa* (Berkeley: University of California Press, 1981); Jennifer Seymour Whitaker, *How Can Africa Survive?* (New York: Harper and Row, 1988), 46; Edmund J. Keller, "The State in Contemporary Africa: A Critical Assessment of Theory and Practice," in Dankwart A. Rustow and Kenneth Paul Erikson, eds., *Comparative Political Dynamics: Global Research Perspectives* (New York: HarperCollins Publishers, 1991), 134–53; and Crawford Young, *The African Colonial State in Comparative Perspective* (New Haven and London: Yale University Press, 1994).
21. John A.A. Ayoade, "States Without Citizens: An Emerging African Phenomenon," in Donald Rothchild and Naomi Chazan, eds., *The Precarious Balance: State and Society in Africa* (Boulder: Westview Press, 1988); Robert H. Jackson and Carl G. Rosberg, "Why Africa's Weak States Persist: The Empirical and Juridical in Statehood," *World Politics* 35 (October 1982): 1–24.
22. Young, *The African Colonial State in Comparative Perspective*, 2.
23. Georges Nzongola-Ntalaja, *Revolution and Counter Revolution in Africa* (London: Zed Books Ltd., 1987), 77.
24. For details, see John Walton and David Seddon, *Free Markets and*

*Food Riots: The Politics of Global Adjustment* (Cambridge, MA: Blackwell Publishers, 1994), 23–54.

25. For details see James Caporaso, "The State's Role in Third World Economic Growth," *The Annals of the American Academy of Political and Social Science* 459 (January 1982) 103–11; Laing Gray Cowan, *Privatization in the Developing World* (New York: Greenwood Press, 1990).

26. Paul Krugman, "Dutch Tulips and Emerging Markets," *Foreign Affairs* 74, no. 4 (July/August 1995): 28-44.

27. Streeten, "Against Minimalism."

28. Streeten, "Against Minimalism"; Joseph E. Stiglitz, *The Economic Role of the State* (Cambridge, MA: Basic Blackwell, Inc., 1989), 33.

29. Milner, *Social Democracy and Rational Choice*, 116.

30. Stiglitz, *The Economic Role of the State.*

31. John R. Freeman, *Democracy and Markets: The Politics of Mixed Economies* (Ithaca: Cornell University Press, 1989), 69–72.

32. Stiglitz, *The Economic Role of the State*, 33–45.

33. Paul Bowles and Xiao-Yuan Dong, "Current Successes and Future Challenges in China's Economic Reforms," *New Left Review* 208 (November/December 1994): 49–76.

34. Rueschemeyer and Evans, "The State and Economic Transformation," 57.

35. Dietrich Rueschemeyer and Louis Putterman, "Synergy or Rivalry?" in Louis Putterman and Dietrich Rueschemeyer, eds., *State and Market in Development: Synergy or Rivalry?* (Boulder and London: Lynne Rienner, 1992), 248.

36. Rueschemeyer and Evans, "The State and Economic Transformation," 47.

37. Rueschemeyer and Putterman, "Synergy or Rivalry?" 256.

38. Zia Onis, "The Logic of Developmental State," *Comparative Politics* 24, no. 1 (October 1991): 109–26.

39. Robert Charlick, *The Concept of Governance and Its Implications for A.I.D.'s Development Assistance Program in Africa* (Washington, D.C.: Associates in Rural Development, 1992).

40. Robert Dahl, "Why All Democratic Countries Have Mixed Economies," in John W. Chapman and Ian Shapiro, eds., *Democratic Community* (New York: New York University Press, 1993), 259–82.

41. Rueschemeyer and Putterman, "Synergy or Rivalry?" 255.

42. Stiglitz, *The Economic Role of the State*, 35.

43. Rueschemeyer and Evans, "The State and Economic Transformation," 47.

44. For such an argument see Donald K. Emmerson, "Capitalism, Democracy, and the World Bank: What Is to Be Done?" in Lual Deng, Markus Kostner, and Crawford Young, eds., *Democratization and Structural Adjustment in Africa in the 1990s* (Madison: University of Wisconsin, African Studies Program, 1991), 9–12.

45. Mahmood Mamdani, "Democratization and Marketization," in K. Mengisteab and B. I. Logan, eds., *Beyond Economic Liberalization in Africa: Structural Adjustment and the Alternatives* (London: Zed Press and SAPES-SA, 1995).

# 6

# The Post-Cold War Global Order and Africa's Autocentric Development

▼  ▼  ▼

## Introduction

The discussion in the three preceding chapters attempted to identify the types of democracy, internal and regional integration, and economic system that will promote autocentric development without neglecting the benefits of globalism. The present chapter places African development within the global context. Given the weak economic and political position of sub-Saharan Africa, including internal fragmentation, excessive dependency, lack of control of the process of capital accumulation, and lack of food self-sufficiency, the global political economy is certain to be a critical factor in whether or not any development strategy, including an autocentric one, succeeds or fails in Africa. Yet the external environment is not necessarily the decisive factor unless African countries allow it to be. The main objectives of this chapter are to examine the most important constraints the external environment imposes on Africa and to explore some opportunities that may enhance its ability to control its development agenda as well as its process of accumulation. The chapter is organized into three parts. The first part briefly discusses the conditions the external environment presented African states during the Cold War era. The second part examines the nature of the emerging post-Cold War global division of labor and global distribution of power and Africa's place therein. The third and concluding section discusses some measures that may enable African states to reverse their growing marginalization from the global system and empower them to ward off some of the adverse impacts of the external environment.

## The Cold War

The Cold War clearly entailed a number of adverse impacts on Africa's socioeconomic development. Conflicts between and within African states were often intensified by the intervention of the two superpowers and their allies. The conflict in the Congo in the early 1960s, the Nigerian civil war, the Ethio-Somali wars, the long Ethio-Eritrean conflict, and the liberation struggles in Zimbabwe, Angola, Mozambique, Guinea Bissau, Namibia, and South Africa are among the obvious examples. Despite their formal membership in the Non-Aligned camp, many African countries, like other countries in the developing world, were sacked into one side or the other of the ideological divide instead of advancing their own cultural identities and pursuing development strategies more conducive to their own conditions. Neither ideological camp proved to be compatible with their socioeconomic interests.

The U.S.-led camp of the capitalist countries essentially applied the carrot and the stick to attract and keep African countries in its sphere of influence. It provided some incentives in the form of economic and military aid to the countries under its influence. The price for siding with the U.S. camp was maintaining the socioeconomic structures left behind by the colonial system. The interests and ideological orientation of this camp, by and large, did not allow fundamental changes in the existing social order. Nationalist liberation movements or governments with an agenda to control the process of accumulation were often subjected to protracted counterinsurgency or subversive interventions, economic sanctions, and other destabilizing measures under the guise of containing left-wing and pro-Soviet movements.

The socialist revolution originated with the goals of liberating oppressed and exploited people and creating an alternative international system by changing socioeconomic relations and by controlling the process of accumulation. The Soviet camp, especially initially, was generally supportive of liberation struggles. Even in the 1970s some liberation movements, notably those in Angola, Mozambique, and Zimbabwe, benefitted considerably from the support of the Soviet camp in gaining their independence as well as in staying in power. However, Soviet support often proved inconsistent with the objective of liberating people. Preoccupied with advancing its own hegemonic interests and competition for power and influence against the U.S.-led bloc, the Soviet Union began to lure Third World regimes that were sympathetic to it and those that had fallen from the grace of the U.S. camp irrespective of their commitments to democracy and the liberation of their peoples. In fact, the camp harbored some of the worst dictators Africa has seen, such as Mengistu Hailemariam of Ethiopia, simply because they adopted the rhetoric of socialism and proclaimed themselves "anti-imperialist."

Implementation of socialism, which, in contrast to Marx's predictions, was attempted in less advanced countries, encountered a number of problems, including absence of such preconditions as advanced democratic institutions and developed economies. Often the leadership of the countries where socialist revolutions were attempted became a self-serving elite which, despite its rhetoric, was antiliberation and antidemocratic. The absence of democratization and the rise of a new elite, in turn, undermined the popular alliance essential for creating an alternative economic system with a socialist development strategy.[1] The socialist camp operated largely within the capitalist camp, despite the destabilizing hostilities and economic sanctions it faced from the U.S.-led capitalist camp. The Soviet-supported African (Afro-Marxist) states, for instance, failed to bring about any notable changes in their economic structures or to promote control over the process of accumulation, despite some static redistributive measures such as land tenure reforms.

The Cold War global environment was not, however, entirely adverse to the interests of African countries. Despite being squeezed by the forces of the two blocs, which essentially discouraged autonomous social change, and despite intensification of internal conflicts due to external intervention, African countries, like other developing countries, were able to derive some benefits from the rivalry between the two camps. The Cold War facilitated the decolonization of African states in the early 1960s. Colonial monopolies were largely incompatible with the U.S.-led global liberal economic regime and the alliance among the former colonial powers that formed the anti-Soviet bloc. In spite of concerns that the vacuum left by the disintegration of empires may be filled by communists, the United States was, for the most part, opposed to colonialism in favor of universal free trade.[2]

The European powers, especially Britain, saw the colonies as a means of restoring lost glory and attempted to block decolonization. These intentions were evident from the following 1948 statement by the then foreign minister of Britain, Mr. Bevin:

> . . . to develop our own power and influence to equal that of the United States of America and the USSR. We have the material resources in the Colonial Empire, if we develop them, and by giving a spiritual lead now we should be able to carry out our task in a way which will show clearly that we are not subservient to the United States of America or to the Soviet Union.[3]

Such aspirations were, however, unattainable. Britain simply did not have the resources necessary to maintain its colonies. Resistance to decolonization was also likely to intensify the anticolonial struggle which would have given the Soviet Union more chance to influence nationalist forces in Africa and elsewhere in developing countries. This made relatively peaceful decolonization an essential requisite for collaboration between Africa and the European colonial powers and a mechanism of forestalling "communist penetration."[4]

The Cold War also enabled African countries and other developing countries to exercise some degree of autonomy.[5] Moreover, it allowed them to exert some influence on the international system. The Non-Aligned movement, the UN General Assembly, the United Nations Conference on Trade and Development (UNCTAD), and the United Nations Industrial Development Organization (UNIDO) were among some of the principal international forums that developing countries used in their efforts to influence the global agenda and to participate in the global decision-making process. Although it ultimately failed, UNCTAD, for example, represented an effort by developing countries to obtain better terms of trade and to establish a new international economic order in which their interests were better represented. The European Economic Community–African, Caribbean, and Pacific (EEC-ACP) agreements and the generalized system of preferences of the General Agreements on Tariffs and Trade (GATT) were some concessions of the Cold War era from which African states derived some modest benefits. Needless to say, these concessions were not significant enough to considerably improve their process of accumulation. The self-serving African leadership also largely squandered any benefits that were derived from these concessions.

Nevertheless, the Cold War—at least until the early 1970s when its full steam was mitigated by *detente*—was accompanied by relatively favorable commodity prices and terms of trade partly triggered by rather rapid economic growth in the industrialized countries. As indicated in Table 6.1, African countries experienced a modest economic growth during this period. They were also able to expand their infrastructure and health and educational services for about a decade and half after their independence.

## The Post-*Detente* Cold War Era

The bargaining power of African states in particular and those of developing countries in general and the benefits they derived from playing off the super powers and the two blocs against each other began to decline during the post-*detente* stage of the Cold War era. Declining commodity prices precipitated partly by synthetic substitutes to many primary products and partly by the recessions in many industrialized countries following the two oil crises of the 1970s, worsening terms of trade, mounting debt and debt-service obligations, shrinking resource inflows, rising OECD trade barriers, and more stringent conditionalities imposed by the multilateral financial institutions in accordance with the economic liberalization counterrevolution of the 1980s, were among the many devastating characteristics of this period.

Partly triggered by the debt crisis, which has eluded any solution, the 1980s also saw a rapid growth in the export of capital from the developing countries to the countries of the North. Broad and Cavanagh,[6] for example, estimate that in 1986 a 30-percent decline in less-developed countries' (LDCs) terms of trade resulted in a $94-billion transfer of income to the developed world. All this culminated in a widespread decline in rates of economic growth and drastic increases in poverty in most developing countries. African countries in particular fared extremely poorly during the last decade of the Cold War era (see Table 6.1).

The economic crisis of the 1980s was also accompanied by widespread political crisis. Failing to shelter its citizens from the crisis, the state in Africa increasingly lost its legitimacy and came to be perceived as a predatory institution acting as a middleman between society and the international system instead of as an apparatus that safeguards and promotes the interests of society.[7] Often it has also been regarded as partial in the competition for and

**Table 6.1**
**Africa's Average Annual Growth Rates (in %)**

|                | 1965–73 | 1973–80 | 1980–90 |
|----------------|---------|---------|---------|
| GDP            | 5.9     | 2.5     | 1.8     |
| GNP per capita | 2.9     | 0.1     | -1.1    |
| Agriculture    | 2.2     | -0.3    | 1.7     |
| Industry       | 13.8    | 4.3     | 1.2     |

*Sources*: International Monetary Fund, *World Economic Outlook: October 1993* (Washington, D.C.: IMF); UNDP, *Human Development Report* (New York: Oxford University Press, 1994); World Bank, *World Development Report 1994* (Oxford: Oxford University Press, 1994).

distribution of meager resources among different regions, ethnic groups, religious entities, and social classes within countries. As a result, various conflicts have intensified during the decade of the 1980s and they remain a major threat to national integration and state-building in many African countries.

Africa's political and economic crises have by the end of the 1980s culminated in increased marginalization of the continent from the global system despite its relative wealth in resources and the large size of its rapidly growing population, presently estimated at about 600 million (see Table 6.2). The following *New York Times* report underscores Africa's deepening marginalization in the global economic system.

> Africa's share of world trade . . . is now closer to 2 percent. That is so marginal it is almost as if the continent has curled up and disappeared from the map of international shipping lanes and airline routes that rope together Europe, North America and the booming Far East. Direct foreign investment in Africa is so paltry it is not even measured in the latest World Bank study.[8]

Africa's image has also been tarnished, exacerbating its marginalization. The economic downturn and the general political crisis and ethnic conflicts have continued in the early 1990s despite some promising changes such as the liberation of South Africa and the settlements of some conflicts, including the Ethio-Eritrean conflict and Mozambique's civil war. As already noted, the state has disintegrated in Liberia, Somalia, Rwanda, and Sierra Leone. Some other countries, particularly Zaire, Burundi, and the Sudan, also find themselves dangerously on the brink of disintegration. How

**Table 6.2**
**Sub-Saharan Africa's Share in Aggregate GDP, Exports, and Debt as Percent of Totals of the World and of LDCs (1990)**

| Total GDP | | Total Exports | | Total Debt |
|---|---|---|---|---|
| LDCs | World | LDCs | World | LDCs |
| 4.4 | 1.5 | 3.3 | 0.7 | 8.7 |

*Source*: International Monetary Fund, *World Economic Outlook: October 1993* (Washington, D.C.: IMF, 1993), 125.

is the post-Cold War global order likely to affect the African condition?

## The Emerging Post-Cold War Global Order

Whether the end of the Cold War represents a watershed in the global system and signifies a beginning of a fundamentally different global order is debatable.[9] There is little doubt, however, that the conclusion of the Cold War has signaled a new configuration of global power. The bipolar system of the Cold War has vanished. The global liberal economic order, which was championed by the United States during the Cold War, has also been intensified. Rapid globalization, indicated by increased mobility of capital and production facilities across borders and growing liberalization of trade, has become the hallmark of the post-Cold War order. With globalization, the state has also increasingly disengaged from economic activity. Wide-ranging deregulation, privatization, and retrenchment of expenditures on social programs are among the manifestations of the state's growing disengagement.

The post-Cold War global power configuration is still in a formative stage and it is too early to determine its nature with a reasonable degree of certainty. However, as Krauthammer notes, the current period of transition is essentially characterized by a "unipolar moment" under U.S. dominance.[10] Many analysts have argued that a unipolar system is untenable and that the global system is headed toward a multipolar system.[11] A detailed discussion on how long a unipolar system might last or what type of a multipolar system is likely to emerge is beyond the scope of this chapter. The primary concern here is rather to examine the possible implications of each scheme for Africa's socioeconomic development. The possible scenarios for the emerging global distribution of power include a unipolar system under U.S. preponderance, a managed multipolar system, and a competitive multipolar system. Although less likely in the near future, there is also a fourth possibility—what Samir Amin refers to as a polycentric system.[12] This fourth order will be discussed in the last section of the chapter.

## Africa in a Unipolar World Order

Following the collapse of the Soviet Union, the United States clearly emerged as the sole super power in the world. President Bush's declaration in his 1992 State of the Union address that "a world once divided into two armed camps now recognizes one sole and pre-eminent power: the United States of America," was not merely wishful thinking. There are also considerable indications that the U.S. administration envisions and intends to create a world order in which the bipolar global system is replaced by a unipolar U.S. hegemony.

As Layne notes,[13] the Pentagon's Defense Planning Guidance (DPG) for fiscal years 1994–1999 and the 1991 summer study organized by the Pentagon's Director of Net Assessment indicate a vision of a unipolar world order and a view that a multipolar system is dangerously unstable. Among other things the Pentagon's DPG proposes for the United States to:

1. Ensure that no rival superpower arises anywhere in the world;

2. Discourage advanced industrial nations from challenging American leadership;

3. Use military force, if necessary, to prevent proliferation of nuclear weapons;

4. Threaten retaliation in kind against any country that uses such weapons; and

5. Form coalitions with other nations where possible, but to act independently where such coalitions are not forthcoming.

Another indication of America's hegemonic interests is its resistance to peacekeeping activities by regional powers such as

Russia and the Conference on Security and Cooperation in Europe (CSCE). As manifested by the crisis in Bosnia, the other powers have also not been able to formulate and implement any credible conflict resolution measures without U.S. leadership.

A unipolar system faces a number of difficulties, including doubts as to whether the United States has the economic muscle to impose and sustain it. Its share of world income, which was around 50 percent in the 1950s, has been cut by half and it is likely to continue to decline as new economic powers rise. Its economy is also vulnerable to external pressures due to its massive budgetary and trade deficits.[14] As Gergen suggests,[15] the victory in the Gulf War, which seemed to be "a magical restoration of America's greatness," was quickly undermined by persistent economic problems and a lingering recession. The country's determination to form a unipolar hegemony also faces widespread popular apprehension about becoming the world's policeman. The Pentagon's 1991 Summer Study, however, reinforces the vision of U.S. preponderance and a world in which there is no threat to America's super power role.[16] With the recovery of the U.S. economy from the recession while the economies of other industrialized powers, especially those of Japan and Germany, continued to experience a number of difficulties has also given impetus to the unipolar hegemonic aspirations of the United States.

Despite its economic vulnerability evidenced by its dependence on foreign capital, the United States has presently established a unipolar preponderance, although the degree of its dominance and its likelihood to last are questionable. There are a number of factors that would seem to enable the United States to sustain a hegemonic power. Its military superiority is uncontested. It has also maintained its structural power as it still establishes the rules of the global economic system.[17] Furthermore, the United States continues to exercise decisive influence over the MFIs and has the powerful tool of denying to contenders and adversaries access to its huge capital and product markets.[18] Moreover, in cases where existing regional balance of power appeared to be threatened, as in the cases of Iraq and North Korea, it has shown little hesitation to act. With its present unipolar position, the United States also appears to have strengthened the global liberal economic regime. We now examine the implications of a unipolar system and intensification of the global liberal regime for developing nations in general and for Africa in particular.

## A Unipolar Hegemony and Global Resource Distribution

In the Gramscian sense two types of hegemony may be identified.[19] One is when the hegemonic power exercises a function of political and moral direction in the international system. In this case the hegemon takes into account the interests and aspirations of allied groups of countries and renounces part of the narrow economic corporate benefits which its position might enable it to acquire.[20] The second type of hegemony is essentially an imperialistic domination based on force and fraud and not on the consensus of other countries or groups of countries. Under the second type of self-serving hegemony the international system is unlikely to be stable for long.

Given these two broad categories, the characteristics of the emerging global order can provide a clue as to the likely nature of U.S. hegemony. In the 1950s and the 1960s, the global liberal regime was accompanied by rapid growth. Since the 1980s the global regime has entered a new era that Robert Cox characterizes as "new capitalism" whose "thrust is deregulation, privatization, and the dismantling of state protection for the vulnerable elements of society."[21] Unlike in the 1950s and 1960s, the intensified global liberal regime has been plagued by stagnation of real wages, growing job insecurity, and, in many cases, rising rates of chronic unemployment. It has also intensified income disparity: "the rich are getting fewer and richer and the poor poorer and more numerous" all over the world.[22]

With freer mobility of capital and production facilities, and more countries competing to offer lower wages, less regulations, and attractive tax breaks to multinational corporations, the United States has lost its competitive edge in some industries. It has also seen a decline in standard of living partly due to the large military expenditures during the Cold War. Many of the country's leaders have attributed the country's economic problems to unfair trading by other countries, overlooking internal factors.[23] As a result, there has been growing pressure to violate the laissez-faire liberalism the country has championed since the 1940s. This is evident from the protectionist measures the United States has imposed on a number of products in which it has lost competitiveness to foreign producers and its vigorous enforcement of the so-called "unfair" trade laws. A 1989 OECD study, for example, found that in the 1980s the

United States had the worst record among the industrialized countries in erecting trade barriers.[24] In light of these inconsistencies, the credibility of the United States as a champion of laissez-faire liberalism has been eroded. A noted economist characterizes U.S. leadership in support of a liberal trade regime in the following manner:

> American trade policy has become increasingly schizophrenic as fear of competition and pressures from special interests influence a variety of sectoral policies even as we continue to assert our support for an open multilateral system.[25]

Despite frequent violations of the liberal economic regime, mainly in an attempt to capture lost dominance and to protect industries threatened by competition, the United States continues to spearhead and intensify the regime, which emphasizes efficiency and economic growth over redistribution. The social classes that benefit from and support globalism have remained stronger than those that support more nationalist capitalism in the country. The United States also continues, directly and through the MFIs, to press developing countries and countries with weak economies, such as those of Eastern Europe and the former Soviet Union, to practice laissez-faire liberalism. Often times these countries are bullied into executing liberal policies more stringently than they are practiced by the industrial powers themselves. Adherence to structural adjustment programs has become a condition for access to private and public loans and other types of economic assistance for developing countries. Imposing economic liberalization and structural adjustment programs on these countries when the appropriateness of such policies, especially for low-income developing countries, is widely contested can hardly be regarded as magnanimous leadership. For many developing countries liberalization has been accompanied by growing debt service, worsening terms of trade, rising transfer of wealth to the North, and accentuation of social polarization between rich and poor.

As Cox[26] and Bienefeld[27] note, the emerging New World Order has reduced the role of the state, especially in the developing world, to adjusting the economy to the less regulated global economy. In these countries the state has faced campaigns that attempt to discredit and dismantle it by "weakening its authority, destroying its morale and diluting its resource base." The United States, the MFIs, and a proliferation of nongovernmental organizations

(NGOs) have all participated in this campaign. To be sure, many NGOs attempt to help and shelter the poor from the cruelties of their own governments and often are opposed to the deregulation of the global market that victimizes the destitute the most. However, many NGOs, especially the most powerful, are active in the campaign against the state and in promoting the emerging new order. Such campaigns are essentially robbing the Third World state of its relative autonomy and weakening its ability to resist the hegemony of the unfolding wild "new capitalism."

There are also a number of other reasons why post-Cold War U.S. hegemony is likely to be the self-serving type.[28] As already noted, the magnitude of U.S. economic dominance over other industrial powers is much smaller at the end of the Cold War than it was at the end of the Second World War. The United States is, therefore, not in a position to be magnanimous when it is engaged in a serious competition with the economies of the other industrial powers which are potential contenders. This weakness is evident in the foot-dragging of the United States in policing conflict areas, such as Bosnia and Rwanda.[29]

Many of the problems that the international system faces in the 1990s and beyond are also unlikely to be managed by hegemonic impositions. The most important global problems, which include poverty in developing countries, environmental problems, and proliferation of nuclear weapons, require a more democratic collective action. Hegemonic powers tend to find solutions not imposed by themselves unacceptable and the United States is not likely to be an exception.

Overcoming the problem of poverty clearly requires joint efforts by countries of both the South and the North. Real solutions to such a problem cannot be imposed by a hegemonic power of the North, especially one that is not magnanimous. The United States is not likely to have either the resources or the political will to champion poverty alleviation in developing countries. Its resistance during the Cold War to the demands by developing countries for a New International Economic Order and lack of serious effort to find solutions for the debt crisis are indications. Its aid commitment, for example, has declined from 0.31 percent of its GNP in 1970 to 0.17 percent in 1991.[30] This level of commitment, which is the lowest of the seven leading industrial powers, also hardly demonstrates leadership in the fight to alleviate poverty. Growing disengagement of the state from economic activity and growing poverty within its own borders further prevent the United States from playing a leading role in this area. Understandably, a growing perspective among its citizens is "we can not take care of the world's poor when we have not taken care of ours." The ideology behind the global liberal economic regime, however, emphasizes growth and productivity and not redistribution.

Similarly, solutions to environmental problems, especially issues of overpopulation, deforestation, and pollution, which are closely related to problems of poverty and maldistribution of income, cannot be imposed by a unipolar hegemon. Rather, meaningful solutions are likely to require collective decisions and measures. Presently the United States government is regarded as a major obstacle to a treaty on global warming while members of its scientific community provide technical leadership on the ensuing dangers of the problem.[31]

Proliferation of nuclear weapons is another global security problem that requires collective effort. While not a direct threat to U.S. security, proliferation, as Jervis points out,[32] constitutes a limitation or a deterrent to its intervention in the regions of proliferators. The United States has clearly an interest in preventing proliferation and its antiproliferation activities have visibly increased since the end of the Cold War, as was evident from the Gulf War and the pressure recently applied to North Korea. The Pentagon's DPG document also encourages the destruction of nuclear facilities of would-be proliferators by military means if necessary. This type of leadership by coercive intervention instead of by example and consensus is also unlikely to be effective in the long run. Countries such as India, for example, support global nuclear disarmament but view the NPT as a discriminatory effort that creates and perpetuates nuclear haves and have-nots.

Considering that the primary interest of the United States is to solidify its hegemonic dominance and to maintain the status quo in the international division of labor, most of the Third World is unlikely to invite a U.S. unipolar hegemony. In the post-Cold War era the great powers of the North also face no credible threat to their security that would cause them to invite a U.S. hegemonic leadership. A U.S. hegemony that maintains the status quo, offers them security and preservation of their privileged standard of living, but they hardly face any imminent danger. If the economic competition among them intensifies, even the Cold War allies are unlikely to continue to embrace U.S. hegemony. For Russia, where patriotism (nationalism) seems to be on the rise in response to its humbling experience following the disintegration of the Soviet

Union,[33] and for aspiring new powers, such as China, a unipolar system implies accepting a subservient position. These countries are also unlikely to invite U.S. preponderance if they can help it.

Under these circumstances, if the United States succeeds in remaining a unipolar hegemon by strengthening its economy and by thwarting all possible challenges and/or by persuading the potential contenders such as the EC, Germany, Japan, Russia, and China to submit to its leadership, it is highly likely that it would become an imperialistic hegemon, at least from the perspectives of the developing world. Since it faces no real rival hegemon, it is also, as Bienefeld notes, less likely to make concessions that would give more space to developing countries to pursue nationalist economic policies.[34] One likely outcome of such hegemony is a collusion of the North against the South in which the United States coordinates and preserves the interests of the North and its continued control over the process of accumulation. This implies a further decline in the bargaining power of the developing countries and a further weakening of their position in the global division of labor.[35]

Under a collusion of the North and with the erosion of the legitimacy, sovereignty, and moral authority of the state in developing countries, the South is likely to be exposed to more explicit and intensive domination by the North, led and coordinated by the United States. The laissez-faire trade system would continue to benefit the North with its advanced production and marketing systems and huge multinational firms.

It is also likely that such an order would have differential impacts on developing countries depending on the level of their manufacturing capability. For the relatively more diversified LDCs, those competitive in the production of low-tech and labor-intensive manufactures, free trade will give them a chance for more access to the markets of the North, although more advanced (high-tech) production is likely to be largely overwhelmed by competition from the North. The World Trade Organization's intellectual property rights agreement is also likely to adversely impact such industries in developing countries. On the other hand, for the least diversified economies such as those of sub-Saharan Africa, imposition of free trade can easily halt their efforts to enter the global market of manufactured exports. Open trade may very well destroy their manufacturing before it is established enough to compete.

A unipolar system under the new order of deregulated global economy is thus unlikely to be favorable to or stable in the South. Growing poverty and inability of the state to address the economic interests of its citizens is likely to increase revolts against the state and even ethnic conflicts. True independence of the United Nations or other NGOs is also not very likely in a unipolar system. The 1992 Jakarta Summit of the Non-Aligned Movement called for strengthening the UN, especially the powers of the Secretary General and the authority of the General Assembly. In the post-Cold War era only the Security Council, which is dominated by the countries of the North with veto power, has been strengthened. The Gulf War, in which the UN was to a large extent used to legitimize U.S. foreign policy, provides a case in point.[36] Those that promote the interests of developing countries, such as UNCTAD and UNIDO, have been weakened. The United States has withdrawn from UNIDO handing that organization a blow. There have also been proposals to dismantle UNCTAD.[37]

## A Multipolar System

As noted earlier, a unipolar system is regarded as untenable by many analysts. One basis for this claim is the realist hypothesis that states struggle for primacy and tend to gang up together in order to counterbalance any preponderance that emerges.[38] According to Waltz, for example, states live in a self-help system and they use their combined capabilities in order to serve their interests.[39] Unipolar preponderance, which is self-serving by definition, is thus expected to breed a balancing opposition by other great and middle powers. It may, however, take considerable time for a balancing opposition to mature, although at least one notable scholar argues that the former anti-Soviet allies are already engaged in a fierce struggle for primacy.[40] Huntington relates Japan's trade policies which he equates with "a strategy of economic warfare" to what he regards as Japan's salient attempts to attain primacy.[41]

This realist (neorealist) hypothesis may be relevant. However, the nature of the different levels of global competition need to be considered in order to determine how likely it is for a multipolar system to emerge and what its nature is likely to be. The Cold War allies are clearly competitors in the areas of trade, investments, and technology. However, the meaning of national competitiveness has become vague as multinational corporations have increasingly lost their national identity.[42] The Cold War allies also constitute an exclusive club of rich countries that perceive a common potential challenge to their privileged position in the global division of labor from the old South (the Third World) and the new South (the formerly Second World) that share aspirations to bring about changes in the global division of labor. Whether the industrial powers challenge U.S. preponderance or voluntarily accept U.S. hegemony, and if they forge a multipolar system whether it turns out to be one with "managed competition" and shared leadership of the global system or it drifts to an adversarial competitive system depends, at least in part, on how they perceive their interests given these different levels of competition. The degree of resistance they face from their populations to the "new capitalism's" polarizing impacts between rich and poor is also likely to have a bearing.

If the rest of the countries of the North view the challenges they face from the South as more threatening to their interests than U.S. preponderance, the competition among them and against U.S. preponderance would become secondary. In this case, U.S. preponderance may become more sustainable and even if a multipolar system emerges, it would likely be one in which intra-North competition is managed and its policies toward the South are coordinated. In this case, the United States would likely remain the *primus inter pares* and the global liberal economic regime would also be strengthened. In addition, the multilateral financial institutions, such as the IMF and the World Bank, and the World Trade Organization, would likely be entrusted to intensify globalization and to continue coordinating the policies of the North toward the South.

The implications for the South in general, and for Africa in particular, of this type of managed multipolar system are not likely to be considerably different from those of a unipolar system. The primary objectives of the North in both scenarios would be maintaining the status quo and its privileged position in the global division of labor.

On the other hand, if the challenge from the South is perceived to be not threatening and internal opposition to the social inequalities generated by the "new capitalism" becomes significant, then there is little reason for the great powers that contend for global dominance to tolerate any disadvantages they may perceive and face from U.S. preponderance and the global liberal economic regime it champions. The disappearance of the "Soviet threat," the danger that intensified globalization poses to the power and sovereignty of states, the growing polarization between rich and poor and protectionist pressures within countries, and the relative decline of Pax Americana are other factors that would contribute to the rise of a true multipolar system with serious intra-North competition. It is also possible that competitive multipolarism may strengthen regionalism with several trading blocs such as the EC, NAFTA, and APEC. The successful conclusion of the Uruguay Round of the GATT negotiations after a long delay, the power of transnational production organization, and the magnitude of the intra-North volume of trade are considerable forces that may mitigate the trend toward regional trading blocs. U.S.-Japan trade, for example, is too important to be given up for regionalism despite the frequent bickering between the two countries. Nevertheless, even if it appears unlikely at the present time, multipolarism with trading blocs cannot be ruled out altogether.

The implications of competitive multipolarism with regionalism to developing countries are mixed. On the one hand, Third World solidarity, even a loose one, might be unlikely as some Third World countries get absorbed into the spheres of influence of the regional powers. Their aspirations for real political and economic independence may also be sacrificed. On the other hand, regionalism may reduce the marginalization of some parts of the South from the international economic system. Regional powers may increase their investments in their spheres of influence. They may also extend freer market access to their Third World partners (subordinates). Some regions of the Third World, sub-Saharan Africa in particular, may, however, be largely left out from membership in any of the possible blocs. This would at least in the short run aggravate Africa's marginalization. In the longer run, however, there may be some positive outcome as African states would have no option but to be autocentric and collectively self-reliant.

Multipolarism without regionalism may also give developing countries the opportunity to exploit the intra-North competition and to secure some improvement in their terms of trade and access to technology and markets. Third World participation in global decisionmaking and the autonomy of the UN system may also be higher under competitive multipolarism than under unipolarism or under managed multipolarism. Multipolarism would also undermine the "new capitalism" and the global liberal economic regime by giving states more room to maneuver. The power of the multilateral financial institutions over developing countries would, for example, be lessened by intra-North competition. There are, for example, some indications that Japan has questioned the appropriateness of the IMF/World Bank-sponsored economic liberalization programs for developing countries.[43] However, it is doubtful, although not inconceivable, that multipolarism would allow significant changes in the control of the process of accumulation and thus in the global division of labor. Anytime such a threat becomes imminent the North can revert to managed multipolarism or even unipolarism to protect the status quo unless the competition between them gets out of hand.

Some argue that the global system has already entered a "postnational" age in which corporations are more central players in global affairs than states.[44] According to this view, the global power configuration of unipolarism or multipolarism would be irrelevant since transnational corporations are replacing the parochialism of states by the "global village." The prospects for Africa and other developing countries are not likely to be any better under such a global order organized and led by capital from OECD countries. It is, however, premature to relegate the state in the industrialized countries to a secondary role. As *The Economist* notes,[45] public spending (33 percent of GDP in the United States, 49 percent in Germany, and 68 percent in Sweden) still remains high and has since 1980 increased, on average, from 36 percent to 40 percent. The ability of some states to tax and to influence income distribution also remains strong. Furthermore, to the extent that democracy survives, the state as the overarching organization of citizens is unlikely to be subservient to private organizations, even ones as powerful as transnational corporations.

## Africa's Options

The foregoing analysis suggests that neither a unipolar nor a multipolar global order creates conditions conducive to socioeconomic development in Africa. Both orders represent "North-centrism"[46] and are undemocratic, although competitive multipolarism gives relatively more space to the countries of the South. It is clear that the unipolar and multipolar systems are reflections of the existing global inequality and that they are mechanisms that perpetuate it. If the global system were more equal it would be something resembling what Amin calls a "polycentric" system. This section of the chapter argues that a world order, one that leads toward polycentrism or a more democratic order, is more suitable for the transformation of the countries of the South. It also argues that such a global order is conceivable in the future through more autocentric development in the South.

Under the existing global division of labor and the predominant development strategies that correspond with it, development in the South is largely dependent on economic conditions in the North. The rise of the "new capitalism" and SAPs and the revitalization of the export-promotion development strategy attempt to preclude alternative development strategies. In line with the prevailing dependent development strategy, the countries of the South have intensified their competition with each other "to offer cheaper, more docile labor forces and more attractive financial incentives to lure transnational corporation (TNC) assembly lines away from other countries and . . . to win scarce export markets."[47] Yet few, if any, have succeeded in emulating the NICs. Excessive reliance on external dynamics in tandem with the fierce competition among them has generally limited the ability of many LDCs to accumulate capital.

There are also no strong reasons to expect that the prospects for the transformation of the South and for the alleviation of global poverty will improve under the unfolding deregulated and export-based system, in which global production is largely driven by consumption in the countries of the North. Every country in the South is engaged in a cut-throat competition for access to the nearly saturated markets of these countries. The export-promotion strategy appears to face the paradox that the more it succeeds initially the more likely its eventual failure becomes. In other words, if some countries succeed it becomes more difficult for others to follow suit, at least in the short to intermediate runs. The more the NICs succeed in expanding and diversifying their exports, for example, the more the pressure for protectionism mounts in the North and the less likely their markets would remain open for other developing countries. In the long run it would seem that the more countries diversify and industrialize, the more the global market expands, creating more opportunities for latecomers. However, mass consumption does not simultaneously expand with industrial production. As a result, there is a time lag that hinders the realization of the potential of the export-propelled development strategy. The 1980s can clearly be characterized as a period in which export promotion in the South and growing protectionism in the North took place concurrently with severe economic problems in much of the South.[48]

As already noted, the "new capitalism" generates a number of problems for the North as well. Increased imports threaten certain low-tech and labor-intensive industries and the jobs they create. By encouraging the exports of capital and assembly lines and by more automation and technological advancement, the strategy also generates loss of jobs, balance-of-payment problems, and loss of tax revenue exacerbating budgetary deficits in the North.[49] It also enhances capital accumulation while it intensifies the polarization between rich and poor. Moreover, the strategy can generate a great deal of conflict between the North and the South. On the one hand, the South associates its problems of poverty and inequality with the North's control of the process of accumulation. The North, on the other hand (at least in popular perception), relates the problems of unemployment and declining real wages to imports from the South and exports of capital to the South.[50]

Under these conditions, an autocentric development strategy that cultivates markets in the largely untapped potential markets of the South by coordinating production with social needs appears to be a viable safety net with considerable potential to alleviate poverty in the South and to stimulate a more rapid global economic development. Africa is the least competitive in the dependent development strategy, as is evident from its marginalization within the global system. It is also a continent where the social classes that benefit from globalism are probably the weakest. These conditions may give Africa the opportunity to explore alternative autocentric development strategies. As emphasized by Amin[51] and throughout this book, autocentric development does not imply autarky nor does it discourage exports or imports. Rather it is a development strategy that emphasizes domestic needs as sources of its dynamics over excessive reliance on external demand and in so doing diversifies the source of dynamism for global development.

Autocentric development is also not antimarket or anticapitalist. In the intermediate run, it is consistent with a mixed economy in which the state actively engages in coordinating production with social needs, thereby to cultivate domestic markets. In the longer run, this strategy advances the market system by integrating largely excluded segments of the global community into the global production and exchange systems. By intensifying reliance on internal dynamics for growth, autocentric development enhances national control of the process of accumulation. Furthermore, by spreading the centers of economic development, and by rehabilitating the legitimacy and sovereignty of reformed states that safeguard the interests of their citizens, it has the potential to lead, in the longer run, to a more polycentric global order in which decisionmaking at the global level as well as at the national level is more democratic.

Clearly, developing countries cannot succeed in creating a polycentric global order by demanding it from the countries of the North as attempted by UNCTAD in the 1970s. Rather they will have to establish its foundations internally by implementing fundamental changes that allow autocentric development and thereby enable them to have more control over the process of accumulation.

At the national level, transforming the peasantry, developing domestic markets, mobilizing the general population through broad popular coalitions, as well as establishing democratic systems are among the essential conditions for autocentric development. The roles of civil society and NGOs are critical in all this. However, civil society and NGOs have diverse and often conflicting interests. Reforming and rehabilitating the state is thus essential since it is the only institution that can mitigate societal conflicts and coordinate a national development agenda. At the regional level, autocentric development involves regional integration to promote not only regional trade but also some degree of production coordination, and establish institutions that would enhance regional collective bargaining. As already noted, in the absence of a rival hegemon, the new global order is less likely to tolerate regimes with a nationalist development strategy. Strong regionalism may provide some degree of protection and more space for such regimes. At the level of the developing world, autocentric development entails close solidarity, cooperation, and increased trade among the countries of the South in order to reduce their dependency on the North and to increase their influence on the global system.

Autocentric development, which involves the empowerment of the poor and the deprived segments of society, faces nearly insurmountable obstacles at different levels. At the national level the elite classes are not likely to easily surrender their privileges in order to create access to resources for the deprived groups. The bourgeois and petty bourgeois classes that are accustomed to a relatively high level of consumption, for example, are not likely to support radical changes that would adversely affect their consumption patterns despite their increased loss of control of the process of capital accumulation. This makes forming broad coalitions an extremely difficult process requiring skillful leadership that mobilizes and convinces the different classes of society that cooperation is imperative, and avoids disruptive conflicts by striking compromises acceptable to all segments of the population.[52] In other words, a political system that avoids winners and losers and instead emphasizes compromises needs to be created to provide a framework for an autocentric development strategy.

Regional cooperation and integration schemes in the South have also generally been undermined by a number of factors, especially the dependent development that has prevented complementarity among their economies. African leaders, for example, recognized as early as the period of decolonization in the 1960s and especially with the Lagos plan of 1980 "that Africa's development could not be merely a passive result of the world system's or evolution of the European Economic Community."[53] However, as discussed in chapter 3, progress in integrating their economies with the ultimate goal of bringing about continental economic union has been very slow. The development strategies they have adopted which promote dependency on the markets of the North and duality within their economies have not made regionalism possible. Despite the existence of the OAU for over three decades, African countries have also not succeeded in advancing their political integration by jointly defining their interests in the global system and harmonizing their position and foreign policies, or in mastering the political will to propel their economic integration.

Similarly, South-South cooperation has been generally unsuccessful, not withstanding the efforts of UNCTAD and the Non-Aligned Movement. The wide differences among the countries of the South and the large number of these countries have made it difficult to have a tight organization that represents their interests. These countries have also faced a number of problems with competition for regional influence among their own ranks. The issue of nuclear proliferation is a case in point. Development of nuclear weapons by regional powers has been viewed by neighbors as a threat to their security and as an indication of intentions for regional domination and not simply as an attempt to deter hegemonic global powers from interference in regional affairs. The cases of India, Pakistan, Iraq, and North Korea are obvious examples. More importantly, the higher a developing country is on the ladder of global hierarchy, the stronger the social classes that benefit from globalism become and the less inclined the country becomes to challenge globalism and the existing global division of labor although it is in a better position to do so.

Despite the identified obstacles, there are a number of factors that can promote autocentric development in the South in general and in Africa in particular. One is the tightening of the North's control of the process of capital accumulation, especially since the mid-1970s with the soaring of the debt crisis and the surge of neo-liberalism. The tighter control of the process of accumulation, which is evident from the increase of capital outflow from the South, has squeezed the benefits of the elite in the South. The stakes to the elite of the South in defending the system may have been undermined. By increasing relative as well as absolute poverty in the South, it has also increased popular pressure for change. As a result, there is reason to anticipate that the forces of change toward a more autocentric development will continue to be strengthened. One of the potential dynamics of genuine democratization is that it can promote more autocentric development by empowering the general population to influence policy.

Another factor is the dilemma inherent in the export-promotion strategy itself. Governments in the North face considerable interest-group pressure to protect labor-intensive industries from competition from the South. Considering that multinational corporations are producing goods and services faster than they are creating purchasing power, this pressure is likely to grow. Despite the Uruguay Round of GATT agreements, a global export-promotion strategy is likely to build pressure for protectionism and to remain an important issue of confrontation. Saturation of the present export-led system and growing marginalization in the international system are likely to push many countries to give an autocentric development strategy a try. If the countries of the North do not impose protectionism to protect jobs and if the conditions of the poor continue to deteriorate with rollbacks of the welfare safety mechanisms, they may face growing internal protests.

Most economic projections under the present system point out that the fate of many developing countries is bleak. Africa's predicament, according to these projections, is particularly alarming. Its very survival is now at serious risk. The search for success stories from structural adjustment programs has so far produced only mirages. The African "success story," Ghana, has at best shown modest improvement which may very well be attributable to the higher level of aid the country has received. Such a level of aid is, however, unavailable to the rest of Africa. A decade of implementation has not won SAPs much support. In fact, a consensus appears to be emerging in Africa that adjustment has failed, despite the insistence of the IMF and the World Bank to the contrary. Under these conditions African states in particular and the rest of the developing countries in general can be expected to attempt to reorganize themselves in order to increase their influence in shaping the global system instead of simply engaging in a perpetual struggle to adjust to a system over which they have little influence. Trying to adjust to the global system without being able to influence it is like aiming at a moving target. By the time these countries adjust to a certain change the system undergoes considerable new changes.

## Conclusion

The end of the Cold War has led, at least in the short run, to further consolidation of the North's control of the global process of capital accumulation and to intensification of the liberal economic regime. The outcome in the South has been burgeoning debt, declining standard of living, and intensification of the level of poverty. African countries are hit by these problems the hardest and are the most marginalized from the prevailing global system. Africa's interests are, in fact, in danger of diverging from those of the rest of the countries of the South. This was evident at the North/South clash which dominated the October 4–6, 1994 annual meeting of the World Bank and the IMF in Spain. Africa was largely reduced to a spectator.[54] Africa thus has a unique responsibility to be the most active in leading change towards an autocentric development approach.

Adjustment and export promotion for African countries at the present stage of their development are no longer sufficient changes. In the first place, it is highly doubtful that they are politically sustainable, considering the widespread political crisis. Second, the strategies have not worked in the absence of diversification of exports. African countries can no longer let the global system determine the prospect of their development and survival. They have to take charge of their own fate and establish internal dynamics for their development. They have to extricate themselves from the feudal hierarchical relations with the multilateral financial institutions. Perhaps they need to devise a means by which they collectively negotiate with these institutions. A revitalized OAU can play a more active role in this regard.

African countries can also no longer afford self-serving authoritarian regimes without culminating in the disintegration of more states and in the starvation of millions of their citizens. It is highly imperative that these countries radically reform the state, mobilize themselves, and build coalitions for survival. An autocentric approach that fosters internal integration, collective self-reliance through regional integration, and foreign policies that promote South-South cooperation seems to be among their best options. If with democratization African countries take steps toward an autocentric approach, there are a number of external factors that may support their efforts. One is that the hegemony of the "new capitalism" which generates massive inequalities both in the North and in the South is likely to generate popular resistance even in the North. Economic diversification of some countries of the South, especially the NICs, also allows African countries to reduce their dependence on the North by diversifying their trading partners.[55] Finally, given the magnitude of their marginalization, African countries may not draw too much intervention, at least not military intervention, from the North if they initiate an autocentric approach to development.

## Notes

1. Amin, *Delinking*.
2. John D. Hargreaves, *Decolonization in Africa* (London: Longman, 1988), 91.
3. Quoted in Hargreaves, *Decolonization in Africa*, 104.
4. Hargreaves, *Decolonization in Africa*, 92.
5. Edmond J. Keller, "The State in Contemporary Africa: A Critical Assessment of Theory and Practice," in Dankwart A. Rustow and Kenneth Paul Erickson, eds., *Comparative Political Dynamics: Global Research Perspectives* (New York: HarperCollins Publishers, 1991), 134–59.
6. Robin Broad and John Cavanagh, "No More NICs," in Gerald Epstein, Julie Graham, and Jessica Nembhard, eds., *Creating a New World Economy* (Philadelphia: Temple University Press, 1993), 382.
7. For a critique of the predatory view of the state, see Dean E. McHenry, Jr., "The State in Africa: A Predator or Contributor? In Decline or Resurgence?" Paper delivered at the 1993 African Studies Association Annual Meeting, Boston, 4–7 December 1993.
8. *New York Times*, 20 June 1994.
9. For details see Hans-Henrik Holm and Georg Sorensen, "Introduction: What Has Changed?" in Hans-Henrik Holm and Georg Sorensen, eds., *Whose World Order* (Boulder: Westview Press, 1995), 1–17; Geoffrey R.D. Underhill, "Conceptualizing the Changing Global Order," in Richard Stubbs and G.R.D. Underhill, eds., *Political Economy and the Changing Global Order* (New York: St.

Martin's Press, 1994), 17–44.

10. Charles Krauthammer, "The Unipolar Moment," *Foreign Affairs* 70, no. 1 (Winter 1991): 23–33.

11. Christopher Layne, "The Unipolar Illusion: Why New Great Powers Will Rise," in Sean M. Lynn-Jones and Steven E. Miller, eds., *The Cold War and After* (Cambridge, MA: MIT Press, 1993), 244–90.

12. Amin, *Delinking*.

13. Layne, "The Unipolar Illusion," 245.

14. Sumitra Chishti, "Systemic Changes in the World-Hegemony and World Economic Order in the Nineties," *The Indian Journal of Social Science* 4, no. 1 (1991): 49.

15. David Gergen, "America's Missed Opportunities," *Foreign Affairs* 71, no. 1 (1991/92): 10–11.

16. Layne, "The Unipolar Illusion."

17. Susan Strange, *States and Markets* (London: Printers Publishers, 1988), 28.

18. Chishti, "Systemic Changes," 51–54.

19. Hegemony is an equivocal concept. For details on its various conceptions see David Wilkinson, "Reconceiving Hegemony," Paper presented at the Annual Meeting of the International Studies Association, Washington, D.C., 28 March–2 April 1994.

20. Enrico Augelli and Craig Murphy, *America's Quest for Supremacy and the Third World* (London: Printer Publishers, 1988), 122.

21. Robert W. Cox, "The Crisis in World Order and the Challenge to International Organization," *Cooperation and Conflict* 29, no. 2 (1994): 105.

22. Cox, "The Crisis in World Order," 106.

23. Some argue that the accusations are not justified since macroeconomic factors and not Japanese protectionism are the explanations for Japanese trade surplus vs. the United States. See Stephen S. Golub, *The United States-Japan Current Account Imbalance: A Review* (Washington, D.C.: IMF Paper on Policy Analysis and Assessment, 1994). Others, however, argue that deliberate Japanese policies emanating from the country's aspirations for primacy are the culprit. See Samuel Huntington, "Why International Primacy Matters," in Sean M. Lynn-Jones and Steven E. Miller, eds., *The Cold War and After: Prospects for Peace* (Cambridge, MA: MIT Press, 1993), 307–22.

24. Gergen, "America's Missed Opportunities," 4–5.

25. Anne Krueger, *American Trade Policy: A Tragedy in the Making* (Washington, D.C.: The American Enterprise Institute, 1995), 6.

26. Cox, "The Crisis in World Order."

27. Manfred Bienefeld, "The New World Order: Echoes of a New Imperialism," *Third World Quarterly* 15, no. 1 (1994): 35.

28. Some have argued that continued U.S. involvement and leadership is essential for world security. See Samuel Huntington, "Why

International Primacy Matters." There is, however, a qualitative difference between active involvement and being preponderant.

29. Despite early resistance the United States could not avoid rather generous humanitarian assistance to Rwandan refugees given the magnitude of the tragedy.

30. UNDP, *Human Development Report* (New York: Oxford University Press, 1993).

31. Gergen, "America's Missed Opportunities," 4.

32. Robert Jervis, "The Future of World Politics," *International Security* 16, no. 3 (Winter 1991/92).

33. Peter Reddaway, "Is Russian Democracy Doomed?" *Journal of Democracy* 5, no. 2 (April 1994): 13–19.

34. Bienefeld, "The New World Order."

35. The Third World is obviously a diverse group of countries and the implications of a unipolar system would not be the same. Nevertheless, the implications would by and large be similar.

36. Stephen Lewis, "A Promise Betrayed," *World Policy Journal* (Summer 1991); Krauthammer, "The Unipolar Moment."

37. Rubens Ricupero, "UNCTAD: Enfant Terrible Hopes for Rebirth," *The World Today* 52, no. 4 (April 1996): 106–107.

38. Layne, "The Unipolar Illusion."

39. Kenneth N. Waltz, *Theory of International Politics* (Reading, Mass.: Addison-Wesley, 1979).

40. Huntington, "Why International Primacy Matters."

41. Huntington, "Why International Primacy Matters," 314.

42. For details see Robert B. Reich, "Who Is Us?" *Harvard Business Review* 68, no. 1 (January-February 1990): 53–64; and Paul Krugman, "Competitiveness: A Dangerous Obsession," *Foreign Affairs* 73, no. 2 (March/April 1994): 28–44.

43. For details see Overseas Economic Cooperation Fund, "Issues Related to the World Bank Approach to Structural Adjustment: Proposal from a Major Partner," OECF Occasional Paper no. 1 (Tokyo: OECF, October 1991), 1–17.

44. Benjamin R. Barber, *Jihad vs. McWorld*. New York: Random House, 1995, 23.

45. "The Myth of the Powerless State," *The Economist* 337, no. 7935, 7 October 1995, 15–16.

46. Bahgat Korany, "End of History, or Its Continuation and Accentuation? The Global South and the 'New Transformation' Literature," *Third World Quarterly* 15, no. 1 (1994): 10.

47. Broad and Cavanagh, "No More NICs," 378.

48. The perception that free trade with developing countries leads to unemployment and lower wages in OECD countries may be unfounded, as noted by Robert Z. Lawrence in IMF, "Trade Has Small Impact on Wages," *IMF Survey* 23, no. 13 (27 June 1994): 211. OECD exports to developing countries have increased faster than

OECD imports from those countries (*IMF Survey* 23, no. 13 (27 June 1994): 211). Even if Lawrence's contentions are valid, interest group pressure for protectionism remains an important obstacle since there are losers from freer trade, and the burden of adjustment is difficult. This is evident from the narrow margin of passage of the NAFTA ratification in the U.S. Congress.

49. Gerald Epstein, "The United States as a Debtor Country," in Gerald Epstein, Julie Graham and Jessica Nembhard, eds., *Creating a New World Economy* (Philadelphia: Temple University Press, 1993), 207.

50. Size may be an important factor in adopting an autocentric development strategy. Small countries may be less successful than large ones. However, collective self-reliance mitigates the problems of small countries.

51. Amin, *Delinking*.

52. Given the global class alliances, class and ideological warfare in African countries is not likely to be won by the lower classes, which may be regarded as having the most to benefit from and to support autocentric development. The petit bourgeoisie and even some of the bourgeoisie may also be benefactors of autocentric development in the long run. With proper consciousness and leadership compromises seem to be possible.

53. Samir Amin, *Maldevelopment: Anatomy of a Global Failure* (London: Zed Press, 1990), 57.

54. "IMF/World Bank: A Challenge from the South," *Africa Confidential* 35, no. 21 (21 October 1994).

55. Jerker Carlsson and Timothy M. Shaw, *Newly Industrializing Countries and the Political Economy of South-South Relations* (London: Macmillan, 1988); Timothy M. Shaw, "The South in the 'New World (Dis)Order': Towards a Political Economy of Third World Foreign Policy in the 1990s," *Third World Quarterly* 15, no. 1 (1994): 17–30.

# 7
## Conclusion:
## Prospects for an Autocentric
## Development Approach

▼   ▼   ▼

## Summary

According to prevailing development models that guide policy in Africa, African development hinges primarily on external dynamics. These models, while attempting to bring about close integration with the global economy and a free-enterprise market system, grossly neglect Africa's internal dynamics. This book has attempted to demonstrate why such development models are inappropriate for the specific structural conditions that characterize African countries. Implementing these models has also proved extremely difficult. One aim of this concluding chapter is to pull together the reasons already given in the foregoing chapters as to why existing development models are largely incompatible with Africa's socio-economic realities, why they have failed to promote development, and why balancing globalism with an autocentric development approach offers a more promising alternative. A second objective is to briefly assess the prospects for successful implementation of an autocentric approach in Africa in the near-to-intermediate future. The second objective attempts to answer two related questions: (1) Can an autocentric approach be a realistic alternative or is it a farfetched dream? And (2) Since some autocentric efforts have been unsuccessful in Africa in the past three decades, why would they be successful in the 1990s and beyond?

There is little doubt that external dynamics can be an important source of development. In some cases they may even be the primary driving force for an economy. Botswana and Mauritius are relatively good examples in Africa. To be successful, externally-driven development requires a number of preconditions, including the ability to attract a considerable amount of foreign investment, the ability to produce competitive export products with reliable external demand, the ability to obtain access to foreign markets, the ability to maintain favorable export prices and terms of trade, a reasonable degree of control over the national process of capital accumulation, and the involvement of significant portions of the general population in the production of tradeables either directly or through linkages. The more diversified and competitive the production system becomes as a result of these conditions, the more integrated the internal and external dynamics of an economy become. In other words, the external dynamics, by promoting economic growth and raising the standard of living, expand internal dynamics to the point that over time the two become closely enmeshed together.

The conditions essential for externally-driven development are largely absent in most of Africa. Africa's access to foreign capital, with the exception of a few countries, is negligible. Most African countries are too small, have insignificant purchasing power, and are often too politically unstable to attract foreign investments. They are also characterized by the absence of adequately developed human resources and infrastructure, which contributes to their weak overall investment climate. Moreover, African countries are disadvantaged by the lack of diversification of their exports and by their inability to exert influence over the prices of these products. As a result, terms of trade are generally tilted against them. These conditions, in tandem with a host of other factors, including technological dependency and lack of food self-sufficiency, have hindered their ability to control the process of accumulation.[1]

The absence of these (pre)conditions at the present time does not necessarily mean that the requisites for successful externally-driven development cannot be created in the future. However, there are a number of almost insurmountable obstacles. First, foreign investments, external markets, and favorable terms of trade are scarce factors for which almost all countries are fiercely competing. African countries are currently among the least competitive in obtaining them. Second, African countries are not likely to be able to bring under control all the factors that hinder foreign investments anytime soon. Third, the image of Africa in the advanced, capital-rich countries is so negative that changing it and cultivating the requisites for externally-propelled development are onerous uphill battles. Last, even if African countries modestly diversify their exports, foreign markets are susceptible to saturation and protectionism, rendering the foreign-demand-propelled development strategy rather risky for countries coming late to industrialization.[2]

In this context, a development model that relies on external dynamics to the near exclusion of internal dynamics (as African countries currently do) amounts to putting all one's eggs in a single highly dubious basket. The experience of the last thirty years in general, and those of the last decade in particular, have solidified the lesson that the prospects for African countries attaining greater prosperity or economic independence while neglecting internal dynamics are rather dim. The rise of the new global order, characterized by deregulation, privatization, and restriction of the redistributive roles of the state, since the late 1970s and early 1980s, has made the prospects even dimmer, since transformation of the peasantry is unlikely without an active state.

Given the present situation of African countries and under the prevailing global conditions, an autocentric approach to development becomes a risk-diversification mechanism for African states. Yet African states are economic midgets that heavily depend on external trade; hence, disengagement from the global system is unrealistic. African countries will also need to keep engaged with the global community and learn from it a number of things, including technology. (There is little need to reinvent the wheel, but African countries would need a technology policy to promote technological self-reliance.) The aim of an autocentric approach, after all is to gear a country's development process primarily to internal and regional dynamics while utilizing external dynamics whenever necessary and available. This strategy gives the developing country itself greater control of both the process and the outcome of development. Cultivating internal dynamism would also improve the (aforementioned) prerequisites to the success of externally-driven development, thereby reversing Africa's growing marginalization within the global economy.

An autocentric approach to development promotes internal dynamism in several ways. One critical priority of this approach is ending the fragmentation and duality that characterize African economies by transforming the subsistence sector into an active

181

exchange economy. Transforming the peasantry is, of course, tied to transforming the agricultural sector. At least initially, an autocentric approach involves rural-biased (agricultural-biased) resource-allocation patterns. Extension services that promote the productive capacity of the peasantry are among those critical initial priorities. Such measures mobilize the productivity of a large segment of the population and thereby cultivate an internal market.

A related characteristic of an autocentric approach is promoting agriculture-linked industrialization. With the peasantry becoming a more active participant in the exchange economy, agriculture-led industrialization that primarily services social needs becomes a more promising option. These industries are likely to begin as small scale but they are the type of industries that are positioned to grow with the communities around them. With regional integration their growth potential becomes even greater.

This approach seems to differ markedly from the approach of some of the NICs, which identified certain industries with potential to become globally competitive and provided them with a variety of supports.[3] These industries, as leading sectors of the economy, then provided considerable stimuli to the rest of the economy through a number of linkages.

The NICs approach is more difficult now than it was at the time when those countries undertook it. As noted earlier, the competition for foreign investments and for access to foreign markets is much heavier now. African countries also lack the level of technical advancement and infrastructure needed to successfully engage in similar ventures and compete globally. Given these constraints, agriculture-linked industrialization, which an autocentric approach encourages, becomes a strategy that reduces the duality of African economies. Moreover, if a given country succeeds in attracting foreign investments and in obtaining market access or if private firms can compete internationally, an autocentric approach does not prevent such developments from coexisting with the inward-looking approach. As I have stressed throughout this book, an autocentric approach does not, by any means, imply or promote autarky; rather, it is a mechanism that bases development on the most promising opportunities, diverts risks by utilizing both internal and external dynamics, and thereby expands control of the national process of capital accumulation. As already noted, beyond a certain stage of development the distinctions between the two sources of dynamism are likely to become increasingly blurred.

## Autocentric Approach and
## Regional Integration

Another essential aspect of an autocentric approach is promoting regional integration. African countries are too small for an autocentric approach to be successful solely on the basis of self-reliance. Countries that attempt such an approach individually may also be ostracized by the countries and agencies of the North that espouse the "new capitalism" and the new global order. To have a chance for success an autocentric approach would have to be rooted in regionalism and collective self-reliance. This involves a number of changes, including restructuring Africa's extroverted production, transportation, and communication systems inward in order to serve internal needs and to foster regional integration. It also requires some form of production coordination to best utilize their meager resources and a system of payments for intra-African trade that does not necessitate hard currency. Intra-African trade is unlikely to grow appreciably as long as African countries rely on currencies of OECD countries to conduct trade with each other. African exporters are not currently competitive in either the quality or the pricing of their manufactured products. They are also unlikely to be competitive in extending credit to importers. Devising a system of payments that avoids the need for hard currency may, however, give them an edge that would enable them to compete in African markets. Countertrade also needs to be explored carefully since it may be a useful mechanism that can, at least partly, alleviate the problem of payments of intra-African trade.[4]

By transforming the peasantry and promoting agriculture-linked industrialization, an autocentric approach can advance some of the essential preconditions for regional integration. Transforming the peasantry implies some expansion of internal and regional markets which can in turn enable African economies to support selected import-substituting industries. Agriculture-linked industrialization together with selected import-substitution industrialization could also promote complementarity among African economies.[5] An autocentric approach thus has the potential to mobilize the presently stagnant regional integration schemes in Africa. In addition, regionalism has the mechanism to allow African states to export to each other and eventually to the rest of the world and thereby to combine export-promoting and import-substituting strategies as two aspects of the same process. Industries that may substitute imports from outside Africa can be export industries within Africa.

As noted, an autocentric approach runs counter to the ideological orientation of the post-Cold War global order. As such, it is likely to draw opposition from the dominant powers as well as the MFIs. African countries have a better chance of resisting such opposition if they act collectively or if they develop mechanisms by which they protect their members from undue external pressure, perhaps through the OAU.

## Market-State Relations in an Autocentric Approach

Another strength of an autocentric approach is that it is market-friendly. It allows the price system to operate and it safeguards market-based private allocation of resources. The state, however, plays an active role in areas such as poverty alleviation and human resource development and in promoting sectors of the economy that are promising for national development by creating externalities. In the case of the NICs—and even Japan—the state promoted certain export-oriented industries through a host of measures. In the African case, transforming the subsistence sector and promoting internal integration are likely to be the economic activities that generate crucial economic externalities initially. State support for such activities cannot be regarded as hostile to the market system.

There is, of course, legitimate concern about state intervention, since not all interventions and not all states are poverty-alleviating or market-creating. The history of state intervention in Africa has not been encouraging. There is little doubt that intervention by the present "African state," which for the most part is dominated by self-serving authoritarian regimes, cannot be regarded as poverty-alleviating or market-promoting. This has led many analysts to support the neo-liberal marketization drive as a second-best choice. There are, however, serious problems with the second-best argument in this case. First, the market cannot be a substitute for good government. The market by itself, does not, for example, bring about the transformation of the subsistence sector or do all the market-creating activities, such as supporting selected industries that a good government can. Second, there is little chance that the market will be allowed to operate freely under self-serving authoritarian regimes even if such regimes do not openly and formally oppose the marketization drive.

Instituting good governance through a process of democratization is, thus, an essential precondition for an autocentric approach to development. In Africa it is also critical for creating a sustained and properly operating market system. Again, this argument appears to contradict the experiences of some countries, such as those of the NICs and Chile, where functional market systems emerged under authoritarian regimes. However, the market system in these countries was to a large extent supported by external dynamics, which, as already noted, is not likely to happen in the case of Africa. Moreover, one cannot determine *a priori* if an authoritarian regime is going to be market-promoting or self-serving. In other words, while there is a possibility that some authoritarian regimes can engage in market-promoting activities as well as become developmentalist, the danger of them becoming self-serving is even greater. It is too risky for Africa to rely either on dictators or on outside saviors to pull it out of its present general crisis. Only democratic reorganization—which can unleash popular participation, mobilization, and internal dynamism—is a dependable prospect.

## Democracy in an Autocentric Approach

This brings us to the question of what type of democracy is consistent with an autocentric approach to development and compatible with African conditions. In responding to this question, this study has taken into consideration the problems of state-building (nation-building)[6] that have paralyzed many African states. These countries are largely characterized by fragmentation between the modern and subsistence sectors, the deprivation of the latter, and widespread animosity among ethnic and religious groups, due to uneven development and a host of other reasons. The extroverted extractive nature of African economies, which bypasses many segments of the population, has contributed to the uneven development of African countries. Many African states have faced active ethnonationalist responses that have threatened to tear them apart. Inability of the self-serving state to deal with these challenges has led to chronic ethnic and religious conflicts, growing poverty, environmental degradation, fundamentalism, anarchy, and growing criminal activity.

185

Given these problems, the type of democracy that is likely to be more appropriate for African countries is one that promotes a system of governance in which all the different ethnic and religious entities participate in setting the rules of the game, including the terms of integration of the different entities, how decisions are to be made, and where the boundaries between public and private decisions are to be drawn. The rules of the game are not likely to be accepted by the general populace and the different entities if they are imposed by any one group, even if it constitutes the majority. They are also much less likely to become operational if they are imposed by coercion or copied from an external cultural or socioeconomic context. Africa has to invent its own democratic procedures out of its historical and cultural context. It has to revisit its grassroots consensual decision-making tradition. It may not be possible to transplant in modern African states the traditional African village-level consensual democracy. Traditional forms of decision making can, however, still serve as bases for developing a democratic system more suitable for African societies than the majoritarian system that many seem to be trying to adopt at present.

*Limitation of executive power* and *power-sharing among different political parties* in association with *extensive decentralization* are mechanisms that approximate the traditional African grassroots democracy.[7] Considering the disparity of incomes and of access to resources and political power among ethnic and social groups as well as the level of competition for resources among different ethnic groups, rules of governance established through consensus-building compromises are also unlikely to define rigid spheres of private and public decisionmaking as the minimalist liberal democracy does. Rather it is likely to be flexible, allowing the state to play an active role in redistributive measures as well as in market-creating activities. Indications from the pro-democracy movements in Africa are that the state is expected to be active in poverty alleviation and other redistributive measures.[8] A type of democracy with a mixed economy base and a consensus-building framework is essential for Africa's socioeconomic development. This type of democracy (essentially a hybrid of consensual [consociational] and social democracy) differs significantly from liberal democracy in its minimalist form. State-building in Africa is difficult to conceive without such a flexible arrangement.

As some have argued,[9] liberal democracy (by far the most widespread form of democracy) may be easier to implement than

186

most other forms of democracy, including the one proposed here. Limiting the state's role in economic activity and adopting the winner-take-all type of majoritarian decision-making formula are clearly easier than the process of consensus building or the meddling of the state in economic activity. However, liberal democracy in its minimalist form has not been successful in overcoming the problems of state-building in societies divided along ethnic lines. Countries such as India and Sri Lanka provide obvious testimonies.[10] Even more established democracies such as the United Kingdom and Spain show that problems of ethnonationalism have persisted despite the entrenchment of the liberal democratic tradition. Overcoming Africa's state-building problems along liberal democratic lines is even less likely.

## Prospects for an Autocentric Approach

Africa is facing a myriad of trends that seriously endanger the survival of millions of people and threaten to fragment many states. Disintegration of the state, as in Rwanda, Somalia, Liberia, and Sierra Leone, and civil wars such as those of the Sudan and Angola can easily recur in several other states, with catastrophic cost of human life. With growing poverty, African states are also facing breakdowns in their educational and health-care systems as well as in their infrastructure, which gravely exacerbate their development crisis. In addition, African countries find themselves seriously threatened by the spread of epidemics such as AIDS and many other infectious diseases. Dissatisfaction with the existing conditions and development strategies is mounting as Africa's general crisis intensifies.

However, even if an autocentric approach appears to be a more appropriate alternative, as this analysis suggests, it does not necessarily mean that it is likely to be widely adopted. The next section of this chapter explores the prospects for its implementation in the not-too-distant future by assessing factors that impede and promote its adoption.

## Obstacles to an Autocentric Approach

As already noted, some forms of autocentric development, such as Tanzania's self-reliance and *ujamaa* villagization, were tried and failed in Africa. Collective self-reliance efforts through regional integration schemes have also been unsuccessful. These efforts failed due to a confluence of factors, among which was underdevelopment of human resources. African countries emerged from colonialism with a minimal number of educated people. There were few skilled bureaucrats and technocrats to manage such development programs. The balance of class relations was also decidedly against the masses. The elite in close cooperation with the elite of the former colonial powers largely maintained the status quo while often paying lip service to the prospect of change and the cause of the impoverished masses. Under these conditions and given the ideological tensions of the Cold War, autocentric development efforts had little chance of success. Even in the present post-Cold War era, adoption of an autocentric development approach in Africa is hampered by the lack of a number of requisites: one is absence of the necessary levels of education, consciousness, and political organization on the part of the masses, especially the peasantry, who would be expected to be its major beneficiaries and supporters. Such qualities could enable the masses to become a force in establishing the political system and rules of governance as well as restructuring policy. However, the African peasantry remains largely marginalized, with limited impact on policymaking. Moreover, the population at large is often fragmented along ethnic or religious lines which impede collective action and solidarity in enhancing its influence on policymaking.

In the absence of popular influence on policy, visionary leadership with a high level of understanding of the nature of development problems and a high degree of commitment to promoting development could create conditions for an autocentric approach by at least partly compensating for the weaknesses of the masses. The disasters that threaten Africa are, after all, no longer limited to the poor masses. Many of the pending dangers of the crisis clearly involve and impact the elite. We have also seen that the benefits of existing development strategies to the elite are increasingly eroded by the changes in the global environment. Unfortunately, quality leadership is also rather rare in the African scene. The grip on power by self-serving authoritarian regimes is still formidable, as indicated by the intensity of the struggle for democratization and by the reversals of the democratization process in some countries over the last few years. Civil society that has championed the current wave of the democratization struggle is also characterized by contradictory interests. While some segments and

188

classes are strongly opposed to SAPs and excessive reliance on external dynamics, others are strongly in favor of such conditions.

Lack of diversification of African economies and their internal fragmentation also undermine an autocentric approach. As already noted, these problems also impede greater integration and collective self-reliance among African countries.

An autocentric approach also faces formidable external impediments. The neo-liberal orientation of the emerging post-Cold War global order may constitute the most serious obstacle to an autocentric approach. In line with the neo-liberal doctrine, the MFIs continue to actively impose policy through a number of conditionalities and under the auspices of adjustment mechanisms on financially strapped countries. These institutions have become major defenders of many externally-oriented strategies that are incompatible with African realities. In addition, they have contributed to the undermining of the state's autonomy and legitimacy by appropriating its policymaking powers.

## Factors for Optimism

Despite the persistence of formidable obstacles, the prospects for successful implementation of an autocentric approach are much better now than they were at the time of independence and they are improving. There are a number of factors that have improved the prospects for successful adoption of an autocentric approach. First, African peoples are now, for all practical purposes, engaged in a struggle for survival. As already noted, even the benefits for those who have been perpetuating the prevailing extroverted political economy have been considerably discounted by the recent changes in the global environment, especially the end of the Cold War. If present trends continue, projected calamities in terms of food shortages and violence are frightening. With their backs against the wall, it can be expected that African societies would look for inner strength and resourcefulness for survival as they have done through other crises in the past. If African societies succeed in averting the disasters facing them, it is going to be essentially through internally developed and self-reliant survival strategies and not through dependency on external salvation. Survival strategies are essentially autocentric in nature.

A second reason for optimism is the intensive democratization struggle underway in much of the African continent. Clearly, as

Michael Chege notes,[11] the struggle for democratization is a long way from being won. This is evident from the cases of Zaire, Cameroon, Kenya, Guinea, Gabon, Rwanda, Sudan, Togo, and Nigeria. Even where a multiparty system has been established, as in Zambia, a number of weaknesses are visible in the democratization process. One weakness is that the process is largely urban-dominated. Another weakness is that there is little indication that the new leadership is any more committed (or even inclined) to an autocentric approach than the previous regimes. According to one analyst,[12] Zambia's new leadership, for example, has given little signs of distancing itself from existing dominant ideologies. Instead it depends heavily on foreign sources of funding and support and its programs are largely designed to meet the demands and ideological dictates of the west. The post-Kaunda leadership in Zambia has clearly been more receptive to the directives of the MFIs than Kaunda's regime was.

Yet a civil society that was largely absent at the time of independence in the 1960s has begun to emerge in Africa. As noted before, although the peasantry largely remains marginalized, over the last three decades Africa has seen the emergence of a small "middle class," which includes educated professionals, students, and urban dwellers. As Bagachwa and Stewart note,[13] African small enterprises, including blacksmiths, carpenters, tailors, craft workers, and vehicle, shoe and electrical repairers (which are the future of African entrepreneurship) are on the rise. Africa is indeed undergoing a "silent revolution," to borrow Cheru's phrase.[14] These social groups, which have become the backbone of the pro-democracy movement, have begun to impact Africa's political landscape. The nature of class relations in Africa is now different and more complex than it was at the time of decolonization. Democratization, thus, cannot be written off, even though ups and downs are to be expected in such a struggle. Besides, several countries, including Zimbabwe, Benin, Uganda, Senegal, Mauritius, Botswana, South Africa, and Ethiopia have shown notable progress towards democratization.

Even ethnonationalism has a democratizing aspect in Africa. As James Scarritt notes, few such movements are secessionist in Africa.[15] Movements such as the SPLM in Southern Sudan and the Oromo Liberation Front in Ethiopia, for example, have resisted secessionist tendencies. The predominant demands of most ethnonationalist movements in Africa are decentralization of decisionmaking, equity of access to resources and political power, and cultural self-determination. Given the mounting pressure from the populace at large and ethnonationalist movements, African states do not appear to have the power to resist for long. More states are likely to move towards decentralization and democratization merely in order to survive. In other cases, it can be expected that authoritarian regimes will continue to be forcibly removed from power.

The global trend is also toward democratization although it encourages liberal democracy which has serious limitations in Africa. Yet once the procedures of democracy (such as political parties, competition for public offices, and elections) are consolidated, it is unlikely that the substance of democracy will remain restricted to a liberal form, given the African context. Ethnic and class polarization and the absence of a hegemonic bourgeois class are likely to pull it toward more consociational and social democratic forms of democracy. Political parties are, for example, more likely to adopt policies that are more reformist and pro-peasantry in order to win the peasantry's support in elections.

Another reason for optimism is the widespread support for regionalism, especially among the African intellectual community. Ratification of the 1991 Abuja Treaty, which aims at establishing a continental common market by the year 2025, indicates such support. Needless to say, the African elite has not shown much commitment to implementing the agreements beyond the signing stage. However, if progress is made in the area of democratization, a parallel progress toward regionalism can be expected to take place for several reasons. One is that genuine democratization (as noted in Chapter 4) contains forces that promote internal integration. To the extent that democratization promotes popular influence on policymaking, it can be expected to better coordinate production with social needs and, thereby, improve rural standards of living. Such improvements, in turn, encourage the development of internal markets and foster complementarity of African economies.

The African intellectual community has regarded regionalism and collective self-reliance as requisites for African development. It is also developing a consensus that successful development needs to be based on the transformation of the peasantry, since neglect of the peasantry has undermined any sustained, internally-propelled development. Democratic governments can be expected to act on such unified intellectual leadership. Furthermore, there seems to be an emerging consensus among Africa's intellectual community in particular and the "middle class" in general that

Africa's development requires the empowerment of its peoples to determine their own destinies and to control policymaking as well as the national process of accumulation. If the democratization process succeeds, it can be expected that these sentiments will begin to be reflected in policy.

Despite the magnitude of its general crisis, Africa has also produced a growing number of skilled bureaucrats and technocrats. Clearly, Africa is far from meeting its needs in these areas; however, capability has expanded considerably, improving the prospects for successful implementation(s) of an autocentric approach.

Another factor that can facilitate an autocentric approach is the significant diversification of the economies of some countries of the South, especially the NICs, Brazil, China, and India. South-South trade is now more possible than ever, since these countries can become suppliers of manufactured goods to—and even a great deal of the technological needs of—the rest of the South. Their impacts as markets to the rest of the South will be limited; nevertheless, they can reduce the monopolistic impact of the North in some areas and give the countries of the South a little more room to maneuver.

Finally, as noted in Chapter 6, the emerging global order of "new capitalism" poses new challenges for Africa. However, some of the changes in the global environment (including the end of the Cold War and reduction of ideological tensions) have created some opportunities for it. These changes appear to have reduced the likelihood of external military intervention in African conflicts. The autocentric approach envisioned here is also market-friendly, democratic, and characterized by low-key ideological rhetoric. The types of democratization and marketization consistent with an autocentric approach differ markedly from those projected by the new global order. Yet the magnitude of Africa's marginalization and the democratic and market-friendly nature of the autocentric approach greatly mitigate the likelihood of external military intervention in Africa. However, policy intervention (especially by the IMF, the World Bank, and the World Trade Organization) as well as military intervention by proxy can be expected to continue until African states collectively develop mechanisms to shield themselves from such measures.

The balance between the factors that promote the implementation of an autocentric approach and those that obstruct it cannot be determined with reasonable accuracy. It is also clear that changing the extroverted and extractive nature of African economies, entrenched since about the thirteenth century, is a formidable task. However, given the ongoing "silent revolution" and the not-so-silent struggle for democratization, there are strong indications that the forces of revival are on the rise and that, at the very least, the conditions for change in the direction of autocentric development are ripening. What remains to be seen is whether civil society, which was largely absent three decades ago, forges working compromises among its different components—or fails to do so, and fragments. If it fails in forging compromises and the existing development strategies continue, then the gloomy prophecies that are often made about Africa—e.g., that it is a continent committing a "slow suicide"[16] or that "if God gave it [Africa] to you and made you its economic dictator, the only smart move would be to give it back to him"[17]—will likely come true. If civil society manages to forge compromises, however, democracy can be expected to be successful at least in some countries. Under genuine democracy, it is inconceivable that the political and economic exclusion of the masses will continue. The extractive enclaves, the self-serving state functionaries, and the external domination of policymaking can all be expected to give way to internally more integrated economies and an autonomous state that promote societal interests, which are essential for an autocentric approach. An autocentric development approach is no longer an unrealizable dream. It is rapidly becoming a credible alternative, although it remains a difficult one. However, the alternatives are neither easier nor more promising. Even establishing the requisites for proper integration with the global economy is not likely to occur without cultivating internal dynamics through an autocentric approach. Finally, this book has concentrated on the political-economy aspects of an autocentric approach; to be successful, however, the approach has to be ingrained in all facets of African societies, including culture.

## Notes

1. Samir Amin, *Delinking: Towards a Polycentric World* (London: Zed Books, Ltd., 1985).
2. The Uruguay Round of GATT Agreements may reduce the rise of protectionism, but even this undermines industrialization efforts of latecomers by subjecting them to competition before they are ready and able to compete.
3. Mrinal Datta-Chaudhuri, "Market Failure and Government Failure,"

*Journal of Economic Perspectives* 4, no. 3 (Summer 1990): 25–39.

4. Berhanu Mengistu, "Counter-trade as a Strategy for Regional Economic Cooperation: The Case of the PTA," in Kidane Mengisteab and B.I. Logan, eds., *Beyond Economic Liberalization in Africa: Structural Adjustment and the Alternatives* (London: Zed Books, Ltd., 1995), 273–87; Frances Stewart, *North-South and South-South: Essays on International Economics* (New York: St. Martin's Press, 1992), 162–87.

5. F. Stewart, S. Lall, and S. Wangwe, "Alternative Development Strategies: An Overview," in F. Stewart, S. Lall, and S. Wangwe, eds., *Alternative Development Strategies in Sub-Saharan Africa* (New York: St. Martin's Press, 1992), 143.

6. State-building here refers to bringing about national integration of countries by creating a political economy that accommodates the demands of the various ethnic groups in a country.

7. Basil Davidson, "What Development Model?" *Africa Forum* 1, no. 1 (1991): 13–16.

8. Yusuf Bangura, "Authoritarian Rule and Democracy in Africa: A Theoretical Discourse," in P. Gibbon, Y. Bangura, and Arve Oftsad, eds., *Authoritarianism, Democracy and Adjustment* (Uppsala: Scandinavian Institute of African Studies, 1992); Thandika Mkandwire, "The Political Economy of Development with a Democratic Face," in Giovanni Andrea Cornia, Rolph van der Hoeven, and Thandika Mkandawire, eds., *Africa's Recovery in the 1990s* (New York: St. Martin's Press, 1992).

9. Richard Sandbrook, "Liberal Democracy in Africa: A Socialist-Revisionist Perspective," *Canadian Journal of African Studies* 22, no. 2 (1988): 240–67.

10. Dennis Austin, *Democracy and Violence in India and Sri Lanka* (New York: Council on Foreign Relations Press, 1995).

11. Michael Chege, "What's Right with Africa?" *Current History* 93, no. 583 (May 1994): 193–97.

12. Julius Ihonvbere, "Democratization and Civil Society in Zambia," in Kidane Mengisteab and Cyril Daddieh, eds., *Democratization and State-Building in Africa* (forthcoming).

13. M.S.D. Bagachwa and Frances Stewart, "Rural Industries and Rural Linkages in Sub-Saharan Africa: A Survey," in F. Stewart, S. Lall, and S. Wangwe, eds., *Alternative Development Strategies in Sub-Saharan Africa* (New York: St. Martin's Press, 1992), 169–80.

14. Fautu Cheru, *The Silent Revolution in Africa: Debt, Development and Democracy* (London: Zed Books, 1989).

15. James R. Scarritt, "Communal Conflict and Contentions for Power in Africa South of the Sahara," in Ted Robert Gurr, ed., *Minorities at Risk: A Global View of Ethnopolitical Conflicts* (Washington, D.C.: United States Institute of Peace, 1993), 252–89.

16. "A Continent's Slow Suicide," *Readers' Digest*, May 1993, quoted in

Chege, "What's Right with Africa?"

17. Lester Thurow, *Head to Head: The Coming Struggle Among Japan, Europe and the United States* (New York: William Morrow, 1992), 216.

# References

Adedeji, Adebayo, "Sustaining Democracy," *Africa Report* (January-February 1992): 29–32.

Adepoju, Aderanti, *The Impact of Structural Adjustment on the Population of Africa* (London: UNFPA, Heinemann and James Currey, 1993).

*Africa Confidential* 35, no. 20 (7 October 1994).

*Africa Recovery* 5, no. 4 (December 1991): 20–21.

*Africa Recovery* 6, no. 3 (November 1992): 35.

*Africa Recovery* 8, no. 3 (December 1994): 8.

African National Congress, *The Reconstruction and Development Programme: A Policy Framework* (Johannesburg: Umanyans Publications, 1994).

Ake, Claude, "How Politics Underdevelops Africa," in Adebayo Adedeji, Owodunni Teriba, and Patrick Bugembe, eds., *The Challenges of African Economic Recovery and Development* (London: Frank Cass, 1991), 316–29.

Ake, Claude, "Rethinking African Democracy," in Larry Diamond and Marc F. Plattner, eds., *The Global Resurgence of Democracy* (Baltimore: Johns Hopkins University Press, 1993), 70–82.

Amin, Samir, *Delinking: Towards a Polycentric World* (London: Zed Books Ltd., 1985).

Amin, Samir, *Maldevelopment: Anatomy of a Global Failure* (London: Zed Press, 1990).

Anjac, Henri, "Cultures and Growth," in Mitchell A. Seligson, ed., *The Gap Between Rich and Poor* (Boulder: Westview Press, 1984), 38–52.

Araka, John et al., "Farmers Adjust to Economic Reforms," *African Farmer* 3 (April 1990): 5–15.

Asamash, Obed, "A New Role for ECOWAS," *Africa Report* 35, no. 5 (October 1990): 17–20.

Ashiabor, A., "Emerging Complementarities in African Economies," in *The Long-Term Perspective Study of Sub-Saharan Africa*, vol. 4, Proceedings of a Workshop on Regional Integration and Cooperation (Washington, D.C.: World Bank, 1990), 96–101.

Augelli, Enrico and Craig Murphy, *America's Quest for Supremacy and the Third World* (London: Printer Publishers, 1988).

Austin, Dennis, *Democracy and Violence in India and Sri Lanka* (New York: Council on Foreign Relations Press, 1995).

Ayoade, John A.A., "States Without Citizens: An Emerging African Phenomenon," in Donald Rothchild and Naomi Chazan, eds., *The Precarious Balance: State and Society in Africa* (Boulder: Westview Press, 1988), 100–18.

Bagachwa, M.S.D. and Frances Stewart, "Rural Industries and Rural

Linkages in Sub-Saharan Africa: A Survey," in F. Stewart, S. Lall, and S. Wangwe, eds., *Alternative Development Strategies in Sub-Saharan Africa* (New York: St. Martin's Press, 1992), 145–84.

Balassa, Bela, "Adjustment Policies and Development Strategies in Sub-Saharan Africa," in Moshe Syrguin, Lance Taylor, and Larry E. Westphal, eds., *Economic Structure and Performance* (New York: Academic Press, 1984), 316–40.

Bangura, Yusuf, "Authoritarian Rule and Democracy in Africa: A Theoretical Discourse," in P. Gibbon, Y. Bangura, and Arve Ofstad, eds., *Authoritarianism, Democracy and Adjustment* (Uppsala: Scandinavian Institute of African Studies, 1992).

Barber, Benjamin, *Jihad vs. McWorld* (New York: Random House, 1995).

Bartlett, Bruce, "The State and the Market in Sub-Saharan Africa," *The World Economy* 12, no. 3 (September 1989): 293–314.

Bates, Robert H., *Markets and States in Tropical Africa* (Berkeley: University of California Press, 1981).

Bayart, Jean-Francois, "Civil Society in Africa," in Patrick Chabal, ed., *Political Domination in Africa: Reflections on the Limits of Power* (Cambridge: Cambridge University Press, 1986).

Beetham, David, "Liberal Democracy and the Limits of Democratization," *Political Studies* 40 (Special Issue, 1992): 40–53.

Bentsi-Enchill, Nii K., "Breaking the Expatriate Grip on Africa," *Africa Recovery* 7, no. 1 (June 1993): 13.

Bentsi-Enchill, Nii K., "NGOs Widen Anti-adjustment Action," *Africa Recovery* 6, no. 3 (November 1992): 26–27.

Berlin, Isaiah, *The Crooked Timber of Humanity: Chapters in the History of Ideas* (New York: Alfred A. Knopf, Inc., 1992).

Bhagwati, Jagdish, "Regionalism Versus Multilateralism," *The World Economy* 15, no. 4 (September 1993): 535–55.

Bienefeld, Manfred, "The New World Order: Echoes of a New Imperialism," *Third World Quarterly* 15, no. 1 (1994): 31–48.

Bondestam, Lars, "People and Capitalism in North Eastern Lowlands of Ethiopia," *Journal of Modern African Studies* 12, no. 3 (1974): 432–39.

Bowles, Paul and Xiao-Yuan Dong, "Current Successes and Future Challenges in China's Economic Reforms," *New Left Review* 208 (November/December 1994): 49–76.

Bowles, Samuel and Herbert Gintis, *Democracy and Capitalism* (New York: Basic Books, 1986).

Bowles, Samuel and Herbert Gintis, "Democracy and Capitalism," in Philip Green, ed., *Democracy: Key Concepts in Critical Theory* (Atlantic Highlands, NJ: Humanities Press, 1993), 168–74.

Bratton, Michael, "Beyond the State: Civil Society and Associational Life in Africa," *World Politics* 41, no. 3 (April 1989): 407–30.

Bratton, Michael, "Civil Society and Political Transitions in Africa," in John W. Harbeson, Donald Rothchild, and Naomi Chazan, eds., *Civil Society and the State in Africa* (Boulder and London: Lynne Rienner

Publishers, 1994), 51–81.

Breuilly, John, *Nationalism and the State* (New York: St. Martin's Press, 1982).

Broad, Robin and John Cavanagh, "No More NICs," in Gerald Epstein, Julie Graham, and Jessica Newbhard, eds., *Creating a New World Economy* (Philadelphia: Temple University Press, 1993), 326–90.

Cabral, Amilcar, *Revolution in Guinea: An African Peoples' Struggle* (London: Monthly Review Press, 1969).

Callaghy, Thomas, "The State as Lame Leviathan: The Patrimonial Administrative State in Africa," in Zaki Ergas, ed., *The African State in Transition* (New York: St. Martin's Press, 1987), 87–116.

Caporaso, James, "The State's Role in Third World Economic Growth," *The Annals of the American Academy of Political and Social Science* 459 (January 1982): 103–11.

Caporaso, James A. and David P. Levine, *Theories of Political Economy* (Cambridge: Cambridge University Press, 1993).

Cardoso, Fernando Enrique, "On the Characterization of Authoritarian Regimes in Latin America," in David Collier, ed., *The New Authoritarianism in Latin America* (Princeton: Princeton University Press, 1979).

Carlsson, Jerker and Timothy M. Shaw, *Newly Industrializing Countries and the Political Economy of South-South Relations* (London: Macmillan, 1988).

Carter, A., "Industrial Democracy and the Capitalist State," in G. Duncan, ed., *Democracy and the Capitalist State* (London: Cambridge University Press, 1989).

Carter Center, "The Promise of Democracy," *Africa Démos* 3, no. 4 (March 1995): 1–4.

Cawson, A., "Is There a Corporate Theory of the State," in G. Duncan, ed., *Democracy and the Capitalist State* (London: Cambridge University Press, 1989).

Chabal, Patrick, *Power in Africa: An Essay in Political Interpretation* (New York: St. Martin's Press, 1992).

Chang, Ha-Joon and Ajit Singh, "Public Enterprises in Developing Countries and Economic Efficiency," *UNCTAD Review* 4 (1993): 45–82.

Charlick, Robert, *The Concept of Governance and Its Implications for A.I.D.'s Development Assistance Program in Africa* (Washington, D.C.: Associates in Rural Development, 1992).

Chazan, Naomi, "Between Liberalism and Statism: Africa Political Cultures and Democracy," in Larry Diamond, ed., *Political Culture and Democracy in Developing Countries* (Boulder and London: Lynne Rienner, 1993), 67–105.

Chege, Michael, "What's Right with Africa?" *Current History* 93, no. 583 (May 1994): 193–97.

Cheru, Fautu, *The Silent Revolution in Africa: Debt, Development and Democracy* (London: Zed Books, 1989).

Chishti, Sumitra, "Systemic Changes in the World-Hegemony and World

Economic Order in the Nineties," *The Indian Journal of Social Science* 4, no. 1 (1991): 45–57.

Cline, William R., *Exports of Manufactures from Developing Countries: Performance and Prospects for Market Access* (Washington, D.C.: The Brookings Institution, 1984).

Cohen, John M., *Integrated Rural Development: The Ethiopian Experience and Debate* (Uppsala: Scandinavian Institute of African Studies, 1987).

Cohen, John M., "Land Tenure and Rural Development in Africa," in Robert H. Bates and Michael F. Lofchie, eds., *Agricultural Development in Africa: Issues of Public Policy* (New York: Praeger, 1980).

Connor, Walker, *Ethnonationalism: The Quest for Understanding* (Princeton: Princeton University Press, 1994).

Cordell, Dennis D. And Joel W. Gregory, eds., *African Population and Capitalism: Historical Perspectives* (Boulder: Westview Press, 1987).

Cornia, A. Giovanni and Frances Stewart, "Country Experience with Adjustment," in G.A. Cornia, R. Jolly, and F. Stewart, eds., *Adjustment with Human Face*, vol. 1 (Oxford: Clarendon Press, 1987), 105–27.

Cowan, Laing Gray, *Privatization in the Developing World* (New York: Greenwood Press, 1990).

Cox, Robert W., "The Crisis in World Order and the Challenge to International Organization," *Cooperation and Conflict* 29, no. 2 (1994): 99–113.

———, "Global Restructuring: Making Sense of the Changing International Political Economy," in Richard Stubbs and Geoffrey R.D. Underhill, eds., *Political Economy and the Changing Global Order* (New York: St. Martin's Press, 1994), 45–59.

Curry, Robert L., Jr., "Regional Economic Co-operation in Southern Africa and Southeast Asia," *ASEAN Economic Bulletin* 8, no. 1 (July 1991): 15–28.

Da Costa, Peter, "A New Role for ECOWAS," *Africa Report* 36, no. 5 (September 1991): 37–40.

Daddieh, Cyril, "Structural Adjustment Programs and Regional Integration: Compatible or Mutually Exclusive," in K. Mengisteab and B.I. Logan, eds., *Beyond Economic Liberalization in Africa* (London: Zed Press, 1995).

Dahl, Robert, "Why All Democratic Countries Have Mixed Economies," in John W. Chapman and Ian Shapiro, eds., *Democratic Community* (New York: New York University Press, 1993), 259–82.

Datta-Chaudhuri, Mrinal, "Market Failure and Government Failure," *Journal of Economic Perspectives* 4, no. 3 (Summer 1990): 25–39.

Davidson, Basil, "What Development Model," *Africa Forum* 1, no. 1 (1991): 13–16.

De la Torre, Augusto and M.R. Kelly, *Regional Trade Arrangements* (Washington, D.C.: International Monetary Fund, 1992).

De Melo, Jaime and A. Panagariya, *The New Regionalism in Trade Policy* (Washington, D.C.: World Bank, 1992).

References

Diamond, Larry, "Class Formation in the Swollen African State," *The Journal of Modern African Studies* 25 (December 19871): 567–96.

Diamond, Larry, "Promoting Democracy," *Foreign Policy* 87 (Summer 1992): 25–46.

Dietz, L. James, "Overcoming Underdevelopment: What Has Been Learned from the East Asian and Latin American Experiences?" *Journal of Economic Issues* 26, no. 2 (June 1992): 373–83.

Dolny, Helena, "The Challenge of Agriculture," in John S. Saul, ed., *A Difficult Road: The Transition to Socialism in Mozambique* (New York: Monthly Review Press, 1985), 211–52.

Douglass, Mike, "Global Opportunities and Local Challenges for Regional Economies," *Regional Development Dialogue* 13, no. 2 (Summer 1992): 3–21.

Duncan, Alex and John Howell, "Assessing the Impact of Structural Adjustment," in Alex Duncan and John Howell, eds., *Structural Adjustment and the African Farmer* (London: Overseas Development Institute, 1992), 1–13.

Economic Commission for Africa, *Economic Report on Africa 1990* (Addis Ababa: ECA Secretariat, 1990).

Edwards, Sebastian, "Openness, Trade Liberalization, and Growth in Developing Countries," *Journal of Economic Literature* 31, no. 3 (September 1993): 1358–1393.

Eicher, Carl K., "African Agricultural Development Strategies," in Frances Stewart, Sanjaya Lall, and Samuel Wangwe, eds., *Alternative Development: Strategies in Sub-Saharan Africa* (New York: St. Martin's Press, 1992), 79–102.

Ellis, Frank, *Peasant Economies* (New York: Cambridge University Press, 1989).

Emmerson, Donald, "Capitalism, Democracy, and the World Bank: What Is to Be Done?" in Lual Deng, Markus Kostner, and Crawford Young, eds., *Democratization and Structural Adjustment in Africa in the 1990s* (Madison: University of Wisconsin, African Studies Program, 1991), 9–12.

Engedayehu, Walli, "Ethiopia: Democracy and the Politics of Ethnicity," *Africa Today* 40, no. 2 (Second Quarter, 1993): 29–52.

Epstein, Gerald, "The United States as a Debtor Country," in Gerald Epstein, Julie Graham, and Jessica Nembhard, eds., *Creating a New World Economy* (Philadelphia: Temple University Press, 1993), 199–220.

Eshag, E., "Some Suggestions for Improving the Operation of IMF Stabilization Programmes," *International Labor Review* 128, no. 3 (1989): 297–319.

Etzioni-Halevy, Eva, *The Elite Connection: Problems and Potential of Western Democracy* (Cambridge, UK: Polity Press, 1993).

Fakuyama, Francis, "The End of History," *The National Interest* 16 (September 1989): 3–18.

FAO, *Atlas of African Agriculture* (Rome: FAO, 1986).
———, *The State of Food and Agriculture 1990* (Rome: FAO, 1991).
Fashoyib, Tayo, "Nigeria," in Aderanti Adepoju, ed., *The Impact of Structural Adjustment on the Population of Africa* (London: UNFPA, Heinemann and James Currey, 1993).
Fatton, Robert, Jr., *Predatory Rule: State and Civil Society in Africa* (Boulder and London: Lynne Rienner, 1992).
Feder, Gershon, and Raymond Noronha, "Land Rights Systems and Agricultural Development in Sub-Saharan Africa," *The World Bank Research Observer* 2, no. 2 (July 1987): 143–69.
Feierman, Steven and John Janzen, eds., *The Social Basis of Health and Healing in Africa* (Berkeley: University of California Press, 1992).
Femia, Joseph V., *Marxism and Democracy* (Oxford: Clarendon Press, 1993).
Fetter, Bruce, "Health Care in Twentieth Century Africa: Statistics, Theories, and Policies," *Africa Today* 40, no. 3 (1993): 9–24.
Forontan, Faezeh, "Regional Integration in Sub-Saharan Africa: Post Experience and Future Prospects," in Jaime de Melo and Arvind Panagariya, eds., *New Dimensions in Regional Integration* (Cambridge and New York: Cambridge University Press, 1993), 234–71.
Freeman, John R., *Democracy and Markets: The Politics of Mixed Economies* (Ithaca: Cornell University Press, 1989), 69–72.
Friedman, Milton, *Capitalism and Freedom* (Chicago: Chicago University Press, 1962).
Gergen, David, "America's Missed Opportunities," *Foreign Affairs* 71, no. 1 (1991/92): 10–11.
Gershenkron, Alexander, *Economic Backwardness in Historical Perspective* (New York: Praeger, 1962).
Ghai, D. and L. Smith, *Agricultural Price Policies and Equity in Sub-Saharan Africa* (Boulder: Lynne Rienner, 1987).
Godfrey, M., "Trade and Exchange Rate Policy: A Further Contribution to the Debate," in T. Rose, ed., *Crisis and Recovery in Sub-Saharan Africa* (Paris: OECD, 1985), 168–79.
Goldin, Ian, Odin Knudsen, and Dominique van der Mensbrugghe, *Trade Liberalization: Global Economic Implications* (Paris and Washington, D.C.: OECD/World Bank, 1993).
Golub, Stephen S., *The United States-Japan Current Account Imbalance: A Review* (Washington, D.C.: IMF Paper on Policy Analysis and Assessment, 1994).
Gonzaleaz-Vega, Claudio, "Cheap Agricultural Credit: Redistribution in Reverse," in Dale W. Adams, Douglas H. Graham, and J.D. von Pischke, eds., *Undermining Rural Development with Cheap Credit* (Boulder: Westview Press, 1984), 120–32.
Gramsci, Antonio, *Selections from Prison Notebooks*, ed. and trans. Quentin Moore and Geoffrey Nowell Smith (London: Lawrence and Wishart, 1971).

Green, Reginald H., "Economic Integration/Co-ordination in Africa," in James Pickett and Hans Singer, eds., *Towards Economic Recovery in Sub-Saharan Africa* (London and New York: Routledge, 190), 106–28.

Gunn, Gillian, "The Angolan Economy: A Status Report," in Helen Kitchen, ed., *Angola, Mozambique and the West* (New York: Praeger, 1987).

Hagos, Tecola W., *Democratization? Ethiopia (1991–1994): A Personal View* (Cambridge, MA: Khepera Publisher, 1995).

Hardin, Garett, "The Tragedy of the Commons," *Science* 162 (1968): 1243–48.

Hardy, Chandra, "The Prospects for Intra-regional Trade Growth in Africa," in Frances Stewart, Sanjaya Lall, and Samuel Wangwe, eds., *Alternative Development Strategies in Sub-Saharan Africa* (New York: St. Martin's Press, 1992), 426–44.

Hargreaves, John D., *Decolonization in Africa* (London: Longman, 1988).

Harsch, Ernest, "Privatization: No Simple Panacea," *Africa Recovery* 2, no. 3 (August 1988): 12–14.

Hassen, Mohammed, "Ethiopia Missed Opportunities for Peaceful Democratization Process," paper presented at the Annual Meeting of the African Studies Association, Toronto, 1994.

Hawkins, A.M., "Can Africa Industrialize?" in Robert J. Berg and Jennifer S. Whitaker, eds., *Strategies for African Development* (Berkeley: University of California Press, 1986), 279–307.

Hayek, F.A., *The Constitution of Liberty* (London and Henley: Routledge and Kegan Paul, 1960).

———, *The Road to Serfdom* (London: Routledge and Sons, 1944).

Henderson, David, "International Economic Integration: Progress, Prospects and Implications," *International Affairs* 68, no. 4 (1992): 633–53.

Holm, Hans-Henrik and Georg Sorensen, "Introduction: What Has Changed?" in Hans-Henrik Holm and Georg Sorensen, eds., *Whose World Order* (Boulder: Westview Press, 1995), 1–17.

Hughes, Helen, "Does APEC Make Sense?" *ASEAN Economic Bulletin* 8, no. 2 (November 1991): 125–36.

Huntington, Samuel, "Democracy's Third Wave," in Larry Diamond and Marc F. Plattner, eds., *The Global Resurgence of Democracy* (Baltimore: Johns Hopkins University Press, 1993), 3–25.

———, "Why International Primacy Matters," in Sean M. Lynn-Jones and Steven E. Miller, eds., *The Cold War and After: Prospects for Peace* (Cambridge: MIT Press, 1993), 307–22.

———, "Will More Countries Become Democratic?" *Political Science Quarterly* 99, no. 2 (1984): 205.

Husain, Ishrat, *The Evolving Role of the World Bank: The Challenge of Africa* (Washington, D.C.: World Bank, 1994).

Hyden, Goran, "The Resilience of the Peasant Mode of Production: The Case of Tanzania," in Robert Bates and M.F. Lotchie, eds., *Agricultural Development in Africa* (New York: Praeger, 1980), 218–43.

Ibeanu, Okechukwu, "The Deteriorating Condition of the Nigerian Peasantry," in Okwudiba Nnoli, ed., *Dead End to Nigerian Development: An Investigation of the Social, Economic, and Political Crisis in Nigeria* (Dakar, Senegal: CODESRIA, 1993), 124–53.

Ihonvbere, Julius, "Democratization and Civil Society in Zambia," in Kidane Mengisteab and Cyril Daddieh, eds., *Democratization and State-Building in Africa* (forthcoming).

"IMF/World Bank: A Challenge from the South," *Africa Confidential* 35, no. 21 (21 October 1994): 1–3.

International Monetary Fund, "Asian Model Attests to Value of Openness and Minimal Policy-Induced Distortions," *IMF Survey* 22, no. 21 (8 November 1993): 338–41.

———, "Camdessus Cites Ways to Ease Transition to Market Economies," *IMF Survey* 22, no. 13 (28 June 1993), 194–97.

———, "Liberalization and the Role of the State Highlighted at World Bank Conference," *IMF Survey* (31 May 1993): 172–76.

———, "Poverty Reduction and Structural Adjustment Discussed at IMF Seminar," *IMF Survey* (14 June 1993): 178–82.

———, "Trade Has Small Impact on Wages," *IMF Survey* 23, no. 13 (27 June 1994): 210–11.

Jackson, Robert H. and Carl G. Rosberg, "Why Africa's Weak States Persist: The Empirical and Juridical in Statehood," *World Politics* 35 (October 1982): 1–24.

Jervis, Robert, "The Future of World Politics," *International Security* 16, no. 3 (Winter 1991/92): 39–73.

Johnson, Bryan T. and Thomas P. Sheehy, *1996 Index of Economic Freedom* (Washington, D.C.: The Heritage Foundation, 1996).

Johnson, E.G. Omotunde, "Economic Integration in Africa: Enhancing Prospects for Success," *Journal of Modern African Studies* 29, no. 1 (1991): 1–26.

Kahama, C. George, T.L. Maliyamkono, and Stuart Wells, *The Challenge for Tanzania's Economy* (London: James Currey, 1986).

Kamuzora, C.L., "Towards Understanding Low Contraceptive Prevalence in African Societies," *The African Review* 19, nos. 1 and 2, 1992: 1–9.

Kapur, Ishan, Michael T. Hadjimichael, Paul Hilberts, Jerald Schiff, and Philippe Szymczak, "Ghana Adjustment and Growth, 1983–1991," IMF Occasional Paper No. 86.

Keller, Edmond J., "The State in Contemporary Africa: A Critical Assessment of Theory and Practice," in Dankwart A. Rustow and Kenneth Paul Erickson, eds., *Comparative Political Dynamics: Global Research Perspectives* (New York: HarperCollins Publishers, 1991), 134–59.

Korany, Bahgat, "End of History, or Its Continuation and Accentuation? The Global South and the 'New Transformation' Literature," *Third World Quarterly* 15, no. 1 (1994): 7–15.

Krauthammer, Charles, "The Unipolar Moment," *Foreign Affairs* 70, no. 1 (Winter 1991): 23–33.

Krueger, Anne, *American Trade Policy: A Tragedy in the Making* (Washington, D.C.: The American Enterprise Institute, 1995), 6.

Krugman, Paul, "The Case for Stabilizing Exchange Rates," *Oxford Review of Economic Policy* 15, no. 3 (Autumn 1989): 28–44.

———, "Competitiveness: A Dangerous Obsession," *Foreign Affairs* 73, no. 2 (March/April 1994): 28–44.

———, "Dutch Tulips and Emerging Markets," *Foreign Affairs* 74, no. 4 (July/August 1995): 28–44).

———, "Regionalism Versus Multilateralism: Analytical Notes," in Jaime de Melo and Arvind Panagariya, eds., *New Dimensions in Regional Integration* (Cambridge and New York: Cambridge University Press, 1993), 58–79.

Kuznets, Simon, "Economic Growth and Income Inequality," *American Economic Review* 45, no. 1 (March 1995): 1–28.

———, "Towards a Theory of Economic Growth," in Robert Levachman, ed., *National Policy for Economic Welfare at Home and Abroad* (New York: Doubleday and Co., Bicentennial Conference Series, 1955), 12–85.

Laishley, Roy, "Faster Growth But No Economic Turnaround," *Africa Recovery* 8, nos. 1 and 2 (April/September 1994): 11.

Landau, Daniel, "Government and Economic Growth in Less Developed Countries," in *The Report of the President's Task Force on International Private Enterprise: Selected Papers* (Washington, D.C.: U.S. Government Printing Office, 1984).

Lappe, Frances Moore and Rachel Schurman, *Taking Population Seriously* (Oakland, CA: Institute for Food and Development Policy, 1990).

Layne, Christopher, "The Unipolar Illusion: Why New Great Powers Will Rise," in Sean M. Lynn-Jones and Steven E. Miller, eds., *The Cold War and After* (Cambridge, MA: MIT Press, 1993), 244–90.

Lehmbruch, Gerhard, "Consociational Democracy and Corporatism in Switzerland," *Publius* 23, no. 2 (Spring 1993): 43–60.

Lele, Uma, Robert E. Christiansen, and Kundhavi Kadiresan, *Fertilizer Policy in Africa: Lessons from Development Programs and Adjustment Lending, 1970–1987* (Washington, D.C.: World Bank, 1989).

Levitt, Kari, "Debt, Adjustment and Development: Looking to the 1990s," *Economic and Political Weekly* 25, no. 29 (21 July 1990): 1585–94.

Lewis, Arthur W., *Politics in West Africa* (London: Allen and Unwin, 1965).

Lewis, Stephen, "A Promise Betrayed," *World Policy Journal* (Summer 1991): 539–49.

Lewis, Stephen R. Jr., "Africa's Trade and the World Economy," in Robert J. Berg and Jennifer S. Whitaker, eds., *Strategies for African Development* (Berkeley: University of California Press, 1986), 476–504.

Lijphart, Arend, "Majority Rule in Theory and Practice: The Tenacity of a Flawed Paradigm," *International Social Science Journal* 129 (August 1991): 483–93.

Lindblom, Charles E., "The Market as Prison," *Journal of Politics* 44, no.

2 (May 1982): 324–36.

——, *Politics and Markets: The World's Political Economic Systems* (New York: Basic Books, 1977).

Lipumba, Nguyuru H.I., *Africa Beyond Adjustment* (Washington, D.C.: Overseas Development Council, Policy Essay No. 15, 1994).

—— and Louis Kasekende, "The Record and Prospects of the Preferential Trade Area for Eastern and Southern African States," in Ajai Chhibber and Stanley Fischer, eds., *Economic Reform in Sub-Saharan Africa, A World Bank Symposium* (Washington, D.C.: World Bank, 1991), 233–44.

Lutlala, M., M. Kintambu, and M. Mvudi, "Zaire," in Aderanti Adepoju, ed., *The Impact of Structural Adjustment on the Population of Africa* (London: UNFPA, Heinemann and James Currey, 1993).

Macpherson, Crawford B., *Democratic Theory: Essays in Retrieval* (Oxford: Clarendon Press, 1973).

——, *The Real World of Democracy* (Oxford: Oxford University Press, 1966).

Maizels, Alfred, "The Impact of Currency Devaluation on Commodity Production and Exports of Developing Countries," University College London, Discussion Paper No. 86–07, 1986.

Mamdani, Mahmood, "Democratization and Marketization," in K. Mengisteab and B.I. Logan, eds., *Beyond Economic Liberalization in Africa: Structural Adjustment and the Alternatives* (London: Zed Press and SAPES-SA, 1995), 17–22.

——, "Peasants and Democracy," *New Left Review* 156 (March/April 1986): 48.

Manglapus, Raul S., *Will of the People: Original Democracy in Non-western Societies* (New York: Greenwood Press, 1987).

Mansoor, Ali and Andras Inotai, "Integration Efforts in Sub-Saharan Africa: Failures, Results and Prospect—A Suggested Strategy for Achieving Efficient Integration," in Ajai Chhibber and Stanley Fischer, eds., *Economic Reform in Sub-Saharan Africa, A World Bank Symposium* (Washington, D.C.: World Bank, 1991).

Mbaku, John Mukum, "Bureaucratic Corruption and Policy Reform in Africa," *The Journal of Social, Political and Economic Studies* 19 (Summer 1994): 149–75.

McClelland, David C., "The Achievement Motive in Economic Growth," in Mitchell A. Seligson, ed., *The Gap Between Rich and Poor* (Boulder: Westview Press, 1984), 53–69.

McHenry, Dean E., Jr., "The State in Africa: A Predator or Contributor? In Decline or Resurgence?" Paper delivered at the African Studies Association Annual Meeting, Boston, 4-7 December 1993.

Mengisteab, Kidane, *Ethiopia: Failure of Land Reform and Agricultural Crisis* (New York: Greenwood Press, 1990).

——, "Responses of Afro-Marxist States to the Crisis of Socialism: A Preliminary Assessment," *Third World Quarterly* 13, no. 1 (1992):

77–87.

———— and B.I. Logan, "Implications of Liberalization Policies for Agricultural Development in Sub-Saharan Africa," *Comparative Political Studies* 22, no. 4 (January 1990): 437–57.

Mengistu, Berhanu, "Counter-trade as a Strategy for Regional Economic Cooperation: The Case of the PTA," in Kidane Mengisteab and B.I. Logan, eds., *Beyond Economic Liberalization in Africa: Structural Adjustment and the Alternatives* (London: Zed Books, Ltd., 1995), 273–87.

Michels, Robert, "Political Parties," in Philip Green, ed., *Democracy: Key Concepts in Critical Theory* (Atlantic Highlands, NJ: Humanities Press, 1993), 68–73.

Milner, Henry, *Social Democracy and Rational Choice: The Scandinavian Experience and Beyond* (London: Routledge, 1994).

Mkandwire, Thandika, "The Political Economy of Development with a Democratic Face," in Giovanni Andrea Cornia, Rolph van der Hoeven, and Thandika Mkandawire, eds., *Africa's Recovery in the 1990s* (New York: St. Martin's Press, 1992).

————, "The Road to Crisis, Adjustment and De-industrialization: The African Case," *Africa Development* 13, no. 1 (1988): 5–31.

Monteil, Peter J. and Jonathan D. Ostry, "The Parallel Market Premium: Is It a Reliable Indicator of Real Exchange Rate Misalignment in Developing Countries?" *IMF Staff Papers* 41, no. 1 (March 1994): 55–75.

Mwega, F.M., and J.W. Kabubo, "Kenya," in Aderanti Adepoju, ed., *The Impact of Structural Adjustment on the Population of Africa* (London: UNFPA, Heinemann and James Currey, 1993).

Neuberger, Benjamin, "Federalism in Africa: Experience and Projects," in Daniel J. Elezar, ed., *Federalism and Political Integration* (Tel Aviv: Turtledove Publishers, 1973), 171–88.

————, "State and Nation in African Thought," in John Hutchinson and Anthony D. Smith, eds., *Nationalism* (Oxford: Oxford University Press, 1994), 232–35.

Nnoli, Okwudiba, "Deadend to Nigerian Development," in O. Nnoli, ed., *Dead End to Nigerian Development: An Investigation on the Social, Economic, and Political Crisis in Nigeria* (Dakar, Senegal: CODESRIA, 1993).

Nurske, R., *Problems of Capital Formation in Under-developed Countries* (Oxford: Oxford University Press, 1953).

Nyerere, Julius, *Ujamaa: Essays on Socialism* (Dar es Salaam: Oxford University Press, 1968).

Nzongola-Ntalaja, Georges, *Revolution and Counter Revolution in Africa* (London: Zed Books, 1987).

Nzouankeu, Jacques-Mariel, "The African Attitude to Democracy," *International Social Science Journal* 128 (May 1991): 373–85.

Onis, Zia, "The Logic of Developmental State," *Comparative Politics* 24, no. 1 (October 1991): 109–26.

Orridge, A.W., "Uneven Development and Nationalism," *Political Studies* 29, no. 1 (1981): 1–15, no. 2 (1981): 181–90.

Ottaway, Marina, *Democratization and Ethnic Nationalism: African and Eastern European Experiences* (Washington, D.C.: Overseas Development Council, 1994).

Overseas Economic Cooperation Fund, "Issues Related to the World Bank Approach to Structural Adjustment: Proposal from a Major Partner," OECF Occasional Paper no. 1 (Tokyo: OECF, October 1991), 1–17.

Owens, Edgar, *The Future of Freedom in the Developing World* (New York: Pergamon Press, 1987).

Owusu, Maxwell, "Democracy and Africa—A View from the Village," *The Journal of Modern African Studies* 30, no. 3 (1992): 369–96.

Park, Yung Chul, "Development Lessons from Asia: The Role of Government in South Korea and Taiwan," *The American Economic Review* 80 (May 1990): 118–21.

Pearson, Scott R. And William D. Ingram, "Economies of Scale, Domestic Divergences, and Potential Gains from Economic Integration in Ghana and the Ivory Coast," *Journal of Political Economy* 88, no. 51 (1980): 994–1008.

Przeworski, Adam, *Democracy and the Market: Political and Economic Reforms in Eastern Europe and Latin America* (Cambridge, MA: Cambridge University Press, 1991).

———, "Democracy as a Contingent Outcome of Conflicts," in John Elster and Rune Slagstad, eds., *Constitutionalism and Democracy* (Cambridge: Cambridge University Press, 1988).

Ravenhill, John, ed., *Africa in Economic Crisis* (London, New York: Basingstoke, 1986).

Reddaway, Peter, "Is Russian Democracy Doomed?" *Journal of Democracy* 5, no. 2 (April 1994): 13–19.

"Regionalism and Trade," *The Economist*, 16 September 1995, 23–27.

Reich, Robert B., *The Work of Nations: Preparing Ourselves for the 21st Century Capitalism* (New York: Alfred A. Knopf, 1991).

———, "Who Is Us?" *Harvard Business Review* 68, no. 1 (January-February 1990): 53–64.

Ricupero, Rubens, "UNCTAD: Enfant Terrible Hopes for Rebirth," *The World Today* 52, no. 4 (April 1996): 106–107.

Rothchild, Donald, *Politics of Integration—An East African Documentary* (Nairobi: East African Publishing House, 1968).

Rueschemeyer, Dietrich and Peter Evans, "The State and Economic Transformation: Toward an Analysis of the Conditions Underlying Effective Intervention," in P.B. Evans, D. Rueschemeyer, and T. Skoçpol, eds., *Bringing the State Back In* (New York: Cambridge University Press, 1985), 44–77.

Rueschemeyer, Dietrich and Louis Putterman, "Synergy or Rivalry?" in Louis Putterman and Dietrich Rueschemeyer, eds., *State and Market in Development: Synergy or Rivalry?* (Boulder and London: Lynne Rienner, 1992).

Sachs, Jeffrey D. and Andrew Warner, "Economic Reform and the Process of Global Integration," *Brookings Papers on Economic Activity* 1 (1995): 1–118.

Sahn, David E., "Public Expenditures in Sub-Saharan Africa During a Period of Economic Reforms," *World Development* 20, no. 5 (1992): 673–93.

Sandbrook, Richard, "Liberal Democracy in Africa: A Socialist-Revisionist Perspective," *Canadian Journal of African Studies* 22, no. 2 (1988): 240–67.

Sartori, Giovanni, "Rethinking Democracy: Bad Polity and Bad Politics," *International Social Science Journal* 129 (August 1991): 437–50.

Scandizzo, Pasquale L. And Dimitris Diakosawas, *Instability in the Terms of Trade of Primary Commodities 1900–1982* (Rome: FAO Economic and Social Development Paper No. 64, 1987).

Scarritt, James R., "Communal Conflict and Contentions for Power in Africa South of the Sahara," in Ted Robert Gurr, ed., *Minorities at Risk: A Global View of Ethnopolitical Conflicts* (Washington, D.C.: United States Institute of Peace, 1993), 252–89.

Schejtman, Alexander, "The Peasant Economy: Internal Logic, Accumulation and Persistence," in Charles K. Wilber, ed., *The Political Economy of Development and Underdevelopment* (New York: Random House, 1988), 364–92.

Schumpeter, Joseph, *The Theory of Economic Development* (Cambridge, MA: Harvard University Press, 1934).

Segal, Aaron, "Africa's Population and Family Planning Dynamics," *Africa Today* 40, no. 3 (1993): 25–38.

Sen, Amartya, "Development—Which Way Now?" in Charles K. Wilber, ed., *The Political Economy of Development and Underdevelopment*, 4th ed. (New York: Random House, 1988).

Sharer, Robert, Christian Schiller, and Miftah Ahmad, "Uganda's Sustained Structural Reforms Yield Broad Gains," *IMF Survey*, 24 January 1994, 21–24.

Shaw, Timothy M., "The South in the 'New World (Dis)Order': Towards a Political Economy of Third World Foreign Policy in the 1990s," *Third World Quarterly* 15, no. 1 (1994): 17–30.

Shaw, W., "Towards the One-Party State in Zimbabwe: A Study in African Political Thought," *Journal of Modern African Studies* 24 (1986): 373–94.

Shivji, Issa G., *Class Struggles in Tanzania* (New York: Monthly Review Press, 1976).

Sklar, Richard, "Developmental Democracy," *Comparative Studies in Society and History* 23, no. 4 (1987): 686–714.

Sorensen, Georg, *Democracy and Democratization* (Boulder: Westview Press, 1993).

Sowa, Nii Kwaku, "Ghana," in Aderanti Adepoju, ed., *The Impact of Structural Adjustment on the Population of Africa* (London: UNFPA, Heinemann and James Currey, 1993).

Steinhart, Peter, "Beyond Pills and Condoms: As Africa's Population Mounts, What More Can Be Done?" *Audubon* 93, no. 1 (1991): 22–25.

Stewart, Frances, *North-South and South-South Essays on International Economics* (New York: St. Martin's Press, 1992), 162–87.

———, Sanjaya Lall, and Samuel Wangwe, "Alternative Development Strategies: An Overview," in Frances Stewart, Sanjaya Lall, and Samuel Wangwe, eds., *Alternative Development Strategies in Sub-Saharan Africa* (New York: St. Martin's Press, 1992).

Stiglitz, Joseph E., *The Economic Role of the State* (Cambridge, MA: Basic Blackwell, Inc., 1989).

Strange, Susan, *States and Markets* (London: Printers Publishers, 1988).

Streeten, Paul, "Against Minimalism," in Louis Putterman and Dietrich Rueschemeyer, eds., *State and Market in Development: Synergy or Rivalry?* (Boulder: Lynne Rienner, 1992), 15–38.

Taylor, Lance, "Economic Openness: Problems to the Century's End," in Tariq Brown, ed., *Economic Liberalization: No Panacea: The Experiences of Latin America and Asia* (Oxford: Clarendon Press, 1991), 99–141.

Teeple, Gary, *Globalization and the Decline of Social Reform* (Toronto: Garamond Press, 1995).

Thurow, Lester, *Head to Head: The Coming Struggle Among Japan, Europe and the United States* (New York: William Morrow, 1992).

Touraine, Alain, "What Does Democracy Mean Today?" *International Social Science Journal* 128 (May 1991): 259–68.

Underhill, Geoffrey R.D., "Conceptualizing the Changing Global Order," in Richard Stubbs and G.R.D. Underhill, eds., *Political Economy and the Changing Global Order* (New York: St. Martin's Press, 1994), 17–44.

UNDP, *Human Development Report 1991* (New York: Oxford University Press, 1991).

———, *Human Development Report* (New York: Oxford University Press, 1993).

———, *Human Development Report 1994* (New York: Oxford University Press, 1994).

UN Economic Commission for Africa, *African Alternative Framework to Structural Adjustment Programmes for Socio-Economic Recovery and Transformation* (Addis Ababa: E/ECA/CM.15/6/Rev. 3).

United Nations, *Trends in International Distribution of Gross World Product* (New York: Department for Economic and Social Information and Policy Analysis Statistical Division, 1993).

United Nations Industrial Development Organization, *Foreign Direct Investment to Developing Countries* (New York: United Nations, 1990).

———, *African Industry in Figures* (Vienna: UNIDO, 1993).

U.S. Committee for Refugees, *World Refugee Survey* (Washington, D.C.:

USCR, 1994).

Vengroff, Richard, "The Transition to Democracy in Senegal: The Role of Decentralization," *In Depth* 3, no. 1 (Winter 1993): 23–51.

Wade, Robert, *Governing the Market: Economic Theory and the Role of Government in East Asian Industrialization* (Princeton: Princeton University Press, 1990).

Walton, John and David Seddon, *Free Markets and Food Riots: The Politics of Global Adjustment* (Cambridge, MA: Blackwell Publishers, 1994), 23–54.

Waltz, Kenneth, *Theory of International Politics* (Reading, Mass.: Addison-Wesley, 1979).

Wangwe, S.M., "A Comparative Analysis of the PTA and SADCC Approaches to Regional Economic Integration," in World Bank, *The Long-Term Perspective Study of Sub-Saharan Africa*, vol. 4, Proceedings on a Workshop on Regional Integration and Cooperation (Washington, D.C.: World Bank, 1990).

Weeks, John, *Development Strategy and the Economy of Sierra Leone* (New York: St. Martin's and Macmillan, 1992).

Whitaker, Jennifer Seymour, *How Can Africa Survive?* (New York: Harper and Row, 1988).

White, Gordon, ed., *Developmental States in East Asia* (London: Macmillan, 1988).

Wilkinson, David, "Reconceiving Hegemony," Paper presented at the Annual Meeting of the International Studies Association, Washington, D.C., 28 March–2 April 1994.

Wolf, Eric R., *Peasants* (Englewood Cliffs, NJ: Prentice Hall, 1966).

Wood, Adrian, *Global Trends in Real Exchange Rates, 1960 to 1984*, World Bank Discussion Paper No. 35 (Washington, D.C.: World Bank, 1988).

Wood, Ellen Meiksins, *Democracy Against Capitalism* (Cambridge: Cambridge University Press, 1995).

World Bank, *Adjustment in Africa: Reforms, Results and the Road Ahead* (Oxford: Oxford University Press, 1994).

——, *The East Asian Miracle: Economic Growth and Public Policy* (Washington, D.C.: World Bank, 1993).

——, *Global Economic Prospects and Developing Countries* (Washington, D.C.: World Bank, 1994).

——, *Global Economic Prospects and the Developing Countries* (Washington, D.C.: World Bank, 1995).

——, *Global Economic Prospects and the Developing Countries* (Washington, D.C.: World Bank, 1996).

——, *Sub-Saharan Africa: From Crisis to Sustainable Growth* (Washington, D.C.: World Bank, 1989).

——, *Trends in Developing Economies* (Washington, D.C.: World Bank, 1993).

——, *World Bank Annual Report* (Washington, D.C.: World Bank, 1991).

——, *World Development Report 1994* (Oxford: Oxford University Press,

1994).

——, *World Development Report, 1995* (Oxford: Oxford University Press, 1995).

—— and UNDP, *Africa's Adjustment and Growth in the 1980s* (Washington, D.C.: World Bank, March 1989).

Wunsch, James S. and Dele Olown, "The Failure of the Centralized African State," in James S. Wunsch and Dele Olown, eds., *The Failure of the Centralized State: Institutions and Self-Governance in Africa* (San Francisco: Institute for Contemporary Studies, 1995), 1–22.

Yeats, Alexander J. "What Are OECD Trade Preferences Worth to Sub-Saharan Africa?" *African Studies Review* 38, no. 1 (April 1995): 81–101.

Young, Crawford, *The African Colonial State in Comparative Perspective* (New Haven and London: Yale University Press, 1994).

Zartman, William, "Introduction: Posing the Problem of State Collapse," in William Zartman, ed., *Collapsed States: The Disintegration and Restoration of Legitimate Authority* (Boulder: Lynne Rienner, 1994).

Zolberg, Aristide R., "The Specter of Anarchy: African States Verging on Dissolution," *Dissent* 39 (Summer 1992): 303–11.

# Index

controls, 41, 49, 51, 57, 136
decontrols, 17, 29, 35, 52, 53, 57, 72
export, 183
farm gate, 57
incentives, 53, 142
mechanism, 139
policy, 139
producer, 41, 51, 52, 71
system, 139, 141, 184
private enterprise, 31, 33, 34, 49, 98, 129, 130, 132, 138-141, 144
privatization, 10, 29, 34, 57, 157, 160, 181
production, 14
coordination, 80-83, 88, 170, 171, 183, 191
global, 7, 17
relations, 9
proliferation, 163
of nuclear weapons, 158, 162, 163, 172
proportional representation, 104, 108, 109, 114, 115
protectionism, 36, 69, 169, 173, 181
regional, 68
protectionist, 75
barriers, 83
measures, 160
pressures, 166
Przeworski, Adam, 103, 117, 130
public expenditures, 33, 41, 53, 54, 57
anti-, 33
retrenchment of, 29, 53, 157
public sector, 31, 37, 48, 97, 98, 136, 139
Putterman, Louis, 146

Ravenhill, John, 86
Reconstruction and Development Program, 112
redistribution, 32
of productive services, 52
redistributive

and regulatory roles of the state, 31, 34, 57, 58, 100, 101, 136, 181
measures, 31, 53, 102, 128, 153, 186
reforms, 103
reform
agrarian, 102, 118
land, 102
regimes, 13, 16, 161
authoritarian, 4, 101, 102, 116, 118, 119, 185, 191
democratic, 101
developmentalist, 102
global liberal, 159, 160
global liberal economic, 153, 159, 163, 166, 167
liberal democratic, 103
liberal economic, 161, 174
liberal trade, 161
self-serving authoritarian, 33, 105, 114, 174, 184, 185, 188
self-serving repressive, 24
socialist, 96
regionalism, 67, 69, 71, 79, 86, 87, 143, 167, 171, 172, 183, 191
regulation, 34, 35, 130, 160
deregulation, 34, 36, 157, 160, 162, 164, 169, 181
of prices, 33, 136
policy, 41
regulatory
involvement, 98
role, 31, 34, 57
welfare state, 99
revolution, silent, 22, 190, 193
Rueschemeyer, Dietrich, 144
rural
-biased development strategy, 142
industrialization, 142
poverty, 142
transformation, 142
Russia, 129, 159, 164
Rwanda, 4, 40, 41, 43, 46, 50, 55,

sustainable growth, 47
Swaziland, 43

Taiwan, 36, 73, 101
Tanzania, 15, 40, 41, 43, 46, 49,
50, 52, 69, 83, 107, 187
tariff, 75, 81, 86, 129
barriers, non-, 39, 75
levels, 39
protection, 83, 138
protective, 129
rates, 75
sheltering, 83
Taylor, Lance, 69
terms of trade, 4, 11, 21, 49, 52,
56, 74, 76, 78, 135, 154, 155,
161, 167, 180
unequal, 48
Togo, 40, 41, 43, 46, 50, 54, 93,
190
trade, 15, 84, 85, 165, 167, 171,
183
barriers, 75, 83, 155, 161
black-market, 84
deficits, 159
disequilibrium, 11
external, 181
foreign, 75, 81
free, 69
global, participation in, 84
integration, 80-82, 84, 88
intra-African, 17, 84, 87, 183
laws, 160
liberalization, 83
open, 164
partners, 68, 175
policies, 165
regime, 161
regional, 70, 85, 167, 171
trading bloc, 70, 167
unions, 21
trickle-down, 55, 101, 105, 136
process, 32, 53, 54, 101, 132
Tunisia, 74

Uganda, 6, 31, 38, 40, 41, 43, 46,

50, 54, 135, 190
*ujamaa* villagization, 15, 187
UN Economic Commission for
Africa (ECA), 3, 4, 38, 69, 85
UN Food and Agricultural
Organization (FAO), 38
Union Douanière et Economique
de l'Afrique Centrale (UDEAC),
68, 85
unipolar
global order, 168
hegemony, 159, 160, 163
moment, 157
position, 159
preponderance, 159, 165
system, 157-159, 164 166, 168
U.S. hegemony, 158, 159, 163,
164
world order, 158
unipolarism, 167, 168
United Kingdom, 13, 187
United Nations, 165
autonomy of the UN system,
167
General Assembly, 165
Secretary General, 165
Security Council, 165
UN General Assembly, 154
United Nations Conference on
Trade and Development
(UNCTAD), 38, 154, 171, 172
United Nations Development
Programme (UNDP), 32, 38, 42
United Nations Industrial
Development Organization
(UNIDO), 154, 158
United States, 67, 129, 152-154,
157-164, 166, 168
Congress, 55
dominance, 157, 159, 161-163
economy, 159
foreign policy, 165
hegemony, 158, 160, 162, 163,
166
leadership, 158, 159, 161, 163,
164